Henry Edwards

The Polish captivity

An account of the present position of the Poles in the kingdom of Poland

Henry Edwards

The Polish captivity
An account of the present position of the Poles in the kingdom of Poland

ISBN/EAN: 9783337274825

Printed in Europe, USA, Canada, Australia, Japan

Cover: Foto ©ninafisch / pixelio.de

More available books at **www.hansebooks.com**

THE

POLISH CAPTIVITY:

AN ACCOUNT OF THE

PRESENT POSITION OF THE POLES

IN

THE KINGDOM OF POLAND, AND IN THE POLISH PROVINCES OF
AUSTRIA, PRUSSIA, AND RUSSIA.

BY SUTHERLAND EDWARDS.

"Poles, we appreciate and admire the greatness of soul, the sensitiveness and the firmness which distinguish your national character, and which have been displayed in your efforts to recover the political existence of your country, which you love above everything."—ALEXANDER I., IN 1815.

"My grandmother and the King of Prussia, Frederick II., in partitioning Poland, committed a fault. . . The ruling Powers will never be able to enjoy these strange acquisitions in peace. The existence of Poland is something natural and indispensable. It would be superfluous to discuss the means of re-establishing it, for when a thing is natural and indispensable it arrives of itself."—THE ARCHDUKE FERDINAND OF AUSTRIA, IN 1848.

IN TWO VOLUMES.—VOL. I.

LONDON:
WM. H. ALLEN & CO., 13, WATERLOO PLACE, S.W.
1863.

ADVERTISEMENT.

A PORTION of this work has already appeared in *The Times*, in the shape of Letters from Warsaw, Cracow, Lemberg, Posen, Kovno, St. Petersburg, and Moscow, and is now reprinted by permission of the Proprietors.

CONTENTS.

CHAPTER I.
	PAGE
FINIS POLONIÆ	1

CHAPTER II.
| TOWARDS WARSAW . . . . | 8 |

CHAPTER III.
| WHERE IS POLAND? . . . . | 24 |

CHAPTER IV.
| ORDER IN WARSAW . . . . | 31 |

CHAPTER V.
| LIFE AND DEATH IN POLAND . . . . | 45 |

CHAPTER VI.
| MANIFESTATIONS AND SIGNS . . . | 67 |

CHAPTER VII.
| THE MONUMENTS OF WARSAW . . . . . | 77 |

CHAPTER VIII.
| ON THE RUSSIFICATION OF POLAND . . . . | 92 |

CHAPTER IX.
| ON DRESS AND OTHER DISTINCTIONS IN POLAND . . | 106 |

CONTENTS.

CHAPTER X.
Proprietors and Peasants . . 136

CHAPTER XI.
The Last Conquest of Poland . 160

CHAPTER XII.
Firm Foundations . . . 183

CHAPTER XIII.
Effect of Persecution on the Poles . . 207

CHAPTER XIV.
Effect of Persecution (continued).—"The Martyrs" . 218

CHAPTER XV.
How Poland Fell 233

CHAPTER XVI.
How Poland Fell (continued).—The Elective Sovereignty . 258

CHAPTER XVII.
The Restoration of Poland, according to Kosciuszko, 1815; General Chlopicki, 1830; and Count Andrew Zamoyski, 1862 293

APPENDIX I.
Extracts from "A Statement of Facts and Arguments on the subject of Poland". 320

APPENDIX II.
Viscount Palmerston to Lord Heytesbury. . . 341

APPENDIX III.
Translation from Mickievicz, by Mrs. Eleanor Orlebar . 352

LIST OF ILLUSTRATIONS.

VOL. I.

PARTITION OF POLAND. *Frontispiece.*	PAGE
ORDER IN WARSAW	30–31
SCENE IN THE CARPATHIANS	38–39
POLISH MOUNTAINEERS	82–83
PEASANTS OF MAZOVIA	106–107
UNIVERSITY OF CRACOW	140–141
VAULTS OF THE CATHEDRAL OF CRACOW	200–201
LELEWEL, THE POLISH HISTORIAN	270–271
CATHEDRAL OF CRACOW	298–299

THE POLISH CAPTIVITY.

CHAPTER I.

FINIS POLONIÆ.

This book is not written in order to prove that what Joseph Lemaistre, probably the greatest Conservative and supporter of order, and, at the same time, one of the greatest admirers of Russia that ever existed, called "the execrable partition of Poland" was indeed execrable; or, to come to what concerns England in a more direct manner, that Russia, Austria, and Prussia have all violated the treaties of 1815, first in the most perfidious, and latterly in the most open and cynical manner. Both these points must be touched upon, and especially the latter, even at the risk of telling the reader what he already knows. The author's chief object, however, is to give a plain, matter-of-fact account, from his own personal observation, of

Poland as it actually exists, and of the position of the Poles, considered both as subjects of the three partitioning Powers and as children of the country partitioned.

It is now ninety years since the first dismemberment of Poland was effected; and in spite of this and of half-a-dozen subsequent divisions and subdivisions of Polish territory among foreign invaders; in spite of massacres, confiscations, banishments, and tortures of all kinds inflicted on the Poles with the view of destroying their nationality, they are more united in feeling, and more thoroughly national at the present moment, than they were in 1772. Poland was believed to be dead, or, at least, reported dead, long since by its murderers, who even went so far as to put "*Finis Poloniæ*" into the mouth of the wounded and fainting Kosciuszko.* But dead countries have

---

* Several French newspapers have lately reproduced a letter addressed by Kosciuszko to the Count de Ségur (author of *La Décade Historique*, &c.) in which the following passages occur:—" Ignorance, or bad faith, persists in putting into my mouth the words '*Finis Poloniæ*,' which I am said to have pronounced on that fatal day of Maciéiovicé. In the first place, before the end of the battle, I was all but mortally wounded; and only recovered my senses two days afterwards, when I found myself in the hands of my enemies. Moreover, if such an expression would be foolish and criminal in the mouth of any Pole, it would be a great deal more so in mine. The Polish nation, in calling upon me to defend the country's integrity, independence, dignity, glory, and liberty, knew very

no history; and we all know whether that of Poland finished with the third partition. It is not too much to say, that many persons who take the warmest interest in the fate of the Poles know them only by their history during the last three-quarters of a century; under Kosciuszko, fighting for their independence; under Kniazevicz, Dombrowski, and Poniatowski, fighting for Napoleon, with a view to their independence—in Italy, in St. Domingo, in Spain, in the Duchy of Warsaw, and throughout the campaign against Russia, the first at Borodino, the last at Leipsic; under the Generals of 1830, fighting against the armies of Nicholas, the violator of their Constitution; then in Siberia, and scattered in exile all over Europe. For a time as

well that I was not the *last* Pole, and that with my death, on the field of battle or otherwise, Poland could not and would not *end*. All the Poles have done since then in the glorious Polish legions, and all they will yet do in the future, to recover their country, must be regarded as proofs that though we, the devoted soldiers of this country, are mortal, Poland is immortal; and no one has a right to say or repeat the outrageous expression, '*Finis Poloniæ*.' What would the French have said if, at the fatal battle of Rosbach in 1757, Marshal Charles de Rohan, Prince of Soubise, had cried out— '*Finis Galliæ*,' or if such cruel words had been attributed to him by his biographers? I shall be obliged to you, then, not to speak of this '*Finis Poloniæ*' in the new edition of your work; and I hope that the authority of your name will silence all who in future may think of repeating that expression, and of attributing to me a piece of blasphemy, against which I protest with all my soul."

if their country was in the grave, and themselves plunged, certainly, in mortal sadness; but with their national bards, Miçkiewicz, Bogdan Zaleski, and Krasinski, to give them such consolation as they could receive, and to encourage them with such hopes as have, indeed, never entirely deserted them. Poland has had a literary, quite as much as a military history, since the dismemberments of the eighteenth century; and it could easily be shown that, counting from its supposed death, it has produced more great poets and warriors than Russia, Prussia, and Austria combined.

Is it not remarkable, too, how many of the modern Polish chiefs, worthy successors of Sobieski, have been men of cultivated intellect, and often of high literary talent—not Bluchers and Platows, but Cæsars and Xenophons? Dombrowski (who owed his life at the battle of the Trebbia to a volume of Schiller's *History of the Thirty Years' War*, which he carried in his breast) occupied himself in his retirement with writing the *History of the Polish Legions*. Morawski and Goreçki, the former a general the latter a colonel in the army of 1830–31, are reckoned among the best poets and fabulists of their time. What have Kosciuszko and Poniatowski, fighting apart, in common with the ordinary run of modern generals? In Poland, since the moral revival caused by the destruction of the country in a political sense, we find poets, historians, politicians, men of distinction of all kinds, serving in the army, not because they had been bred soldiers, but because they were born patriots.

In another sphere, modern Poland has produced a fair number of legists, economists, and other men of science and learning; indeed, an immense number, when we take into consideration the facts that the universities of Warsaw and Wilna were suppressed, and their libraries carried off to St. Petersburg, after the insurrection of 1830–31; that the university of Cracow, the most ancient in Poland, has long been converted into a German academy; and that no superior instruction of any kind, in the Polish language, has been open to the Poles of the present generation.

France owes her system of credit-institutions to a Pole, M. Wolowski, of the French Institute; and the best work on the resources of Russia is by a Pole, M. Tengoborski. For even when a Polish writer or professor is not driven into exile to avoid death, like Lelewel, the great Polish historian, he can find no use for his talent in his own country. There are no universities, and there is a most intolerant censorship. Indeed, in every part of Poland newspapers and reviews are sometimes either directly suppressed, or ruined and destroyed by repeated prosecutions, for no assignable reason than because they are published in the Polish language, and because they take notice, no matter in how guarded a manner, of Polish events.

It is sometimes said by thoughtless persons that the Polish leaders are fit only to head insurrections, and that they do not know how to act within the limits of legality. But look at the line of conduct pursued, and the real influence exercised by Dr. Smolka at Vienna, and by Messrs. Niegolewski and Bentkowski at Berlin, in the Austrian and Prussian assemblies. Think, above all, of Count Zamoyski at Warsaw, and of what the short-lived Agricultural Society of the Kingdom of Poland was able, in the face of obstacles of all kinds, to effect— nothing less than the elaboration of a scheme for emancipating the peasant from task-labour, which, the Russian Government, now that it finds its own plan next to impracticable, would do well to adopt for the Empire generally.

No! there is life in Poland, and a life that grows fuller each day. Everything has been tried that could possibly extinguish it. Perhaps, at last, the most formidable of the partitioning Powers will admit its indestructibility, and find it good policy to reckon with it. At present, however, the Poles are persecuted and beaten down everywhere. Heaven knows whether they suffer most in Russian, Austrian, or Prussian Poland. I have seen them under torture in all three, and have heard their complaints. For the present, I will only say that in Warsaw the Russian tyranny passes for the worst, in Cracow and Leopol the Austrian, and in Posen, the Prussian.

CHAPTER II.

TOWARDS WARSAW.

THE first signs I saw of Poland were at Breslau, the capital of Silesia, which, before being an Austrian, was a Polish province, and which, as every one knows, was taken from Austria by Frederic the Great. Breslau is now connected with Warsaw, by rail, and is the ordinary halting-place for Polish travellers to and from the Kingdom. The whole province is completely Germanized, in so far that the immense majority of the population is German; but no receipt has yet been discovered for turning a Pole into an Austrian or a Prussian, and those who were Poles, and whose fathers and grandfathers were Poles, are Poles still. Wherever Germans and Poles are found together, it is undeniable that there are infinitely more Poles who learn German, than there are Germans who learn Polish; and thus, far beyond Breslau, and beyond the Russo-Polish frontier, and half-way to Warsaw, and in Warsaw itself, we find plenty of Poles speaking German fluently, whereas scarcely any of the

Germans in Breslau speak Polish at all. Indeed, German being the invariable language of the Prussian administration—even in Posen, in spite of treaties which bind Prussia to govern her Polish subjects as Poles—it follows that a man meaning to live in any part of Prussia must understand German, or be prepared to submit to many inconveniences and disadvantages. On the other hand, there is no part of Poland in which it is not a positive recommendation, in the eyes of the governing Power, to be ignorant of Polish.

In Silesia there is no injustice, in the present day, in making German the official and educational language in all the towns. In many of the country districts, however, the case is very different. The German peasants are prosperous and contented enough. But the Polish peasants of Lower Silesia, who are still Poles and speak the Polish language, and that only, are in a miserable position. For them there are no schools. They have no intercourse with their superiors. They feel as much that they are subjected to a foreign Government as the Poles of Posen, and with this additional disadvantage—that they have to deal exclusively with German proprietors. They form a class apart, and though nominally not serfs, are treated like slaves. The home of their hearts is still Poland, and in the annual pilgrimages to the Polish religious places, such as Czenstochow and Calvarya, the peasants of Silesia may still be seen in company with those of Poland proper, Lithuania, and the Ukraine.

Breslau, however, is a town of many tongues. The shopkeepers proclaim their trades in German, Polish, Russian, Hebrew, French, and occasionally English; and the day I took my departure for Warsaw, a professor at the University was to maintain a thesis in the Latin language, and against all comers, *de fistulâ*. It is a town, too, of strange costumes and types; of pike-bearing watchmen, of droschky-drivers in helmets, and of dandified sweeps, with black faces like other sweeps, but also with a romantic bearing, evident pretensions to elegance of attire, and waists like wasps or like Prussian officers. There, too, as in Poland, you may see the genuine Israelite dressed, not in cheap imitation of the Christian swell, but in his own Israelitish gaberdine—

"His beard a foot before, his hair
A yard behind"—

—or, if not behind, in two long ringlets, one on each side.

Even in Breslau, there were reminders both of the brutal persecution of the Poles by the Russians, and of the persecution of a more legal kind (at least as regards form) carried on against them by Prussia.

In the shop-windows were engravings of the

bloody scenes that had just been enacted in Warsaw. At the *table d'hôte* of the Hotel of the "Golden Goose," the Polish gentlemen wore their national costume, proscribed by the Russians, and the bright-eyed, soft-complexioned Polish ladies were dressed in the deepest mourning, and had little crosses of black jet hanging round their necks, and portraits of Kosciuszko in their brooches. Polish newspapers from Cracow, where everyone has a right to say as much as he pleases against the Russian Government, and indeed any Government except that of Austria, were handed about and eagerly caught up. Then a Pole came in, who had just arrived from Warsaw, and who brought with him the ghastly photographs of the first victims of the Russian soldiery in the late disturbances; the five men who were shot in the massacre of the 27th February, and who were half-stripped, and photographed with their wounds and their horribly distorted faces, soon after they fell. The day of the funeral, when all Warsaw was hung with black, and everyone in the city followed the procession, these terrible mementoes were distributed by thousands. For a long time afterwards—perhaps even now, though I have read that the photographer was afterwards imprisoned—they could be purchased almost publicly in Warsaw, and I found them in every house that I visited in Russian, Austrian, and Prussian Poland.

At the confectioners' shops, the only news-rooms to be met with from Berlin to Moscow, I found the Poles complaining of the seizure of the last number of the Posen newspaper, the *Djiennik Poznanski*. Perfect liberty of the press exists everywhere in Prussia, and especially in the Grand Duchy of Posen. But there are certain administrative difficulties in the way of publishing a newspaper in the Polish language; and the one Polish newspaper which has contrived to force its way into existence at Posen is perpetually interfered with and checked by the police, on pretexts which are doubtless well-meant, but which somehow or other have invariably to be overruled when they come to be examined by the light of the law. Liberty of the press triumphs in the end, but in the meanwhile Polish editors get arrested rather often, and editions of their journals rather often get confiscated. This course of proceeding does not alter the fact that liberty of the press is recognized as a principle by the Prussian law; only it is hoped that the law can be so applied as to have the effect of silencing and destroying the *Djiennik Poznanski*.

From Breslau to Warsaw, by rail, is a good day's journey. But what a journey, if you divide it and stop the night at Sosnovicz, the first station beyond the Prussian frontier! The Russians, for the sake of their Government, and the Poles for the credit of their country, ought to unite for once and subscribe a few copecks and groszy, so as to enable the inn-keeper of the place to offer a decent room to the traveller, condemned by an ill-regulated time-table to remain there from nine in the evening until half-past six the next morning. It would be absurd to ask for a well-furnished chamber, and unreasonable to expect such ordinary accommodation as may be met with in the cottage of many an English peasant; but there might be blinds to the windows, and there might be beds long enough for a man of moderate stature, and warranted not to break down if laid upon. On the beds there might be clean bed-clothes; and in case the astronomical arrangements of the night should not allow the traveller to go to bed by the light of the moon, some waxen or stearine substitutes might be provided for the feeble torches of ill-smelling tallow with which the savage host of Sosnovicz at present supplies his faint and weary guests.

It is ridiculous for travellers who go out of beaten tracks to complain of want of accommodation at hotels. But on the high road from Breslau to Warsaw, one cannot help fancying that the half-way house ought to be something better than a pig-stye, furnished in very bad imitation of a human dwelling-place. Never mind the food; there are plenty of fowls running about the Sosnovicz caravanserai, and you can get new-laid eggs. Besides, black bread alone, if it will not satisfy, will, at least, tire the appetite. And you can have a glass of very weak tea at Sosnovicz for sixpence; and after washing out the glass with the first tea, you can get another supply stronger, and proportionately nastier, but which seems, at first, to have a better effect on the nerves, for sixpence, and something extra. You cannot get milk at Sosnovicz, because there are no cows there, but they will give you some kind of rum to mix with your tea, which, if it does not greatly improve the taste, at least changes it. The great crime of the host of Sosnovicz consists in his giving, not too little, but too much. Why, for instance, put dirty bedclothes on a bedstead, when a bedstead alone would be so infinitely preferable? Is it to deter people from going to bed, so as to save trouble to the chambermaid? The notion is ingenious; but if "Freedom shrieked when Kosciuszko fell," I wonder what Cleanliness does when a traveller in a Polish inn, after carefully covering the bed with railway wrappers and great coats, lies down in his clothes on the bedstead, dislocates it in every joint, and brings it down with him into the dirt, which covers the floor so thickly, that mustard and cress might grow in it?

"So this is Poland," one reflects, after rising from the floor and taking a seat at the window, which commands a view of a magnificent wood. The bedless guest stares at the admirable moon-illuminated pine-trees, the shadows of which fall upon the outer walls of the caravanserai. The moon stares into the curtainless room, lights up the remains of the bedstead, and casts a melancholy gleam over a little heap of dirt (it might be larger were the housemaid more industrious) which has been swept into one of the corners, and left there, as much as to say, "There is an end at least of *that* job." The traveller wonders whether there are any wolves in the forest, and says to himself that if they are half as ferocious as certain smaller animals which infest the room, it would not be desirable to encounter them.

No: this is only a part of Poland. Still it is part of it, as a dirty finger-nail is part of a man's hand, a dirty hand part of a man's body. If first impressions were everything, what an idea one would have of Poland from Sosnovicz! Unfortunately (as I afterwards found out) precisely the same idea that one would form of it from making its acquaintance at Graniça, the frontier village between the Kingdom of Poland and the Polish dominions of Austria; or at Kovno, the frontier town between Prussia and Lithuania. Poland is certainly not careful about her extremities. England, France, and Germany, all keep their hands and feet in a much more becoming state. Nor in a journey along the borders of Hungary, nor even in Russia, did I ever see anything to equal in uncleanliness the uncleanliness of Kovno, nor, above all, of Sosnovicz.

The two Sosnovicz servants are worthy of the inn. The inn is "worthy of them both." The chambermaid is without shoes or stockings. She does not, can not change the sheets, but she is ready to bring clean towels if ordered to do so in Little Russian or Ruthenian, and it is quite gratifying to hear her abuse the proprietor in the language of the Ukraine for his various short-comings and crimes of inhospitality.

The "boots" is bootless. He kisses the traveller's hand at night, and in the morning proves his zeal by waking him from his chair, or from his tumble-down couch, at four o'clock, that he may catch the train at half-past six. He commences boot-cleaning in the bedroom, and, when ejected by force, commences the operation immediately outside the door. He uses no blacking, properly so-called, but what he *does* apply, he carries in his salivary glands.

There is no trouble in getting the bill in the morning. It is not heavy, compared with the charges at the best hotels on the Continent. The use of the room with the broken bed is put down at a sum equivalent to one thaler. The youthful boots embraces the traveller's knees by way of a hint that attendance is not included. The poor little chambermaid bows her head, seizes the traveller's hand, and bears it affectionately to her lips. The feet of these domestics are muddy, and, as there are no carpets, or rugs, or mats, or even scrapers about the place (though scrapers would certainly not be nice things for persons without shoes or stockings to use), they bring a great deal of wet mould with them out of the court-yard into the rooms. But they are not without heart, and they respond to a small gratuity by reviling the proprietor in the most obliging manner. The proprietor appears in person, at the last moment, to receive the ironical thanks of the guest for the inattention that has been shown him. He is disposed of, however, by his own servants, who tell him he ought to be ashamed of himself, and so on, and who have so little fear of him, that it is evident he gives them no wages.

Can the general civilization of a country be judged of by its inns? I hope not, for the sake of Poland. But, in any case, it must be remembered that Polish civilization has been in some respects checked, in others greatly thrown back (especially among the poorer classes) by the Partitions and by the wars, confiscations, and educational and commercial restrictions which were their natural consequences. By the accounts of all travellers, the lower orders in Poland were in a miserable position at the period of the first dismemberment, but the Constitution of 1791 provided for the gradual emancipation of the peasantry, and, by conferring representative rights on citizens and traders, encouraged the formation of a respectable middle class. The Poland of 1791 was, in a political sense, at least half a century before either of the States which united to invade and destroy it; and since the ruin of their country the Poles have had to go back and wait for the very slow development of Prussia, Austria, and Russia. Even now, in Prussia and Austria, they can only profit by the advantages of constitutional government by forsaking their ancient national culture and becoming Germans.

Of the effect of political institutions, and especially of such an institution as serfdom, on the condition of a population, some notion may be formed by comparing the Polish peasants of Prussia and Austria, where serfdom no longer exists, with those of Russia, where, in the kingdom, the task-work system is only now being discontinued; and where, in the Polish provinces forming part of the Russian Empire, the position of the peasant, until the recent edict of emancipation appeared, was almost that of a slave. The Polish peasant of Prussia is decidedly the highest, as the Polish peasant of Russia is decidedly the lowest, in the scale of civilization.

The country between Sosnovicz and Warsaw is as dull as it is flat. It is less woody than the immense tract of wilderness between Moscow and St. Petersburg, along which it used to be said that a squirrel could leap from tree to tree without once touching the ground. But the forests one passes are far more interesting than the fields, cultivated by peasants so miserable that it is impossible to wonder at their laziness, and so lazy that they could not well be otherwise than wretched. I am not going to generalize on the subject of agriculture in Poland from what I saw of it during a day's railway travelling through the country, but I affirm that from half-past six in the morning to five in the afternoon all the labourers I passed were ragged and dirty; that at least four-fifths of them were lying down on the ground; that not one in ten was doing any work; and that the few who seemed to be seriously occupied were employed on the railway. The contrast between the appearance of the Prussian and that of the Polish peasant is most striking. Gradually, as you proceed eastward, the labourer seems to sink lower and lower, and in Poland Proper he appears, indeed, in a most pitiable condition.

Afterwards, in the immediate neighbourhood of Warsaw, I saw plenty of well-clad, prosperous-looking peasants, and I was assured that those whose appearance and attitude on the ground had struck me as expressing the last degree of wretchedness and laziness were abstaining from labour on high political grounds and by reason of the new law which changed their system of tenures and required them to substitute money payments for task-work. All the Polish proprietors had declared that it would be impossible to make them pay rent for their land in hard cash, and the Agricultural Society had recommended that their farms should be made over to them in freehold, the proprietors receiving an indemnification from the Government in bills bearing interest, for the payment of which it was proposed to levy a land-tax. The Government, however, through a committee of bureaucrats, had prepared its own measure, which dissatisfied peasants and proprietors alike, and which will yet have to be modified.

Could the Government possibly have been jealous of the Agricultural Association, which, in preparing a simple and perfectly satisfactory solution of the peasant question, proved that it was fit for the exercise of legislative functions, and gave the lie to those who maintain that the Poles are a frivolous and thoughtless race, because they do not display the patience of the ass under gross ill-usage? It is probable enough that such was the case.

The ordinary Prussian is a reasonable being. He treats with a species of reverence every one who wears a Government uniform. He will allow himself to be run through the body by an officer whom he has or has not provoked, and other Prussians will look on with wonder at the Prussian who has presumed to place himself in such a position that it was necessary for an officer to take the trouble to run him through. If a bill is proposed in the Prussian Chamber of Deputies for placing soldiers and civilians on an equality before the law, the bill is forthwith rejected. In a word, the Prussians are quiet and reasonable, and know the obedience they owe to the corporals and sergeants who govern them.

Look at the Russians again. In the early part of the last century, a Russian nobleman would take a beating from his Emperor (the great Frederick William, too, occasionally caned his courtiers). Russian noblemen, even under the most liberal sovereign that Russia has ever known, have been arrested without accusation, and temporarily exiled without trial, though it is fair to add that there have been but few such instances during the reign of Alexander II.

The Poles, however, have never shown that sort of reasonableness which consists in accepting any amount of tyranny and injustice, against which it may be inconvenient and dangerous to protest.

Before condemning them for their folly in this respect, some allowances ought to be made for their position, their education, their traditions, and their descent. It is not given to every one to bear blows and insults meekly, and, to do so, one must have been brought up specially for it, as for other things. Now, the Prussians have been accustomed more or less to stick-law, ever since the establishment of the Hohenzollerns in Brandenburgh. The Russians owe that powerful instrument of government, the knout, to the Tartars, and have brought up generation after generation under its kindly shadow. But the Poles have never yet for thirty years consecutively put up with the *régime* of the knout and the stick without protesting against it and sealing their protest with their blood. It is difficult to accustom them to it; for these Poles, of whom some hundred thousand have been sent to Siberia since the first partition of their native land, and of whom upwards of fifteen thousand—a tenth part of the entire population —were imprisoned in Warsaw during the first six months of the present year;* these Poles are the sons of the men who voted for the Constitution of the 3rd of May, and who fought under Kosciuszko; they are the great-grandsons of the men who fought, not as conscripts, but as

* See the report of the municipal officers of Warsaw, published in the London newspapers early in August, 1862.

volunteers, under Sobieski, and saved Vienna and the west of Europe from a Turkish invasion.

If the Poles are not reasonable, it will at least appear to Englishmen that there is something natural in their conduct. Dr. Johnson told Boswell one day that he had just passed a fishmonger who was skinning eels, and who "cursed them because they would not lie still;" and he mentioned this as a "remarkable instance of heartless brutality." If we cannot assist Poland in her distress, let us at least admit her right to complain and protest as best she can; and let us not sympathize for one moment with her tormentors, who curse her because she will not lie still.

CHAPTER III.

WHERE IS POLAND?

"*Où donc est la Pologne?*" said poor Madame Dubarry, hearing her royal lover and his ministers speak of the first partition as something not quite to be approved of. I ask the same question now, with a strong impression that many of my countrymen cannot answer me precisely, and with the knowledge that Russians, Prussians, and Austrians will all give different replies.

Diplomatically speaking, and by the treaties of 1815, through which the partition received for the first time the sanction of Europe, "Poland" is simply the little "kingdom" of that name, which the Congress of Vienna placed under Russian sovereignty on the express condition that it should be governed constitutionally. This "kingdom," containing nearly five millions* of inhabitants, is a diminution of the Duchy of Warsaw, formed by Napoleon out of the Polish provinces wrested from

* See the report addressed by Col. Staunton, Consul-General at Warsaw, to the Foreign Office (1862).

Prussia after the battle of Friedland, in 1807, and from Austria after the successful campaign of Prince Poniatowski in 1809.

Russia, with the consent of Napoleon, had gained an additional portion of Polish territory, in 1807, at the expense of Prussia, and, in 1809, at the expense of Austria: in the former instance the district of Bialystock, in Lithuania; in the latter a portion of Eastern Galicia.

In 1815, when the sixth division of Polish territory took place, the Duchy of Warsaw was dismembered, as the ancient kingdom of Poland had been dismembered before. Posen was given back to Prussia; Western Galicia, with the exception of Cracow, was given back to Austria; Cracow was proclaimed a free city; while Russia, besides retaining all the provinces of which she had obtained possession at the first, second, and third partitions—besides Bialystock, which she had acquired from Prussia at what may be called the fourth partition—was allowed to unite to her Empire the whole of the remaining portion of the Duchy of Warsaw. All that Russia lost by the arrangement of 1815 was the little district in Eastern Galicia, which Austria had been forced to cede in 1809 (the fifth partition), and which was now given back to her. What she gained was nearly the whole of that portion of Polish territory, with Warsaw for its capital, which, from the three partitions of the eighteenth century, until 1807 had belonged, by right of theft, to Prussia.

For fifteen years, the "Kingdom of Poland" (as the remnant of the Duchy of Warsaw placed under Russian sovereignty was and is entitled,) was governed more or less in accordance with constitutional forms, though the constitution by which it was declared, in the language of the treaties of the 3rd of May and of the 9th June, 1815, to be "linked to Russia," was often violated. After the insurrection of 1830, the Emperor Nicholas abolished the constitution, and pretended to replace it by an "Organic Statute," which was published, but never put in action. The Kingdom of Poland was made a Russian province, in which the rights of the Polish inhabitants were less respected than the treaties of Vienna intended they should be, even in those Polish provinces which formed no part of the Kingdom, but which had been seized upon by Russia at the first, second, third, and fourth partitions.*

But though the Kingdom of Poland is the only portion of Polish territory which still preserves its ancient name, the European Powers who signed the treaties of Vienna have a right, if they choose

---

* The reader will remember that the fourth partition took place when Napoleon formed the Duchy of Warsaw out of Prussian-Polish territory, and gave the district of Bialystock to Russia.

to exercise it, to demand that the inhabitants of those Polish provinces which have been incorporated with the dominions of Russia, Austria, and Prussia be governed as Poles, and be allowed to enjoy representative and national institutions. The country inhabited by the Poles so cared-for in these treaties is Polish, just as much as Venetia is Italian.

A few months ago, I met with a paragraph in several English newspapers, which, under the head of "Russian Sympathy for Poland," set forth that the population of the "Russian" province of Witepsk had taken to wearing Polish colours and emblems, and that they had been ordered by the Government to discontinue the practice under severe penalties. It seems less astonishing that the people of Witepsk should proclaim themselves Poles when one remembers that that province formed part of ancient Poland, and was only annexed to the Russian Empire by force at the first partition. But the Russians speak now of all Polish territory belonging to Russia and not included in the little Kingdom of Poland as absolutely Russian; that is to say, not merely Russian by its political misfortunes, but also by its population, its traditions, and its national sentiment. History apart, facts are every day presenting themselves which prove this view to be false and absurd (as when, quite recently, it was found necessary to declare all the

Polish provinces incorporated with Russia in a state of siege); but the Russian Government endeavours, in its own peculiar way, to persuade itself and its Polish subjects in the incorporated territory that they *are* Russians nevertheless. It forbids them to use their own language, and punishes them for wearing Polish dresses and even for calling themselves Poles.

If you ask a Russian where Poland is, he will say, "In the Kingdom, in Posen, in Cracow and the surrounding territory, but not in the provinces detached from Poland and united to the Russian Empire prior to 1815."

The Prussian Government maintains, on its side, through speakers in the Chamber of Deputies and through pamphleteers, that there are no Poles in the Duchy of Posen, but only Prussians who happen to speak the Polish language. This language, by the way, is *not* spoken in the public offices of Posen; and in the public schools it is only tolerated in the lower classes. Thus, Prussian Poles have no "national institutions," though they have a representation in the Prussian Chamber, where the debates are of course carried on in German.

If you ask a Prussian where Poland is, he will say, "In the Kingdom, in Galicia, in the Polish provinces incorporated with Russia, but not in Posen, which is part of Prussia."

The Austrian Government appears to have no false theories on the subject of Poland. It contents itself with wronging its Polish subjects practically, but without hypocrisy. It does not pretend that Cracow belongs naturally to Austria, as the Russian Government pretends that Wilna belongs naturally to Russia. It does not maintain that the birth-place of Sobieski is and always has been Austrian, as the Prussians do that the birth-place of Copernicus is Prussian, and the Russians that the native province of Kosciuszko is, and from time immemorial has been, Russian. Austria has endeavoured, by all possible means, to Germanize her Polish subjects, but she has never denied the fact of their being Poles. She turned the ancient academy of Cracow into a German university, but did not seek to justify the act. She provoked and organized a massacre of Polish proprietors, but it was precisely because they *were* Poles that she caused them to be murdered. There has been very little deception about Austria's treatment of her Polish subjects. In addition to persecution of the most sanguinary kind, she has systematically defrauded them, but she has defrauded them openly, without pretending in semi-official newspapers and pamphlets that she was acting honestly by them all the time.

Austria acknowledges that the country partitioned by Russia, Prussia, and herself in 1772, was and is Poland. In the travelling maps of Poland sold in the Austrian dominions, the limits of 1772 are preserved; and though in the ethnological charts of the Austrian Empire, the purely Polish and the Polish and Ruthenian portions of Galicia are differently coloured, and though Polish towns in which there is scarcely a German inhabitant are sometimes coloured with the German hue, yet no serious attempt is made to show that any portion of Austrian Poland is Austrian otherwise than in a political sense.

In fine, according to Russia, Warsaw, Cracow, and Posen are Polish; but not Wilna.

According to Prussia, Warsaw, Cracow, and Wilna, are Polish; but not Posen.

According to Austria, Warsaw, Cracow, Wilna, and Posen are all Polish.

Russia, Prussia, and Austria are all agreed as to Warsaw being Polish, though, when Warsaw was in the hands of the Prussians (from 1795 until 1806) it was governed as a German city.

Let us begin, then, with Warsaw, which happens to have been the first Polish town in which I set foot: Warsaw, the capital both of the old and of the new Kingdom of Poland. Here, at least, we are among Poles. Let us see what sort of life they lead.

ORDER IN WARSAW

CHAPTER IV.

ORDER IN WARSAW.

I ARRIVED in Warsaw about a month after the massacre of April. It was not necessary to have read the newspapers, or to ask the meaning of the bullet-marks which might still be seen on the walls of the Sigismund Place, in order to understand that some terrific calamity had fallen upon the city, and that war was going on between the rulers and the ruled.

Nevertheless, I had not much trouble with my passport, which simply set forth that I was travelling towards Moscow. Every road leads to the Russian Rome, and I reached my destination four months after leaving Warsaw, viâ Cracow, Leopol, the Carpathian Mountains, Posen, Kovno, and St. Petersburg. Englishmen are notorious for not being conspirators, and after answering a few questions as to how long I was going to stay (a week or two), why I had come to Warsaw at all (to see it), and where I was going to put up (at the Hôtel de l'Europe), I was allowed to escape from the crowd of greasy Jews who blocked up all the approaches to the little passport-office attached to the railway station. I had already been informed that tickets of residence were not granted for a longer period than a fortnight, but that they were renewable on personal application, which I found to be a matter very easily arranged, though the formalities to be gone through were a little tedious.

Warsaw was now comparatively quiet, though it abounded in signs of the recent agitation. Soldiers were encamped in the open space around the Sigismund monument, and in the large square opposite the Saxony Gardens. Patrols of Cossacks passed continually down the streets; and at the corners of all the principal thoroughfares police-soldiers were stationed. All the barracks seemed crowded, and there was no street or passage without some sort of military guard. At the same time, this display of force was rendered as little offensive as possible. The soldiers doing street duty were without weapons of any kind, and their behaviour, as far as I could judge from my own observation, was perfectly good. Certainly, there was no reason why their demeanour should have been otherwise than peaceable, for they met with no sort of provocation from the inhabitants, who, indeed, for the most part, seemed to make a point of ignoring their existence. Still, as I had seen it stated that acts of brutality were still constantly committed by the Russian troops quartered in Warsaw, I may as well mention that, during the few weeks I spent there in May and June, I was in the habit of walking and driving about the city in all directions, and was only struck by the excellent discipline in which the soldiers were kept, and by their generally inoffensive attitude.

It was thought, perhaps, that Warsaw had already been sufficiently terrorized; or, perhaps, this was the natural reaction after the violent and sanguinary outburst of the 8th of April, which had excited the indignation of all Europe. Be that as it may, the military occupation of the Polish capital, though doubtless effective enough, looked to me far more like a measure of precaution than of intimidation. It is not much, perhaps, to say in favour of soldiers holding a defenceless city, that they do not insult the townspeople, but, as far as it goes, it is to their credit. Unfortunately, the restraint under which the Russian soldiers were kept for a time, was not maintained very long; and we know that in the autumn, when the state of siege had been declared, they behaved with the greatest brutality in the churches and in the streets.*

* See Lord Carnarvon's speech in the House of Lords, April, 1862; and Mr. Mitchell's *Letter to Lord John Russell*, giving an account of the attack made upon Mr. Mitchell by a party of Cossacks in Warsaw.

From what I had heard of the Russianizing system pursued in the Kingdom of Poland, I was surprised to find that Polish was the language of the public offices in Warsaw almost as much as of every-day life; and that in more than one office it was difficult to find a clerk who understood Russian. My ticket of residence, given by the passport authorities, was in the national tongue; so also was the *visa* obtained at the head-quarters of the police; so also was a paper, acknowledging the receipt of some books which, before being delivered up to me, had to be submitted to the censor. At the post-office, Russian seemed to be an unknown language.

The inscriptions on the Government buildings are usually in Russian and Polish; sometimes in Polish alone, but never in Russian alone. In the official journal, Russian and Polish are used side by side as a rule; but, occasionally, notifications and advertisements are printed in Polish only. I believe that, in theory, the Russian currency was substituted for the Polish long ago by the Emperor Nicholas; but, in practice, Polish coin and notes circulate everywhere, and the shopkeepers all state their charges in the ancient money of the country—though they willingly accept, at a just equivalent, Russian, Prussian, Austrian, or any other ready cash.

All the ladies were in the deepest mourning.

Even when the sun was scorchingly hot, if, by the rarest chance, any white or light-coloured dress was seen, all eyes were turned upon the wearer. As for the Russian ladies, the wives and sisters of the officers quartered in Warsaw, they had, for the most part, left the city, having either gone on to Cracow, or some of the German watering-places, or gone back to what the Poles call "Muscovy."

I occasionally meet with exaggerations in connection with Polish affairs (exaggerations most injurious to the Poles, for all that they require in order to insure sympathy is to have their case fairly stated), but certainly no one has ever exaggerated the grace and beauty of the Polish women. They have given numberless proofs of patriotism; and many of them, with all their delicacy of organization, have not shrunk from encountering great personal dangers for the sake of their country. But whatever noble qualities they may possess, they would probably not have the influence which they actually exercise over their countrymen, if Providence had not also bestowed on them, in a remarkable degree, the gift of beauty. Many of the Polish women are very like our English women of the slender, delicate type, but with paler complexions, and brighter, and generally darker, eyes. I thought it was impossible to see finer and more varied expression than their faces exhibited; for I saw them at a time when their enthusiasm, their indignation, their sorrow, and all their religious feeling were awakened. I had read, in some book, that they were frivolous and changeable; but they have been constant enough to Poland, and dull persons will always mistake animation, quickness of perception, and a light manner of treating light subjects, for frivolity. In every civilized country, women give the tone to society, and this is particularly the case in Poland, where social gatherings are far more frequent than with us, and where there are no entertainments, no pleasure-parties of any kind, at which women are not present. If, however, the Polish ladies cared only for pleasure, instead of placing patriotism above all other considerations; if the balls and bribes offered to them and to their husbands, could make them forget their suffering country; then the Russians would certainly by this time have made some progress in the way of gaining adherents among the Polish families of the Kingdom, whereas, as it is, they have not advanced a step. The Polish mothers bring up the young Poles as patriots, and the Polish wives exclude from society all whose patriotism is even doubtful.

That is to say, the women in Poland do their duty like the men, and nurture the Polish spirit, and keep up the Polish traditions, which the men, according to their opportunities, have to defend.

"In the Middle Ages," says Miçkievicz, "the wife prayed in her oratory for her husband while fighting on the field of battle: she was sure that her prayers bore succour to her husband . . . . . . This is still the case in Poland, where the wife joins conspiracies, accompanies her husband to Siberia, and sometimes mounts on horseback to defend the country." *

The tacit agreement by which the women of Poland undertook, a year and a-half ago, not to dance, and kept, and still keep, that promise in all parts of the ancient kingdom, may appear to some persons not to have been a very important resolve. In itself, however, it was, at least, as great a sacrifice as total abstention from wine would be on the part of many Englishmen. The Polish women have a passion for dancing, and no women dance so well. The Poles have invented, or rather, let us say, the rhythmical genius of the Polish people has produced, three dances and three forms of dance-music (the Mazurka, the Polonaise, and the Cracovienne), which have been adopted or imitated by every modern composer; but a great calamity having fallen upon them, they sat down and wept, put on sackcloth and ashes, and refused

* *Cours de Littérature Slave*, vol. v. p. 250.

to dance their national dances "in a strange land." There were other Polish inventions, such as Lancers and Hussars, to which many of the Poles would willingly have had recourse, but that was impossible and not to be dreamt of.

Of course, the Poles never thought that giving up dancing would "lead to anything," as the phrase is; nor did the Hebrews think that by hanging up their harps they would free themselves from the Babylonians. Nor do sons and daughters who go into mourning imagine that wearing crape will bring back a dead parent. These testimonies of sorrow on the part of the inhabitants of all Poland proceeded from emotion, not from calculation. The effect was not thought of. A spontaneous expression of grief and pain was called forth throughout the length and breadth of the land, by the blow which had been struck at Warsaw. The Poles had no thought of impressing either foreign nations or their own foreign Government, though their unanimity of feeling *did* impress all Europe. I am convinced that even the singing of the national prayer was not intended, in the first instance, as a "demonstration." I have often heard it sung in places where it might be thought there was no one to hear it but the Poles themselves and the Heavenly Protector to whom it is addressed; at night, in a deserted bye-street of Cracow; in front of a convent; in a distant

village; in a church almost too small to be taken notice of by the administrative authorities; and, far away from either church or convent, in the solitudes of the Carpathian mountains.

But the Russians heard the hymn in Warsaw, Wilna, and elsewhere, and knew its ultimate meaning. So, also, did the Austrians and Prussians when it reached *their* ears, and it is not astonishing that none of them liked it, and that they all forbade it. If, beyond doubt, Poland were lost for ever, then the Poles might be allowed to sing their songs in peace. But the Polish Hymn contains a prayer that may be granted, and therefore it irritates and maddens the oppressors of Poland. Not only enthusiasts, but our oldest and most experienced politicians are convinced that Poland will live again, and the visionaries now are those who believe in the continuance of the present order of things in that unhappy country. After the occurrences of 1830-1, of 1846, and of 1848, the Polish cause did indeed appear to be irrevocably lost; but those who know what Poland has been doing of late years, and how thoroughly Polish all Poland remains, and that not one Pole has yet been converted into a Russian, an Austrian, or a Prussian, seem to be chiefly struck by the fact that all the oppression and persecution which this devoted nation has undergone, have only served to fortify its national spirit. If the Polish question was not settled in 1795, when all Poland was divided into three; if it was not settled in 1815, when it was divided into five; * or in 1846, when the annexation of Cracow by Austria left it divided into four; still less is it settled now, when there are such increased facilities of intercourse between the four parts, and when, as a natural consequence, so many more direct expressions of sympathy are constantly interchanged.

An eminent Russian journalist, M. Aksakoff, in a newspaper published at Moscow (of which I shall have to speak again in the second volume of this work) has remarked that, but for the forcible partition, Poland might have died out through the insufficiency of her own institutions, through the development of one class to the exclusion of all others, and through the ultimate corruption of this class. But the touch of the foreign sword revived the spirit of the nation, and in destroying its political existence gave it a fresh moral life, which has never since deserted it. Of two plans—both difficult, almost to impossibility—for obtaining the submission of the Poles, the least impossible, though seemingly, at first sight, the longest, was that of conciliation. But the partitioning Powers evidently thought that if they governed their

---

* The Kingdom of Poland, Russian Poland, Austrian Poland, Prussian Poland, and the "Free City" of Cracow.

Polish subjects as Poles, they would only encourage their hopes of a future reunion and revival. They preferred to drive them at once to despair. Many of the oldest inhabitants of Warsaw at this moment must have lived under four entirely different rules, and have acknowledged by turns Stanislaus Poniatowski, Frederick William of Prussia, the King of Saxony, and the Emperor of Russia, as their sovereign. Being Poles, they had, in 1795, to become Prussians, and after being governed for a dozen years as Prussians, and then being once more allowed to call themselves Poles, they found themselves suddenly called upon by the Emperor Nicholas, after 1831, to turn into Russians. They are expected now to be "loyal" to the Russian crown, as they were expected at the beginning of the century to be "loyal" to Prussia !

The partitioning Powers have really cultivated the enmity of the Poles, and by doing so equally on all sides have brought about that unanimity of feeling which shows itself in an impartial hatred of all three. The three sovereigns who detest the sound of the Polish Hymn have reason to do so, for they suspect that its music may be "the music of the future." They know something of Poland, and are aware that they cannot keep it in its present position. As I said before, our most experienced statesmen, men who have followed the fortunes of Poland for half a century, with a full knowledge of all that was befalling it, of its hopes, its disappointments, and its firm faith under the darkest misfortunes, tell us now that they believe this faith was not misplaced, and that Poland will some day live again.

"Looking to a distant period," said Earl (then Lord John) Russell, in the House of Commons in 1861, "one cannot but think that, for a people endowed with so much courage, and which has so long kept alive the holy flame of national existence, a time is reserved when it may recover its ancient glory, and take its place among the nations of Europe."

"I concur with my noble friend," added Lord Palmerston, "in thinking that a nation which, under such a long course of oppression, has resisted all attempts to destroy its national spirit, must be destined, some day or other, for a better fate."

And what says the calm, prudent M. Guizot? The second volume of his *Memoirs*, published in 1861, contains the following remarkable passage in reference to the Polish insurrection of 1830:—

"Soon a century will have passed away since the first partition of that unhappy country. Innumerable diplomatic acts have acknowledged its new masters. Events of immense importance have changed the destinies and absorbed the interest of Europe. In the midst of so many iniquities and misfortunes, the fate of Poland has never ceased to be regarded and felt as a European crime and calamity. It was the murder of a whole nation; as her friends have said with terrible truth. In vain have their adversaries replied that Poland herself, her detestable institutions, her blind quarrels, her execrable anarchy, led to her overthrow, and that national suicide provoked foreign assassination. The explanations of history are not judicial decision, and argument avails nothing against the strong sentiment of universal conviction. For more than sixty years Poland has ceased to figure among nations, and as often as the nations of Europe rise in agitation, Poland also begins to move. Is it a phantom, or is it a people? I cannot say. Poland may be dead, but she is not to be forgotten. By the side of this striking fact, I have remarked another no less extraordinary. Since the conscience of Europe has been disturbed by the fate of Poland, important changes have been accomplished. Various powerful authorities have disposed of nations. Neither monarchy nor republic, neither conqueror nor congress, has ever seriously attempted to call back Poland from her grave, or to heal this European wound. At the time when this murder was committed, neither old France nor old England raised an arm to prevent it: new France and new England have not acted with more efficacy. The re-establishment of Poland never entered into the real or sincere designs of the French Revolution, or of the Emperor. Words have been uttered, prospects have been opened, devoted patriotism has been called into brilliant display by hopes being excited; but that is all. Extreme misfortune alone has made them find passing illusions in all these falsehoods. The whole world has made use of Poland, but no one has ever assisted her."

CHAPTER V.

LIFE AND DEATH IN POLAND.

THE Hôtel de l'Europe is a magnificent hotel, but it was built by an Italian architect, M. Marconi, and the manager is a German. Still, it was designed for Poles, and it is infinitely superior to the caravanserais, more or less furnished, more or less clean, of St. Petersburg and Moscow. I mention this little fact by way of compensation for what I have been obliged to say about the not merely uncomfortable but really disgraceful condition of the village inns in all parts of Poland.

In Warsaw, Cracow, Leopol, and Posen, the principal hotel-keepers are Frenchmen or Germans, generally the latter. It is all very well for the Poles to sneer at the Germans for their pursuit of material welfare, for their worship of *Brodsinn*, for their calm acceptance of the maxim "*Ubi bene ibi patria;*" but they must allow that if the Germans introduce nothing else worth having into Poland, they at least bring cleanliness with them. It seemed to me that cleanliness among the Poles was confined to the few, and that it had scarcely penetrated at all into the lower ranks of society. To be sure, all the inferior inn-keepers are Jews, but that is no reason why the people who stay for however short a time in their miserable hostelries, should not insist upon being treated like Christians.

The Hôtel de l'Europe, however, is a hotel in which a Christian may reside, though, of course, like everything else in Poland, it has one or more Jews connected with it. I found them civil and obliging, and ought to have spoken of them, in modern Polish phrase, as "persons of the Mosaic confession" instead of calling them by a name which from a name of glory has become one of reproach. From "Child of Judah" to "Jew," there is as great a fall as from "Slavonian" to "slave."

The waiters are, for the most part, Poles, and I thought them equally remarkable for their gentlemanly demeanour and their gross inattention. It is impossible to be *not* waited upon with more affability and courteousness than at a Polish hotel. There are German waiters, to be sure, who do what they are told "right away," as the Americans say. In that, however, there is nothing new. There is some originality about the Poles, who show the most delicate foresight in anticipating your wants, and in suggesting what you, otherwise, might never have thought of, and then disappear, apparently never to return.

But the Hôtel de l'Europe is chiefly remarkable, among all the hotels I ever saw, for the admirable decorations of the principal suites of apartments. The ceilings are painted in a style worthy of any palace, and in some of the rooms the woodwork of the walls and the panels of the doors are also ornamented with the most fanciful and graceful designs. The rich hangings and the luxurious furniture harmonize perfectly with the colours employed in the paintings, and it is evident that architects, artists, decorators, and upholsterers have all worked together, or rather that one architect and artist has superintended everything.

I asked who was in the habit of coming to hotels and taking such apartments as these, which included a reception-room, a dining-room, a drawing-room, and a magnificent ball-room. They were only just finished, but they were intended for wedding parties given by country families who had no town-house, and who, expecting guests from various parts of Poland, made Warsaw the common rendezvous.

But they had had a sad inauguration, and the first guests who were brought into them were not dressed in wedding garments, but in bloody clothes, and with Russian bullets in their bodies.

The Agricultural Society had just held its celebrated meeting, at which the scheme for liberating the peasants from task-work, and giving them their land in freehold was adopted. The hotel was full, and when the bodies of the five men who fell beneath the first fire of the troops were carried there, they were placed in these private apartments, and the next day, the photographs were taken of which the prints have since been spread in countless numbers over all parts of the politically dismembered, but morally united, kingdom. One had been shot through the heart, another through the head, a third had had his jaw shattered, and his face was distorted in a frightful manner. Among the five one was a workman, one a student, and one a landed proprietor. The rich and the poor, the old and the young, had their representatives among the victims, and all classes in Warsaw, indeed, all Warsaw in a mass, attended the funeral. I saw the graves of these unfortunate men two months after they had been buried. They lay side by side, and their tomb, which, as yet, bore no inscription, was covered with wreaths, flowers, and funeral offerings of every kind, which the people of Warsaw still brought at all hours of the day.

The Hôtel de l'Europe was pretty well guarded when I was there. There were sentinels at all the entrances, and in the Saxon Square, which the hotel overlooks, was a camp of about two hundred infantry. I had therefore abundant opportunities of studying the manners and customs of Russian soldiers under canvas. Thus, twice a-day I have seen them stand, spoon in hand, in circles of half-a-dozen, round their soup-pots, and attack the contents one by one, in strict order, and with military precision. I have even, thanks to early rising, and to the sleep-murdering effect of their morning drums, been able to watch them at their daily ablutions and devotions. Every man was his own washhand-stand, jug, and basin, and, after filling his mouth with water, ejected it in a graceful stream into his hands, and applied them to his face. The canvas of the tent served as a towel. Then, still standing up and turning to the east, with many bows and gesticulations and with much solemnity, the soldier said his prayers—after which he was ready to be kicked by his officers at parade.

I have seen hundreds of Russian soldiers at their prayers, and never saw one prepare himself for the day without saying them. "And afterwards," some readers will exclaim, "they break into Polish churches, and shoot defenceless Poles!" They simply obey orders, like other soldiers. That does not alter the fact that they have a strong religious feeling, and the fact is an important one to consider in estimating the fighting power of a Russian army, to take no other view of it.

On each side of the Saxon Square are barracks for cavalry and artillery; at the further end are the Saxon Gardens, the great promenading ground of the Varsovians; in the centre stands what the Poles call "the Russian Somovar;"* a hideous bronze monument, commemorating the fidelity of seven Poles who were unfaithful to Poland, when the insurrection of 1830–31 broke out. Twice a-day troops of lancers go in and out of the barracks, and every morning an artillery train comes from some other quarter of the town to be relieved. Besides an immense artillery camp immediately outside the city, various encampments of infantry in the very heart of it, and several more towards the barriers; besides soldiers of all arms in barracks, in huts, and under canvas on the plains around Warsaw, the castle is itself filled with troops, as are also its stables, its courtyard, and its large garden. Warsaw, then, ought really to be considered safe from the attacks of an unarmed population. We certainly had not such a force at the Alma, not a third of such a force at Inkerman, as the Russians have collected here in order to keep down some hundred and fifty thousand defenceless townspeople—men, women, and

* Tea-urn—literally, "self-boiler."

children; that is to say, from thirty to forty
thousand men of all classes, without organization,
without weapons, and without any intention of
fighting. Cossacks and dragoons ride up and
down the streets, as though to guard against the
possibility of surprise. But if the defenceless,
unarmed ones were to go mad and attack the
castle; and if, the garrison having suddenly become paralyzed, they were actually to take it by
storm, there would still be enough artillery and
ammunition in the citadel to lay Warsaw in
the dust—which the Emperor Nicholas threatened
to do if the city gave the slightest sign of a
second insurrection. The citadel, with its bright-
red walls and buttresses, which form such a vivid
contrast with the rich verdure of the earthworks,
and the banks of the broad moat is in many
respects a remarkable edifice. But its picturesque-
ness is less striking than its position, which gives
it the command of the entire city, at a range
of about half a mile from the outer buildings. In
the open space in the interior stands a statue of
Alexander I., "the Benefactor of the Poles," placed
there by Nicholas, who was certainly not their benefactor. Close to the statue of the Benefactor is a
small field of iron hayricks—an acre or so of cannon
balls, piled in rows of pyramids, with which the
Benefactor's successor meant to destroy Warsaw, if
Warsaw ever gave him the least trouble.

I have said that at the Government offices in Warsaw all the inscriptions are in Russian and in Polish. Above the gates of the citadel this formality has not been observed. There, Russian alone is employed, and on seeing the date of the structure, 1835, one feels that it would be superfluous and quite out of place to offer any words on the subject to the Poles, to whom the citadel is itself an address, and a very intelligible one. Indeed, that there might be no doubt about the meaning of it, the Emperor Nicholas, as I have already mentioned, explained it himself.

On the 16th October, 1835, the Czar, who now appeared in Warsaw for the first time since the insurrection, received the municipal officers of the city, and knowing that they were about to present a conciliatory address, suddenly stopped them, and broke out into the following characteristic speech, preserved in the archives of Russia, and printed by D'Angeberg in his *Recueil des Traités, &c., concernant la Pologne* (p. 972):—

"I know, gentlemen, that you have something to say to me, I even know the contents of your address, and, to spare you a falsehood, I do not wish to hear it. Yes, gentlemen, to spare you a falsehood, for I know that your sentiments are not what you would have me believe them to be.

"How could I put any faith in your words, when you used the same language to me on the eve of the Revolution? Did not you yourselves speak to me, five years, eight years ago, of fidelity and devotion? Did you not make all kinds of fine protestations? Not many days afterwards you violated your oaths, you committed horrors.

"The Emperor Alexander, who did more for you than an Emperor of Russia ought to have done, who loaded you with kindness, who favoured you beyond his own subjects, and rendered you the most flourishing and the happiest of nations—the Emperor Alexander was repaid with the blackest ingratitude.

"You never could be contented with the most advantageous position, and you ended by destroying your own happiness. I tell you the truth now, in order to place our mutual position in a proper light, and in order that you may know what to expect; for I now see and speak to you for the first time since the disturbances.

"Gentlemen, I want deeds, not words! Your repentance must come from the heart. I speak to you without losing my temper; you see that I am calm. I have no feeling of rancour, and I will do you good in spite of yourselves. The Marshal, whom you see at my side, fulfils my intentions, seconds me in my views, and thinks also of your welfare. (*At these words, the members of the deputation bow to Marshal Paskievitch.*)

"Well, gentlemen, what do these bows mean?

The most important thing for you is to do your duty, to behave like honest men. You have to choose, gentlemen, between two courses: either to persist in your illusion of an independent Poland, or to live tranquilly, and as faithful subjects, under my government. If you persist in cherishing your dreams of distinct nationality, of Polish independence, and all such chimeras, you can only draw down great misfortunes upon yourselves. I have erected the citadel here, and I declare to you that at the slightest disturbance I will reduce the town to ashes, I will destroy Warsaw, and am not likely to build it up again.

"It is very painful for me to speak to you in this way; it is very painful for a sovereign to treat his subjects in this way; but what I tell you is for your own good. It is for you, gentlemen, to deserve that I should forget the past; it is only by good conduct, and by devotion to my Government, that you can do so.

"I know that you have correspondents abroad, that ill-intentioned writings are introduced here, and that endeavours are made to pervert your minds. But the best police in the world, with a frontier like yours, cannot prevent clandestine communications; you should be your own police, and should keep the evil away.

"Bring up your children properly, and inculcate to them principles of religion and fidelity to their sovereign, if you wish to remain in the good path.

"In the midst of all the troubles which agitate Europe, of all the doctrines which shake the political edifice, Russia alone remains firm and inassailable.

"Believe me, gentlemen, it is really a happiness to belong to such a country, and to enjoy its protection. If you conduct yourselves well, if you fulfil all your duties, my paternal solicitude will be extended to all of you, and in spite of what has passed, my Government will think of your welfare.

"Mind you remember what I have said to you."

Alexander II. has not yet made use of the citadel, to destroy the city of Warsaw; but it was from the citadel that the cannon answered the signal-rockets of the castle, when the troops, on the 8th of April, 1861, entered the town, and took up their position in all the public places, preparatory to the slaughter of the defenceless people.

Was this a massacre or not, in the exact sense of the word? Can it be compared, for instance, as it has been more than once, by Polish, and also by French writers, to the massacre of the Christians in Syria? Most certainly not; nor even to the massacre of the French in Paris, after the 2nd of December. I was present at the latter, and, without any notice to disperse having been given, saw crowds of well-conducted persons fired upon by the drunken soldiers. I did not see any artillery fired, but I saw the guns at the corner of the Rue Faubourg Montmartre, heard the reports, and saw Sallandrouze's carpet-warehouse immediately afterwards with the windows and walls shattered. I also saw bodies, not singly, but in heaps, lying at the *portes cochères*, on the Boulevard Montmartre; and, walking along this boulevard the same evening, found it, in places, almost impassable from pools of blood. An English druggist was shot, standing at his own door (this was worse than what happened to Mr. Mitchell, in Warsaw); an American gentleman was bayoneted in a wine-shop, where he had taken refuge; the house of M. Brandus, the music-publisher, in the Rue Richelieu, was broken into, and one of his servants murdered. The infantry in the street below had previously fired into the balcony, where several of M. Brandus's friends were smoking. As bullets cannot be guided when they have once left the gun, women and children were, in many places, shot; and I know one instance, in which two young girls were fired upon by a sentinel. I speak only of what I witnessed myself, or of what happened in the Paris massacre of December, 1851, to persons known to me more or less intimately.

Now, if the conduct of Prince Gortchakoff, at Warsaw, be viewed side by side with that of the idol of Poland at Paris, it will be seen that the "Muscovite," the "Tartar," the "Mongol" General behaved with comparative moderation, and that the crusader in the cause of liberty, the promoter of the new law in Europe, the champion of the right of oppressed nationalities, acted like a barbarian. The difference, I admit, is only that which exists between assassination with, and assassination without, extenuating circumstances—between black with a brown shade, and black of the deepest dye; but the distinction is, nevertheless, worth noting—though it would never have occurred to me at all to weigh the guilt of two such crimes, were it not that the worst of the two offenders is looked upon, by a number of tormented, bewildered Poles, as impelled, by the nobility of his nature, to rescue them from persecution, and, indeed, as only prevented from doing so by the backwardness of the English Government, which, notoriously, does not go to war (and which also does not commit massacres) "for an idea."

The worst point about the butchery of Warsaw undoubtedly was, that it had been deliberately arranged the day before. I do not say that the soldiers were brought into the city for the express purpose, whatever might occur, of murdering the inhabitants; but it had been decided at a council of war (in spite of some honourable protests on the part of General Lüders and others), that in case of a large crowd again assembling it should be dispersed by force. The gathering of the crowd might have been prevented, but, once formed, to disperse it except with bloodshed was impossible. The people who had collected in front of the Lieutenant's house, were not there to create a disturbance, but to "demonstrate" their unanimity and earnestness in demanding certain rights which it may have been absurd and out of place to demand in the streets, but which it seemed necessary, nevertheless, to claim in a very public manner; especially as the Emperor had already characterized a petition signed by the President of the Agricultural Association, the Catholic Archbishop of Warsaw, and all the chief representative men, acknowledged as such by the entire population of Poland, as proceeding only from "some individuals." It was not likely that a crowd of enthusiasts assembled to assert their devotion to their country, would disperse at the voice of Prince Gortchakoff, threatening them with such terrors as they have almost ceased to care for, but which do not, for that reason, reflect the less discredit on those who have recourse to them. Morally speaking, they could not retire before the threats or even the entreaties of the Russian commander. They were there to bear testimony to their principles and their patriotism. Undoubtedly, they had the option of saving their lives, but they were in a state of great excitement, or rather "exaltation." They were full of the emotion caused by the recollection of the sufferings and degradation which they had undergone, during the last thirty years, and thought the moment had come for them to stand up, unarmed as they were, and without quoting treaties or referring to guarantees, simply tell their oppressors in the face of Europe, that their life was intolerable.

Here, again, as in the matter of mourning and of the national prayer, I do not believe that the Poles acted with any settled intention, and that they said to themselves, "We will stand up to be shot, so that all Europe may know that our country still lives, and that we are still ready to die for it," though that was really the effect produced by their attitude. They sacrificed themselves from a noble impulse, though with an intuitive perception, perhaps, that the sacrifice would not be in vain.

If the Russians did not commit a massacre, at least the Poles suffered martyrdom. That is to say, the Poles died to attest their devotion to a cause, while the Russians fired upon them not because they desired their death, but because, with their despotic habits, they knew no other mode of dispersing a crowd. I fully believe, from the account given to me by a person who was close to Prince Gortchakoff when he ordered the troops to act and for some time previously, and from another who saw him frequently afterwards and during his last illness, that he would most thankfully have escaped the bloody work in which he found himself engaged, and which he did not know how to avoid.

Why should anyone believe the contrary of a soldier like Prince Gortchakoff? Unfortunately, anyone who fills such a post as he occupied, may feel compelled at a given moment to act in a similar manner. It is no use protesting against "massacres" as isolated facts, when the Poles are subjected to a tyrannical and exasperating system calculated to keep them in a continual state of excitement, such as is sure, from time to time, to take the form of that "material disorder" which the Russian Government declares itself determined not to tolerate, but of which it takes care not to remove the natural causes.

I have tried, by comparing a great many different accounts, verbal, manuscript, and printed, of the horrible affair of the 8th of April, to arrive at something like the truth as to the magnitude of the crowd, and the possibility of dispersing it without employing force; the number of persons killed; the duration of the firing, &c. It seems difficult to decide with precision at what hour the Prussians arrived on the field of Waterloo, and it is known to be impossible, owing to the conflicting entries in the logs of the vessels engaged, to fix the time at which the battle of Trafalgar was commenced. Nor can I, with the many different versions of the Warsaw massacre given to me by eye-witnesses, and by persons possessing written narratives which eye-witnesses had furnished, tell, with accuracy, what took place on that dreadful day, from the firing of the first shot until the Sigismund Square had been cleared by the Russian soldiers of every living being and every dead body. To begin with, however, it is quite untrue that the troops rushed into the town from the citadel and the various camps, and, taking up their positions, began the attack without warning, and without the people being repeatedly summoned to retire.

In spite of a few assertions to the contrary, I am convinced, from abundant and most reliable testimony, that the crowd in the Sigismund Place, in front of the castle, was so numerous and compact, and the persons composing it, though perfectly peaceable, so excited, that threats alone, or the employment of force against a few, could never have broken it up. It might have been prevented from forming, or have been left unmolested until night, and the proper precautions taken against its re-assembling the next day, which was not, like the day of the "massacre," a holyday; but military pedantry and love of authority seem to have been shocked by the aspect of defiance presented by the Poles, and the "demoralizing" consequences which, if not resented in a severe manner, it might have on the troops. Indeed, it is said that the Poles laughed at the soldiers, spoke to them in a bantering tone, and threw cigars to them with a generosity which the Russian generals apparently thought could not fail to shake discipline. These contempt-breeding familiarities were checked by the wanton slaughter of some forty men.

Many Polish accounts say eighty and more; but a writer in *Fraser's Magazine*, who was well acquainted with the history of recent occurrences in Warsaw, and had certainly not the least inclination to under-estimate the ferocity of the Russians, puts down the number of killed at forty.* I forget whether the public official report stated that eight were killed or ten.

The Warsaw correspondent of the *Posen Journal* (*Djennik Poznanski*) declared that the firing lasted three hours. This appeared, to me, utterly incredible; for say that the soldiers were made drunk,

---

* See *Fraser's Magazine* for June, 1862.

as I believe was the case, even then such wholesale butchery, committed in cold blood, without any provocation or any resistance being offered, must have sobered and sickened the veriest savages. The killed and wounded, too, would have been counted not in tens or even hundreds, but in thousands. The time, however, occupied in clearing the Square and the adjoining streets (for when the crowd began to move, the troops, as could be seen from the bullet-marks on the walls, followed it, and still fired) may really have amounted to something like three hours; only the discharges of musketry were not kept up with anything like continuity. The first rank fired. The second rank advanced and collected the killed and wounded. Then there was a pause until, after a certain interval, the crowd, not dispersing, the order to fire again was given. Persons who witnessed this bloody scene declare that instead of producing terror and dismay, the volleys of the Russians at first only excited the indignation of the Poles, and roused in them a species of enthusiasm which may be called the enthusiasm of martyrdom.

Many went down on their knees, but not to their enemies. In some parts of the crowd the more timid were entreated in the name of their country to remain firm, and these appeals were not without effect. Afterwards, when numbers had been shot down and brute force was beginning to triumph, the most determined and desperate among the crowd still cried out that there must be no retreating, and some were seen to join hands so as to prevent those before them from falling back. The preconcerted plan for capturing the bodies shows plainly that the Russian commanders anticipated a resort to arms; but that Prince Gortchakoff courted the opportunity and deliberately allowed the crowd to assemble, that he might (according to an expression attributed to one of his officers) "quell the Polish fever by drawing a pint of Polish blood," I see no ground for believing. The reason assigned for the Russians having taken up the bodies at all is, that they feared they would be carried about the city to inflame the population, and that they would be photographed and the photographs circulated throughout Poland, as doubtless would have been the case had it been possible.

It may appear strange that people should be more affected by the counterfeit presentment of a mangled corpse than by the simple statement in writing that such a one has been murdered; but the Russians certainly dreaded the effect of the bodies of their victims being brought before the eyes of their indignant countrymen in all parts of the dismembered kingdom. Besides, what an answer the photographs of the forty dead men or more, with their wounds upon them, would have been to the lying report published in the official journal!

After what took place on the 8th of April at Warsaw, does it not seem a superfluous task to show that the Poles are cruelly oppressed? Can anything be said on the subject that has not been already proclaimed by their attitude that day under the fire of the Russian troops? If *that* will not convince, what can be expected from the most weighty documents, the most logical arguments on their behalf?

Until justice is done to Poland, we must expect such scenes to be of periodical occurrence. It was an old story fifty years ago, but it may be repeated now, that it is impossible to beat and bayonet the Poles into tranquillity; that permanent order cannot be established in Warsaw by sweeping the streets of the city with musketry, however often the process be repeated; and that there will be no end to insurrections in Poland until the causes of insurrection are removed. Four months before the signing of the Treaty of Vienna, Lord Castlereagh addressed a circular diplomatic note* to the plenipotentiaries of the various Powers, in favour of the re-establishment of Poland as an independent State, in which the following passage (translated) occurs:—

"Experience has proved that by seeking to destroy the usages and customs of the Poles, there can

---

* Kluber, ix. 40; D'Angeberg (*Pologne, Recueil des Traités, &c.*), 644.

be no hope of ensuring the happiness of this nation, and the peace of this important part of Europe. Attempts have been made in vain to make them forget, by means of institutions foreign to their habits and opinions, their existence as a people, and even their national language. These endeavours, pursued with too much perseverance, have been repeated often enough, and have been acknowledged to be unavailing. They have only served to create discontent and a painful feeling of national degradation, and will never have any other effect than that of exciting insurrections, and recalling past misfortunes."

CHAPTER VI.

MANIFESTATIONS AND SIGNS.

"What do the Poles want?" is a question often asked by persons of a practical turn of mind, and with great reason. What the political men of Russian Poland demand is simply that treaties shall be respected; that the "Kingdom" shall be governed in accordance with the provisions of the treaties of Vienna, which declared it "joined to Russia by its constitution;" that in the Polish provinces now incorporated with Russia the inhabitants shall be allowed to enjoy those national and representative institutions which were guaranteed to all the Polish subjects of the three partitioning Powers; and, finally, that the Russian Emperor shall profit by the right stipulated for and secured by Alexander I., of forming one constitutional kingdom out of the kingdom of 1815 and the Polish provinces before mentioned, which were seized at the three great partitions. In the meanwhile, those who make these demands pledged themselves, nearly two years ago, to accept peacefully and loyally any partial concessions that might be offered, "not as payment in full, but as instalments." What the political men of the country, however, think it worth while to aim at under present circumstances, and what the Poles as a nation desire and pray for with all their heart and soul, are two very different things. "Who runs may read;" and a man must be stone blind who can walk through the streets of Warsaw without perceiving that what the Poles aspire to as a people is nothing less than the complete unity and independence of Poland with its ancient frontiers.

In every print-shop, at every photographer's, you may see the portrait of Kosciuszko, but you will find nowhere the likeness of Alexander, Poland's first constitutional Russian king, except in the interior of the citadel. Among the portraits of the Polish kings exposed everywhere for sale I find, naturally enough, that the series closes with Stanislaus Augustus; and, since then, all Polish patriots say that their country has been in the tomb, though they do not despair of its resurrection.

No one, again, cares to record the features of any one of those very few distinguished Poles who have risen to eminence in the Russian service—such, for instance, as the much-detested Marquis

Wielopolski. On the other hand, the most popular photograph of the last year or two has been that of Hiszpanski, the boot-maker, one of whose titles to public sympathy is the fact of his having passed twelve years of his life in Siberia. Hiszpanski was in a very different position before he was exiled, but while there he became a boot-maker, and, having once adopted that honourable calling, did not choose to discontinue it when, profiting by the amnesty granted by the present Emperor, he returned to his native land. Beneath one of his portraits, published in Austrian Poland, I find an inscription to the effect that Hiszpanski is probably so much liked by the people of Warsaw because he recalls to them the memory of Kilinski, the cobbler-colonel, who behaved with so much heroism in the insurrection headed by Kosciuszko. Kilinski possessed great influence with the middle and working classes of Warsaw. He belonged to no party, but during the insurrection was made a member of the Provisional Government, and sat side by side with the greatest men in the country, by whom he was as much esteemed as by the people. At one time, Kilinski was summoned before Prince Repnin, the Russian Ambassador, who governed the city, and whose name was a name of terror. The Prince, finding that he remained perfectly calm, thought he could not be aware in whose presence he was standing.

After questioning him several times on the point, he suddenly threw open his cloak, and, exhibiting his breast covered with crosses and decorations, exclaimed, " Look, cobbler, and tremble ! "

"Your Highness," replied Kilinski, "I see a great many more stars every night in the heavens, and never tremble."

Before joining the insurrection, Kilinski took the Communion. He then wished his wife and family good-bye, and proceeded to his post. He distinguished himself greatly in the fight, and after the capture of Warsaw was condemned to perpetual imprisonment. He was thrown into the fortress at St. Petersburg, and, on the accession of the Emperor Paul, was liberated by that crazy but chivalrous monarch simultaneously with Kosciuszko.

The books in the booksellers' windows (to return to the Warsaw of the present day) are quite as suggestive in their way as the photographs and engravings. Lives of Poland's Casimirs, Sigismunds, and Sobieskis; the works of Miçkievicz and other illustrious and exiled poets; French political pamphlets, written from a Polish point of view against Prussia and Austria, in which the reader has only to change the name in order to imagine that he is reading an attack on a certain other Power; albums, illustrative of national manners and customs, from Wilna, Zitomir (Volhynia), Posen, and Cracow; indeed, literary productions of all kinds from all the chief cities in Poland, whether Russian, Prussian, or Austrian,—these are the wares offered for sale by the booksellers of Warsaw. The popularity of Adam Miçkievicz is immense, and the various editions of his poems are adorned with medallion portraits, full-length portraits, and portraits of the poet on his death-bed, in the national Polish costume. Some of Miçkievicz's works, in which Russia and the Russian Emperor are specially and directly assailed, are only sold (publicly sold, that is to say) in the mutilated state in which they have been left by the hand of the Imperial censor; but any Pole of moderate literary acquirements can repeat by heart the passages which the censor has marked out; and Miçkievicz, throughout his writings, prays for no constitutional Polish kingdom with the limits of 1815, but simply for the restoration of ancient Poland. By the side of the portraits and works of Miçkievicz, who died in Turkey during the Crimean war, while helping to form a Polish legion, may be seen those of Count Sigismund Krasinski, the anonymous poet of Poland,* and Lelewel,

* For an account of the life and writings of Count Krasinski the reader is referred to a very interesting article by a Polish critic in the *Révue des Deux Mondes* of Jan., 1862. Count Vincent Krasinski, father of the "Anonymous Poet," kept with the Russians in 1830. His son was cruelly taunted with this, left the country, and in publishing his poems, during this self-imposed exile, never signed one of them with his name.

the historian, both of whom died, the year before last, in Paris.

I have said that Miçkievicz * was from Volhynia; Krasinski was a member of one of the most illustrious families of Masovia, the ancient Polish province of which Warsaw is the capital; Lelewel was professor of history at the University of Wilna. Each belonged to a different part of Poland differently governed, but all died in exile, which was not the less forced because (except in the case of Lelewel, sentenced to death as a member of the Provisional Government of 1839) it was not the result of any formal decree; and all worked for one object, which was, not to procure reforms for this or that portion of dismembered Poland, but to obtain union and liberty for the whole of the ancient kingdom.

While I was in Warsaw, masses were said in several of the churches for Teleki and Cavour; but services for the repose of the soul of Lelewel were celebrated, not only in Warsaw, but in every impor-

---

* A French translation of all Miçkievicz's poetical works, and of his *Book of the Polish Pilgrims* (written in Biblical prose) has been published by his compatriot, M. C. Ostrowski (Paris: Firmin Didot and Co.). The *Book of the Polish Pilgrims* has also been translated by M. de Montalembert. Miçkievicz's *Course of Slavonian History and Literature*, delivered in French at the College of France, is published in five volumes, under the title of *Les Slaves* (Firmin Didot and Co., Paris).

city in Poland. The Cracow newspapers pro-
ted in Warsaw, but which still find their way
e, as correspondence also finds its way from War-
to Cracow, were full of articles on Lelewel's life
works. The Warsaw journals did not publish a
on the subject; indeed, they are condemned by
censorship to absolute silence on all matters
;ing to Poland ; but, at the funeral service per-
ıed in the church of St. Cross, portraits and
ıoirs of Lelewel, privately printed, were distri-
d plentifully among the congregation.*

he patriotic hymn used at this time to
;ung, every Sunday and fête-day, in all the
·ches. The Government continued to address
onstrances on the subject to the Archbishop,
the Archbishop continued to reply that he
d do nothing in the matter, and that if the
ıle were really breaking the law it was for the
;e and not the clergy to interfere. The hymn in
tion was, of course, not sung during service;

Lelewel's *History of Lithuania and Ruthenia* has been
tly translated into French (A. Franck, Paris and Leip-
ɔy M. Rykaczewski. Unfortunately, it is preceded by an
luction full of such rabid nonsense that, among other wild
·dities (especially on the subject of Napoleon III., the
·ator, &c.), England is accused of complicity in the par-
and oppression of Poland. Educated Poles ought, if
ɔle, to prevent those of their compatriots who have not
he same advantages as themselves from exposing their
ance in this lamentable manner.

but no sooner had the priest left the altar than the congregation began. An amateur went to the organ and played the accompaniment, and the vocal part was sung in unison by all present. Occasionally, those who appeared to be leading the chorus, or who sang with very remarkable energy, were crossed on the back with a piece of chalk by one of the omnipresent spies, and the persons so marked were arrested by the police directly they left the church. These arrests seemed to have no effect in diminishing the enthusiasm of the people, who, in singing the patriotic hymn, evidently felt that they were accomplishing a solemn religious duty.

A word about the hymn itself. This celebrated and now historical composition consists of old and new words to a tune which was first sung in 1815, on the occasion of Alexander the First's entry into Warsaw. I was about to write " triumphal entry," but the money which the municipality wished to devote to the erection of a triumphal arch was, by the Emperor's request, employed for the construction of a chapel. The clergy of Warsaw are said to have represented to the Lieutenant-governor that, in singing the hymn in question, the people were continuing to do only what had been freely permitted to them before. This, in a partial sense, was true, that is to say, true as regards the music, which is still sold publicly at the Warsaw music-

ıs; but every one knows that it is to the words
ʲovernment objects, nor can any reader, however
t his sympathy may be for the Poles, say that
objection is unnatural or unreasonable, after
ing the following, which is a literal translation
he verses, as printed on a very large scale for
ate circulation :—

1.

Lord, who, for so many centuries, didst sur-
.d Poland with the magnificence of power and
y; who didst cover her with the shield of Thy
ection when our armies overcame the enemy;
hy altar we raise our prayer: deign to restore
) Lord, our free country!

2.

Lord, who hast been touched by the woes of
injured land, and hast guided the martyrs
ur sacred cause; who hast granted to us, among
y other nations, the standard of courage, of
emished honour; at Thy altar we raise our
er: deign to restore us, O Lord, our free
ɩtry!

3.

hou whose eternally-just hand crushes the
ty pride of the powerful of the earth; in spite
he enemy vilely murdering and oppressing,
:he hope into every Polish breast! At Thy

altar we raise our prayer: deign to restore us, O Lord, our free country!

4.

May the Cross which has been insulted in the hands of Thy ministers give us constant strength under our sufferings! May it inspire us in the day of battle with faith that above us soars the spirit of the Redeemer! At Thy altar we raise our prayer: deign to restore us, O Lord, our free country!

5.

In the name of His commandments, we all unite as brothers. Hasten, O Lord, the moment of resurrection! Bless with liberty those who now mourn in slavery! At Thy altar we raise our prayer: deign to restore us, O Lord, our free country!

6.

Give back to our Poland her ancient splendour! Look upon our fields soaked with blood! When shall peace and happiness blossom among us? God of wrath, cease to punish us! At Thy altar, we raise our prayer: deign to restore us, O Lord, our free country!

CHAPTER VII.

THE MONUMENTS OF WARSAW.

It was not a time for ordinary sight-seeing when I was in Warsaw. Nevertheless, I bought a little guide-book in the French language, which gave me no information whatever, and another in Russian, which told of the vast improvements that had been effected in Warsaw under the Russian dominion. The Russian guide-book does not, of course, mention that in the suburb of Praga, facing Warsaw, on the left bank of the Vistula, 13,000 men, women, and children, were massacred by Souvaroff* during the great struggle for Polish

---

* Neither do Polish authors mention (what, if it does not justify, at least explains, the barbarous conduct of the Russian general)—that seven thousand Russian soldiers of Igelström's corps were sabred in Warsaw, six months' before, when the insurrection broke out. See note to article "Pologne" in the *Encyclopédie des Gens du Monde*. The article, like all those on Polish subjects in this encyclopædia, is by a Pole; the note is added by J. H. Schnitzler, one of the editors, a writer who has made a special study of Russian and Polish history. The *Encyclopédie des Gens du Monde* is remarkable for the number of excellent articles it contains on Russian and

independence which preceded the third partition, but it assures its readers that the Russian rule has been highly beneficial to the inhabitants of Warsaw, and that among other blessings the Russians have introduced gas and a system of water-works. So certain German publicists point with an air of triumph to the fact that Prussia has constructed a railroad from Posen to Breslau, and from Breslau half-way to Warsaw, and ask whether the partition has not at least been the means of civilizing the country? It is certain that the Poland of 1772 had neither railways nor a good water supply in the towns, nor even gas. For these benefits she has to thank the partitioning Powers. What, then, can be clearer than that the partition was a justifiable and even laudable action?

Polish subjects. Our own encyclopædias are comparatively deficient in this respect. In an ably-written article on "Russia" in the *Encyclopædia Britannica*, the partition of Poland, the most important event of modern times, next to the French Revolution, is not even mentioned. In the present sufferings of the Poles the writer of this article sees a proof of the Divine government of the world, though he humanely adds that their punishment ought not to be eternal! No Russian ever went so far as this. M. Prosper Mérimée hints (in his *Faux Démétrius*, I think) that the Poles should not complain too much of the cruelty of the Russians, because (says M. Mérimée) they were cruel themselves in former times; and, as a general rule, authors who have studied the history of Russia without examining that of Poland, surpass the Russians themselves in their enmity to the Poles. Probably the converse of this proposition is also true.

One thing which is not quite so clear to me as that Poland had no gas in the year 1772, is the ancient Polish mode of building in cities as described in the Warsaw guide-book* already referred to. Such, this work informs us, was the licentious wilfulness of the Polish nobility that, in order to prove that they were free, they would often amuse themselves by erecting houses in the very centre of a public thoroughfare. Fancy a freeman of the City of London taking it into his head to build a house across Ludgate Hill, or a peer of the realm throwing a similar permanent barricade across Piccadilly! Those were sad days, those days of Polish liberty! Happily, and thanks to the Russians, the obstacles which the Polish nobles raised in the streets of Warsaw (but which, somehow or other, escaped the notice of travellers who visited the Polish capital towards the end of the eighteenth century) have now entirely disappeared. Was it the bombardment of Souvaroff in 1795, or of Paskievitch in 1831, that destroyed them?

There were no obstacles in the streets and squares of Warsaw in 1861, except a few infantry tents here, a few pieces of artillery there, and so on.

I had often heard the gardens of Warsaw praised for their beauty and extent; but what I

---

* *Opisanie Varshavi.* Istomin, Warsaw.

chiefly remember of them is that the Saxony Gardens were constantly being closed as the scene of "manifestations;" that in the Krasinski Gardens troops were encamped; that in the gardens of the castle a small army was quartered, and that beneath the soldiers' feet rested the bodies of those who had fallen in the massacre of April; finally, that in the gardens of the Belvedere stood the palace in which Prince Gortchakoff lay dead.

Travellers used formerly to visit the castle, not merely for the interest it offered as an ancient royal residence, but also for the sake of its decorations and its gallery of pictures, including a magnificent series of portraits of the Polish kings. But how could anyone visit the castle when it was crammed full of soldiers, who were to be seen at every window, three and four together; who filled the passages and court-yards below; who were even encamped before and behind the castle, around which they swarmed like bees? In these cool shady gardens, down by the Vistula, the soldiers used to smoke, sing, dance, and disport themselves generally as if they were engaged on no business more serious than that of a picnic. Seen from the bridge over the river, or from the high ground on which the castle stands, this camp, with the white tents gleaming through the green trees, presented an outward aspect which was far indeed from having anything of the horrible in it, though it was from here, from the cavalry barracks which line the narrow road separating the gardens from the castle-yard, that the troops went forth who were foremost in the work of the 8th of April.

The castle is not the heart of Warsaw, but it is the head and front as seen from the suburb of Praga on the other side of the Vistula, which is here broad, shallow, ever-changing in its sandy course, and as divided as Poland herself. It is only after the thaw, when rivers of melted snow come pouring down from the Carpathians, and after the autumn rains, that the Vistula at Warsaw would be navigable for large vessels, if there were any large vessels to navigate it. A Company, however, for introducing steamers on the Vistula, has recently been started by Count Andrew Zamoyski, who, like many other Poles in a high position, is determined, even if he is unable to benefit his country politically, to do, at least, what he can for it by promoting its commerce and agriculture, and by founding industrial enterprises of all kinds. Before this company was established, the only craft seen on the Vistula consisted of boats of the most primitive shape—simply trunks of trees scooped out and pointed at the ends—and wooden rafts of various forms and dimensions. The more important of these rafts are furnished with bulwarks and with little wooden cabins or huts, in which the raftsmen prepare their meals and take their rest. They are usually laden with wheat, which they convey from Cracow, the centre of a great corn-growing country, down the Vistula, to Dantzic. The raftsmen use no oars. They simply sail down the stream with the current, and have nothing to do but to keep the raft in position and at a safe distance from the banks. This they effect by means of a long pole, which they use with great skill, and which stands them in lieu of oars, rudder, and sometimes even of anchor. They are said to eat scarcely anything during the voyage, and you may see them arrive at Dantzic "lean, and long, and brown," like ancient mariners as they are. At Dantzic they deliver up their corn and their raft, which is broken up and sold as firewood, and receive their wage. Then for a few days they lead the life popularly attributed to "fighting cocks," and smoke the Havannah cigar and drink the Dantzic gold-water. Another day and the dream is past, and the river pilgrim starts, a-foot and almost penniless, to reach Cracow by land. Under new arrangements they have only to walk as far as Warsaw. There, at times, you may see them waiting by scores for the unparliamentary train—or whatever the cheap train is called—that runs from the most unparliamentary city in the world to Cracow.

By water as by land, on the Vistula as in

POLISH MOUNTAINEERS

Cracow, Warsaw, and Posen, the Poles are doomed to suffer from the injustice and faithlessness of the partitioning Powers. In the towns they are persecuted in a variety of ways; on the river they are simply robbed. The treaty of Vienna provides that there shall be perfect freedom of commerce between all the parts of the ancient kingdom, and perfect freedom of navigation in the whole length of the Vistula. But the raft which starts from Cracow, after paying dues to the Austrian Government, is stopped when it enters the Russian part of the river and forced to make another payment; and toll is again levied upon it when it enters Prussian water at Thorn. The Prussians seek to excuse themselves on the strange plea that this disgraceful system was commenced by Russia. Whoever began it, it is quite certain that all the three partitioning Powers continue it.

But to return to the castle, which stands high on the Vistula's right bank, and commands, at the back, a view of Souvaroff's massacring-ground, on the Praga side of the river, and, in front, overlooks the fatal square in which the slaughter of the 8th of April took place. In the middle of the square stands the column erected in honour of Sigismund III. by his son, Ladislas IV. The monument bears an inscription, setting forth that in Sigismund's reign, Moscow was taken by the Poles, and Prince Ladislas proclaimed King of

Muscovy. It reminds one that Philaret, the father of the first of the Romanoffs, was carried a prisoner to Poland, and kept in confinement there nine years, for refusing to crown this same Ladislas, and that the most important monument in Moscow is a group in the square opposite the Kremlin, which celebrates the declaration of Russian independence, and the liberation of the Russian capital from its Polish invaders. The same inscription, dictated by Ladislas IV., goes on to glorify his father for having "recaptured" Smolensk, which, however, was "recaptured" again by the Russians (and this time kept), within ten years of the erection of the Sigismund column. The Poles, in this unhappy memento of their past but not forgotten successes over the Russians, narrate the very exploits in which the Russian historians ground their justification of Peter's and Catherine's policy towards Poland. Driven from Moscow, the Poles were still able to hold Smolensk, which was regarded as the key to Moscow. Having regained possession of Smolensk (say the Russians), it was necessary, in order to secure it from future attacks, that Russia, which has no natural boundaries on the west, should advance her frontier as far as possible in the direction of the Polish capital. What a commentary on the inscription of the Sigismund monument, was the encampment of Russian soldiers, at the base of the column, and at twenty yards' distance the castle, built by Sigismund himself, now occupied by a Russian viceroy!

There are two other monuments in Warsaw, which, as bringing back the memory of happier days, must be "a sorrow's crown of sorrow" to the Poles. One is the statue of John Sobieski, who, not a century before the partition, saved Vienna for the House of Austria; the other, that of Copernicus,* who, since Thorn, where he long resided, became Prussian, has been claimed as a compatriot by the Germans, though Humboldt admits that he was a Pole. Copernicus was descended from a Galician family, and studied at the University of Cracow, and wrote "Polonus" after his name, long before Prussia had any existence, except as a fief of the Polish crown.

But if there are public memorials in Warsaw which must sadden the Poles, there are others which can only have the effect of irritating them. There, for instance, is the monument before mentioned in the Saxon Square, the mere sight of which is enough to convince any one that Russia governs Poland as a conquered country, and, apparently, with a Tartar-like conviction that "the conquered can never become the friends of

* This admirable statue was executed and presented to Poland by Thorwaldsen, together with an equestrian statue of Poniatowski. The Emperor Nicholas would not allow the

the conquerors." Perhaps, on this point, as between the Poles and herself, she is not far wrong; but lest there should be any uncertainty about the matter, she seems to have taken care to adopt all possible means of humiliating them, and reminding them, from day to day, of their helpless position. The cruelties of Siberian exile have often been dwelt upon; but it has not been sufficiently noticed, if it has been noticed at all, that Warsaw itself is full of signs of the vengeful spirit of Russia against Poland. One would have thought that, the rebellion suppressed, and its chiefs in forced or voluntary exile, the Emperor's first object, from policy if not from humanity, would have been to conciliate those of his Polish subjects who remained. At least, it might have been expected that, after punishing so many with remorseless severity, he would have refrained from irritating and insulting the rest, so as to take away all possibility of their ever becoming—I will not say loyal, but even tolerably obedient and peaceful, subjects. A few walks through the streets and about the suburbs of Warsaw would suffice to convince anyone of the fallacy of such a supposition. In the very heart of the Polish capital, in the centre of the principal square, stands

latter to be kept in Warsaw; and I am assured that it is now in a Polish provincial town (Modlin, I believe), where it passes officially as a statue of St. George.

the hideous bronze monument which commemorates the fidelity of Polish generals, who endeavoured to prevent their soldiers joining the insurrection of the 29th of November, 1830, and were in consequence torn from their horses and massacred. That, at least, is what the monument professes to commemorate, but it will strike everyone who sees it for the first or for the fiftieth time, as a record of the defeat and humiliation of the Polish nation. Say what we will of the last struggle of the Poles for independence; call it a war, or regard it only as an insurrection, and allow that the insurgents, from beginning to end, were in the wrong; even then it is cruel, and, what in the eyes of some statesmen will appear worse, impolitic, to taunt them publicly and constantly in perennial bronze with their subjection. If there is to be any conciliation at all, it is for the stronger party to begin. Such a monument as that of the Saxony Place might be appreciated at Moscow: it is thrown away on the people of Warsaw, who do not perceive the virtue of those whose virtues it celebrates, and who look upon the whole affair as an insulting reminder of their servitude. Curiously enough, during the greater part of the last three years, it has been found necessary to surround this testimonial to Polish loyalty with an encampment of Russian soldiers.

Then there is the citadel, erected, like everything else that is offensive in Warsaw, by the Emperor Nicholas. The reader will remember that within this fortress, built for no other purpose than that of intimidating, and, if necessary, destroying, Warsaw, the sarcastic founder has raised a statue to the Emperor Alexander I., "the Benefactor of the Poles."

Again, all the plains in which the great battles of 1831 were decided, whether won by the Russians or not, are marked by trophies. Of course, then, there is a conspicuous monument on the field of Wola; fought, by the way, on the very ground where formerly the Polish kings were elected, and which was covered, when I saw it, with remarkably fine corn. A victory gained by a Government over its own insurgent subjects! To be sure, the Poles the year before last kept the anniversary of the battle of Grochow; but the Russians would have an unquestionable right—indeed, it would be their bounden duty—to tolerate no demonstrations on that day, if they would themselves begin by knocking down the Wola column.

But worse by far than the monument which stands in the Wola plain, is the little chapel in the Wola cemetery, which in its present condition is without doubt the most atrocious memorial of modern times. At the close of the action which determined the fate of Warsaw, the feeble garrison who defended the village of Wola, attacked by two Russian corps in front and in flank, concentrated itself in the church, where the commandant, Sowinski, made his troops swear on the crucifix not to surrender. After a heavy and crushing cannonade from two points, the church or chapel was stormed, the Poles who occupied it were slain, and Sowinski himself fell, covered with wounds, at the foot of the altar. One would think that the Russians would have been glad to forget this little triumph of theirs as soon as possible —that they would have been only too thankful if the Poles could have remembered the heroism of Sowinski and his troops, without cursing the memory of their destroyers. But, no: the Wola church is maintained, just as appointed conservators keep up celebrated ruins, as nearly as possible in the state in which it was the day after Sowinski and his immortal garrison were put to the sword. I could not have believed this if I had not seen the building with my own eyes, and counted the sixty odd cannon balls which stick fast in its desecrated walls. The savage memento seemed to have been recently restored; the walls had been painted yellow, which the conservators are perhaps not aware was the colour given in the Middle Ages to buildings that were under a curse. The cannon balls had received a coating of black, and are thus brought into fine relief.

Let me give one final proof that Russia openly repudiates all obligations to govern Poland otherwise than according to her own supreme will. In the Kremlin at Moscow, among other curiosities and antiquities, and by the side of such warlike spoils as the crowns of Kazan and Astrakhan, may be seen a box containing the roll of parchment which was the constitution of Poland. It is surrounded with other trophies taken by the army of the Emperor Nicholas from his own subjects, whom he seems to be delighted to look upon as "the enemy"; and it is to be presumed that this constitution will not be given back until the thrones of the Tartar Princes are restored. If Russia had ever held out the slightest hope of its re-establishment, the case would be different; but she has proclaimed candidly—or cynically, if you will—in her official histories, in her official journals (I can point to the exact number of the *Northern Bee* in which the assertion is made), that she holds Poland simply by right of conquest. It is on this plea that, with a barbarism worthy of the French under Napoleon, she has plundered the libraries and museums of Warsaw to enrich those of St. Petersburg; and she has done this in the face of all Europe, and the ukase has even been published in which the Emperor Nicholas, with an air of wonderful magnanimity, "deigns to order" that a portion of the books and of the numismatic collection be allowed to remain in the Polish capital. Is it not, then, mere waste of time to talk to Russia about the treaties of 1815, and about the Polish constitution therein stipulated? For all this, in the opinion of Russia, is ancient history; we might as well speak to her about the treaties signed between Peter the Great's father and John Sobieski.

CHAPTER VIII.

ON THE RUSSIFICATION OF POLAND.

THE only consolation freely allowed to the Russian Poles is to abuse the Government of the Germans, the German Poles being, of course, equally at liberty to condemn the tyranny of Russia. If the papers of Posen and Lemberg are said by Russia to have published greatly-exaggerated accounts of the ferocity of the Russian soldiers in the Kingdom, Prussia will not admit the truth of the accusations contained in the pamphlets directed against her mode of governing her Polish provinces which are sold everywhere in Lemberg and Warsaw; and we may be sure that Austria is, in her turn, indignant at being held up to odium, in Prussia and Russia, as a Power which oppresses all the nationalities subject to her sway.

Each of the three seems willing to admit that the two others are the worst possible Governments in the world, and each two have that opinion of the remaining one. The general inference to be drawn from this striking similarity of views, is sufficiently obvious. It is indeed certain, that Russia, Austria, and Prussia, separately, and in the case of Cracow collectively, have broken every article relating to Poland in the treaty, or rather treaties of Vienna; but they have not broken them all in the same manner, and it will be interesting to notice the effect of the various violations in the Kingdom, in Galicia, in Posen, and in the provinces incorporated with the Russian Empire.

Russia, to do her a certain sort of justice, has said formally in her authorized histories, and virtually in her diplomatic despatches, that it no longer enters into her plans to conform to the stipulations of the treaties of 1815, in respect to Poland. M. Oustrialoff, the official Russian historian, in the tenth edition of his *History of Russia* (in which he seeks to include Lithuania), for the use of schools in Russia and Poland, after stating that at the general peace "the Duchy of Warsaw was united to the Empire under the title of the Kingdom of Poland as a reward to Russia for her sacrifices," tells us, in his account of the insurrection of 1830, that "such a shameful forgetfulness of the most holy duties having astounded the whole of Russia, the Emperor comforted all minds by informing his faithful subjects that he would instantaneously restore to Russia the country which had been torn away from her by the insurgents, and that he would re-establish it on sound foundations, in accordance with the requirements, and so as to insure the peace, of the entire Empire."

The same cynical or facetious writer, in relating the history of the third partition, has informed his readers that "the inhabitants of all the parts given up to Russia had equal rights and privileges granted them with the other subjects of the Empire;" but even these wonderful advantages, conceded to the Poles in 1795, are denied to them in the present day. Thus, in Russia, in spite of the censorship, the press is allowed a certain amount of freedom, whereas in Poland to print any species of comment on home news is positively forbidden.

The newspapers of Warsaw, such as they are, are thoroughly Polish. To publish a Russian journal in the Polish language at Warsaw, would be, if not an impossibility, at least an absurdity. It would not find a reader. But, finding nothing to praise, and not being allowed to blame, the Warsaw journals have really nothing to say. Even the irony which Russian writers practise with so much skill, is denied to the Poles, whose censors will stand no joking of any kind. Nor indeed, is the favourite literary weapon of the "Muscovites" much in favour with them. The tyranny which has made the Russians ironical, has made the Poles mystical.

Some of the Warsaw newspapers, however, have their recognized devices for protesting in print against the existing state of things in Poland. Thus, they never mention Russia by name, but always speak of her as "a certain Power," and it was once the rule at all Polish printing offices, until the device was noticed and put a stop to, to print the PAST and the FUTURE in capital letters, and the PRESENT in the smallest possible type.

Again, in Russia there are several universities, richly endowed and accessible to all classes, at which the historical, linguistic, and scientific chairs have of late years been occupied by the most learned and able men in the country, while in Poland there are no general educational establishments above the rank of gymnasiums, with a course of study inferior to that of our grammar-schools. Except that the Polish nobility are not obliged, like that of Russia, to enter the State service under pain of losing their privileges if two succeeding generations in the same family fail in that respect,—with this one exception the Poles have no political or other advantage over the Russians, and that they labour under more than one disadvantage, as compared with the other subjects of the Empire, I think I have already proved.

It must not be supposed, however, that the Poles are excluded from State employment in Russia. Far from that; they are encouraged to take it, and, if they do so, are sure of speedy advancement, owing, it may be, to their superior qualifications, though the Russians maintain that the Government favours them from motives of policy. Without questioning the remarkable abilities of the Poles, I think it is quite certain that they would not meet with preferment in the service, unless the Government intended they should do so; but the instances are very rare indeed in which Poles of independent positions enter it, and the manner in which the Marquis Wielopolski is spoken of for accepting office and for sending his sons into the army is not calculated to induce other Polish noblemen to follow his example. A member of one of the great families of Poland cannot serve the Russian Government without endangering (at the present moment, without certainly losing) his good name as a patriot, and accordingly nearly all the important official posts in the Kingdom of Poland have to be filled by Russians. The men of influential names cannot recognize an authority of which they deny the validity, but it is unreasonable to complain afterwards that all the best places in Poland are given to their oppressors. A large party in Poland maintained two years ago that it was the duty of all good Poles to refuse to serve on the new Council of State. To this it was wisely objected that if the Poles did not respond to the Emperor's nomination, he would have no alternative but to appoint Russians, unless, indeed, he decided not to form the Council at all, justifying such a course by the unwillingness of the Poles to assist him in taking the first step towards a possible system of elective representation. Then the inhabitants of the Kingdom would once more have had no legal ground on which to make known their wishes and aspirations, and would again have been reduced to those lamentable street demonstrations which can end in nothing but suppression, with or without "massacre," and which have this further disadvantage—that no one knows who the demonstrants really are. This bad advice, however, was not followed, and the Poles proved that they were quite ready, as a nation, to accept any reforms, however slight, that the Government might choose to offer them.

It was said afterwards that the Polish members of the Council ought to resign their seats as soon as two all-important questions about to be submitted to them had been decided. Such conduct would have been puerile, for do not questions of the highest importance arise from day to day? However this may be, the Council, if it is ever completed (which it cannot be until after the municipal elections have again taken place), will, probably, have to reconsider the unsatisfactory solution arrived at in the affair of the peasants and their liberation from the *corvée*: the project for reforming the system of public instruction, which was to have been submitted to them, has already been introduced. I may again remind the reader that the *corvée*, strictly speaking, has long ceased to exist in Poland; inasmuch as the labour performed by the peasants on the estates of the nobles has, since 1807, been the result of a free contract; but the Government had decided that this system should cease after the 1st of October, 1861, and that the peasants should, from that date, pay in money instead of work. This has been found in many places impracticable, inasmuch as the Polish peasant is not in the habit of saving money, and, in fact, has none to save. He has a couple of strong arms, which he cannot alienate, but no florins.

The reform of the educational system was far from presenting the same difficulties as the peasant question; and from what I have said about the gymnasiums, it will be understood that it was of the utmost importance that the young men of Poland should be provided with some superior means of instruction.

I believe the schools of medicine and of design were never suppressed, but it is difficult to understand how such subjects as history, literature, and political geography can be taught anywhere in Poland so ingeniously and so disingenuously as not to fortify and increase the hatred of the Polish youth for the Russians. A Polish professor once told me that he had seen a whole class throw their books at the feet of a lecturer who had ventured to praise the enterprise of the Russian Government in a matter totally unconnected with the affairs of Poland. Still, the present Emperor is not inclined to neglect, or rather to check, education in the Kingdom after the manner of his predecessor. And we must not forget that since the arrival of the Grand Duke Constantine in Warsaw, the university, broken up by the Emperor Nicholas after the insurrection of 1830, has been re-established, and the number of gymnasiums in the kingdom increased from five to thirteen.

This educational reform, so far as it goes, is certainly creditable to Alexander II., who, at least, has conceded to the Poles some slight undeniable rights which would none the less have been strictly denied to them by Nicholas. It must be remembered that the "Organic Statute," published by the late Emperor, was never acted upon, so that to compare its provisions, as is sometimes done, with those of the statute issued in good faith by the present Emperor, and actually put in force, is equivalent to an attempt to establish a proportion between zero and a positive quantity. Prior to the announcement of the recent reforms, Alexander II. had already re-established Polish as the public language of the country, and this at once made the inhabitants of the Kingdom more Polish, and, to a certain extent, more dependent upon one another than the Poles of Galicia and Posen, who are sadly worried by being constantly brought into contact with German officials and pedagogues, or, in other words, by persistent though unavailing attempts to Germanize them. From 1831 until the accession of the present Emperor, if the Polish tongue was not actually proscribed in the kingdom of Poland, its use was as much as possible discountenanced, and the Government actually attempted to make Russian the medium of communication in the public offices and schools. Thus, a Polish child had not only to learn history and geography according to Russian views (which is still his fate at the present moment), but had to learn them in the Russian language; an infinitely greater difficulty, to say nothing of the humiliation, than Panslavonian theorists are disposed to admit. Let me exemplify the action of this cruel tyranny:—A boy, then, was made to repeat, *secundum* Oustralioff, that the happiness of the Poles prior to the insurrection of 1830 was "unexampled in their previous history," with sneers at the "light-headed gentlemen" (including, perhaps, the pupil's father, working, chained to a barrow, in the mines of Siberia) "who remembered with delight and pride the golden time of the reign of the magnates," and had, moreover, to utter this insulting nonsense in the hated language of his self-styled benefactors.

It would have been, it would be now, more decent and humane to imitate the Prussians, and make the history of Poland a forbidden subject in Polish schools.

What, it may be asked, has been the effect of the Russian system in Poland? Simply that, after a quarter of a century's attempted "Russianizing," Warsaw at the present moment is scarcely more Russian, and in many respects less so than Dresden or Berlin. The boys and girls who were taught everything in Russian at school, have made a point of forgetting that language now, and either cannot, or, at all events, will not, speak a word of it. Even the Russian officers who have been a long time in Warsaw seem to feel that it is uncivil to speak Russian before Poles; and I have seen Russian ladies travelling on a Polish railway who were really afraid to speak their own language until all the Poles had left the carriage. And like all hatreds after a certain point, that of the Poles for the Russians, however natural, has now become so unreasonable and blind, that they speak of the Russians of the present day, who are fairly taking their position in literature, art, and science with the English, French, and Germans, as if they were still the "Muscovites" of the seventeenth century. When a writer of such eminence as M. Prosper Mérimée translates Poushkin and

Gogol; when M. Louis Viardot, M. Xavier Marmier, and half-a-dozen other French writers less widely known, follow in the same path, so that the names of Russian authors now appear in every bookseller's list in France (a country of which I here speak in particular, because it is ranked far above all others by the Poles); when Russian operas are announced in London, and Russian concerts are given at which compositions of the most original and varied kind are applauded by our best critics and connoisseurs—then it seems to me that it is rather late in the day to describe the Russians as they had ceased to be long before the blunders and calumnies of M. de Custine were printed. The Russians have produced many fine works, of which something is known everywhere but in Poland; and they read books of all kinds, and of every nation, and especially those which every one reads in England. I will not say that a nation is necessarily civilized because it enjoys the literature of the *Cornhill Magazine*, but managing to procure in Warsaw two recent numbers of two Russian reviews, I found that one, the *Contemporary*, was publishing *Framley Parsonage*, and the other, the *Messenger*, the *Adventures of Philip;* upon which it occurred to me, that the Russian general reader, taking pleasure in the same books as the English general reader,* must to a great extent possess the same literary tastes, and therefore cannot be set down (at least not by us) as a barbarian. "We know nothing of their literary productions and tastes, and we will not hear a note of their music," is what a Pole would naturally reply; "all we know is, that they tried to force their language down our throats, and that if we protest against their tyranny they shoot us like dogs." In fact, the Russians living quietly among themselves at St. Petersburg and Moscow, and the Russians armed and threatening among the Poles, are quite different people; and the Poles, seeing only the worst side of them, so thoroughly detest them, and so seek to ignore them, that no bookseller in Warsaw will have a Russian book in his shop, nor even a music-seller a piece of Russian music.

The result of this heartfelt antipathy to Russia is in one respect almost comic. I have said that Russian books are banished from the booksellers' shops in Warsaw: indeed, works in the Russian language which may be purchased at the principal foreign publishers of Paris and London, are not to

* Not only are all our best novels, but all our best and latest historical and philosophical works, are read in Russia, in the original and in translations. The works of Macaulay, Grote, Motley, Buckle, and Mill, are all translated into Russian.

be heard of at any of the libraries in the capital of Russian Poland. To supply this want, inasmuch as there are plenty of Russian officers in Warsaw—many of them with their families, who are not averse to reading—the grocers have gone into the book trade. The fact has a burlesque aspect, but it is a fact nevertheless. M. Prudhomme would, doubtless, not believe it, but the *épicier* has turned to literature; and in Warsaw, if you want to read Russian, you must get your books, your newspapers, or your reviews, where you buy your tea and sugar. These very original tradesmen also sell Russian music, Russian caviar (not much relished by the Poles), Russian tea-urns, portraits of the late Prince Gortchakoff, and innumerable representations of the members of the Imperial family. Russian books, pictures, and music, might be advertised in the Polish newspapers as " sold in Warsaw by all respectable tea-dealers." In the interior of one of these literary grocers' you may fancy yourself in Russia; but there are not more than three or four of them in all Warsaw, and as soon as you have left the shop you might, for any signs of Russian *civilization* that meet your eye, be two thousand miles from Moscow. Worse than that, you see the Russian soldiers at the corner of every street, and, perhaps, the Lieutenant-Governor's escort of Circassians whipping their way along the great thoroughfare which leads to the castle, and the Lieutenant-Governor himself forcing little schoolboys to salute him, under pain of being arrested and imprisoned. I remember one very curious instance of a number of pupils of the Government gymnasium incurring, in this manner, the wrath of the Emperor's representative. General Suchozanet, indignant at not being saluted, ordered one of his escort to "take those boys' caps off;" upon which the literal-minded Circassian, to the delight of the Warsaw public, not only removed the caps of the offending students, but brought them back, as if they were the heads of his enemies, and threw them into the carriage at the feet of his lord and master the Imaum of Poland.

CHAPTER IX.

ON DRESS AND OTHER DISTINCTIONS IN POLAND.

I SUPPOSE it is simply because the Poles are forbidden to be Poles, that they love to show themselves in their national dress. Otherwise, they surely would not care to walk about the streets in braided military coats, like the undress uniforms of our infantry officers, lancer-like Kosciuszko caps, and long black boots stitched with white, to be worn over the trousers. I believe, after all, that the costume which possesses in so remarkable a degree the property of irritating Russian generals, governors of towns, and officials of all kinds, is not historical, but a compromise, adopted for the sake of convenience, between the ancient Polish dress and the modern dress of ordinary European life. Except that the trousers do not fit tight to the legs, and with some slight difference as to the braiding of the coat, the Polish costume of the present day is nearly identical with the Hungarian, from which, apparently, it has been borrowed. At least, this style of attire is now worn

PEASANTS OF MAZOVIA.

in Hungary by all classes, except workmen and peasants, whose many-coloured habiliments are of a far more splendid character.

Even in the thoroughly Polish city of Cracow, where there is no prohibition against the national dress, it is a rare thing to see a complete and authentic Polish suit. I remember one old Pole there, however, who, but for the reality of his look, the calm dignity of his manner, and the intimate relations evidently existing between himself and his clothes, might have been taken for a mazurka-dancing Pole out of some Polish ballet, produced with unusual magnificence, and with scrupulous accuracy in the costume department. He was old enough to have seen the Constitution of the 3rd of May adopted, supposing that his father had carried him to the assembly, as Suchorzewski did his son, that he might swear a theatrical oath to slay him on the spot if the wise measure which abolished the *veto*, and made the crown hereditary, became law. The first time I saw this ancient Pole, I found myself looking involuntarily to see whether he still wore the sabre which was formerly the distinguishing sign of a Polish gentleman. No, he had abandoned *that;* but he kept to the silken semi-oriental robe, and to the close-fitting tunic worn beneath, and the silver ornamented girdle, and the long black boots of soft shiny leather, and on great days (such, for instance, as the anniversary of the union of Poland with Lithuania) actually appeared in a species of hussar cap, and made a point, according to the ancient custom, of wearing in his dress the colours of his coat of arms.

The ancient and veritable Polish costume is always assumed by the members of the Galician diet on official occasions, but in private life they attire themselves like gentlemen in other parts of Europe, and wear what the Russian Government in Poland calls "European cylinders" on their heads. I mention this seemingly unimportant point (but which is really worth observing) because the enemies of Poland are very fond of repeating that the Polish nobility alone care for the independence of their native land, and that they do so only because they desire the restoration of certain privileges. A stranger arriving in Cracow, might, by simply making use of his eyes, convince himself in a few hours of the utter groundlessness of such a statement, for he would see all the shopkeepers and shopmen, and many of the workmen, wearing the Polish dress, the symbol of Polish nationality, and the nobility, for the most part, wearing plain clothes. The upper classes in Poland, as in most countries, have but little inclination for "demonstrations." That they are always ready to risk everything for their country—their property, their liberty, their lives—they have sufficiently proved;

but I believe that at present in all parts of Poland they wish to keep strictly on legal ground, and to advance little by little, their immediate aim everywhere being to obtain local self-government and the free use of the national language. Wherever any, even the slightest, opportunity exists of doing political work by authorized means, even if it be only the expression of an opinion or a desire, they are prepared to take advantage of it; but, as a rule, they give no encouragement to scenes and tumults in the streets, and instances might be mentioned in which the most popular and influential men in Poland have exerted themselves, with and without success, to prevent public manifestations of feeling. I remember, on one occasion, when Count Andrew Zamoyski was expected in Cracow to be present at the marriage of one of the members of his family, a procession being arranged to meet him, in which many thousands would have taken part. This would have been the Count's first appearance in Cracow since the dissolution of the Agricultural Society and the firing on the people at Warsaw; but hearing what a "demonstration" was to be made in his honour, and fearing that it might lead to a collision with the Austrian troops, he simply stayed away, and by doing so deprived himself of the gratification of being present at his daughter's marriage.

It is difficult to ascertain the feeling of the

Polish peasantry, and the proprietors have proved more than once that even they know very little about it. It seems improbable that, as a class, they should care enough about an independent Poland whose former existence many of them must have forgotten, to be willing to incur any great risk for its sake. They fear the Government officials, however much they may dislike them, and have long ceased to look upon the proprietor as the representative of any real power. It seemed to me, from what proprietors and others told me in various parts of Poland, that the peasants were on perfectly good terms with the proprietors in Posen, on improving terms with them in Galicia, and not on absolutely bad terms in the Kingdom, where, however, the system of taskwork is only now being abolished. In the Russian provinces, where, until the issue of the recent edict of emancipation, serfdom had been maintained as it existed before the partitions, I should have thought it unlikely that the peasants would show any sort of sympathy for a cause which the officials always represent to them as exclusively that of their masters, had I not found the Government threatening and persecuting the Lithuanian peasants for wearing Polish emblems. Nor can it be doubted that the more the Russian Government punishes the Lithuanian and Ruthenian peasants for the crime of being Poles, the more Polish they will become. If they could understand how many years their emancipation had been delayed by the partitions, that all they gained by being annexed to Russia was liability to military service and subjection to the rapacity of Government functionaries, and that when the prospect of emancipation did, at last, dawn upon them, that the proprietors of Lithuania were the first to welcome it—in that case, how thoroughly Polish they would be already!

In the towns, however, it is evident that all the Poles, from the highest to the lowest, are full of patriotism; and the most demonstrative in that respect are certainly not the upper classes. The partitioners, of course, have an answer to this.

"These shopkeepers and workmen," they say, "who make such a fuss about an independent Poland, are many of them, petty noblemen, whose fathers possessed privileges which the sons would like to see restored."

So inconceivable is patriotism to the advocates of the partitioners, that they have to imagine such explanations as the above in order to account for it! Either they write what they know to be false, or they are really unable to understand how carpenters and cobblers can possibly suffer from their country being subjected to a foreign Power. They are well aware that no one in Poland, for the last half-century at least, has had any thought of putting forward nobility of birth as a qualification for the exercise of electoral privileges—the only one of the ancient privileges of nobility that could now be of the slightest advantage to a poor man. They know that all such ideas have disappeared in Poland; that they have been abandoned, practically as well as theoretically. Under the Constitution of 1815, which was fairly and frankly accepted by the Poles, and which worked as long as it was allowed to work, the elections to the Lower House took place on the basis of a property qualification. At the Agricultural Association of the Kingdom of Poland, founded by the Poles themselves, it was not necessary to be a noble in order to become a member. All that was requisite was to be a landholder and to pay a subscription of 150 Polish florins (£3 15s.) a-year; and peasant-proprietors who fulfilled these conditions were accepted, and took their seats in the assembly. Even as regards ancient Poland, a great many mistakes and mis-statements are made, as to the "aristocratic" form of the Government. This arises from a confusion of terms. A "noble" in ancient Poland, as in Hungary, was simply a freeman. "Nobility" does not necessarily mean aristocracy any more than it does peerage. There existed, no doubt, in ancient Poland what, speaking loosely, may be called an "aristocratic" class, and this class, by obtaining fresh concessions from the Crown at each successive election, at last got all political power into its hands; but it had such an extensive base that it has justly been described as an "aristocratic democracy." All freeholders and descendants of freeholders, without limitation, were nobles; and all nobles took part in elections.

In England the nobility are at the head of the aristocracy. In Poland it is the aristocracy which is at the head of the nobility,* and it forms only a very small portion of it, even as the nobility is constituted now, that is to say, without counting the innumerable descendants of freeholders who have lost their privileges beyond even the desire, and far beyond the possibility, of recovering them. As a rule, when it is said that in such-and-such a province of Poland the nobility alone are discontented, for "nobility" we may read "all the educated classes."

I have said that in the chief towns the traders and the nobles are of one opinion, or rather feeling. It is only Russians, Prussians, and Austrians who are alarmed at the aristocratic tendencies of the Polish nobles; and who, to prevent the possibility

* In Galicia, for instance, I should say that the "magnates" who sit in the Upper Chamber of the Reichsrath belong to the aristocracy, and that the great majority of the "noble" landowners who elect members for the Lower House do not. I should not call Kosciuszko a member of the Polish aristocracy, though he was of noble birth and (to speak of what has, of course, nothing to do with the question) possessed the noblest disposition.

of any class-tyranny, are in favour of keeping
whole population in a state of slavery. It is t
that Poland, like Hungary and like England, is
aristocratic country in so far that it is equa
opposed to democracy and to despotism; to
government of the masses, and to the governm
of an autocrat dependent on the masses alone
support. After the shock of the first partition,
Poles, when they had recovered from its stunn
effect, and were proceeding to reform their consti
tion, facilitated, in various ways, admission to
nobiliary body, so that in time every Pole of wo
would have become a "noble," as with us ev
Englishman of ability and resolution may make h
self an elector. This was certainly a liberal idea
the best sense of the word, but also an aristocra
one. The democratic idea would have been to p
down the nobility to the level of the masses. T
despotic idea would have been to knock it dov
Mr. Cobden, the chief traducer of the Poles in E
land,* would have recommended the former proce
The Emperor Nicholas, when he suppressed
Polish constitution, and sent Polish noblem
chained like felons, to Siberia, adopted the latte

"Talk of Polish freedom!" say those Russia
Prussians, and Austrians, who would justify
conduct of their respective Governments towa

---

* See the portion relating to Poland (full of misreprese
tions and blunders) in *Russia, by a Manchester Manufactur*

the Poles from a "Liberal" point of view; "why, in ancient Poland the nobles alone were free: they alone exercised political power!"

And in Russia, Prussia, and Austria, what was the position of the nobles? They possessed no more political power than any other class. Touching equality! which left all classes powerless alike, and which left the peasants dependent on proprietors who had no sentiment of personal dignity, who were themselves slaves, and who, doubtless, for that reason, never conceived the idea of making their peasants free! Poland began the work of serf-emancipation long before Prussia, Austria, and Russia; and the first proprietors who emancipated their peasants privately, without waiting for any law on the subject, were the Czartoryskis and the Zamoyskis. This was anterior to the French Revolution and the invention of modern democracy.

I do not forget that Radicals, in all parts of Europe, have constantly expressed sympathy for the Poles; but these are, for the most part, warm-hearted, hot-headed men who have been struck by the very evident fact that the Poles are shamefully oppressed, who have not studied Polish history sufficiently to understand the leading traditional principle of Polish government, and who, moreover, are not so narrow-minded as to withhold their sympathy from all who do not entertain the same political notions as themselves. Nevertheless, the thorough-going democrat must always have a stone to throw at the Poles, and it is to ultra-democratic principles that the "Diabolical Trinity" now appeal whenever they seek to justify their tyranny in Poland.

We must not forget that the three liberal-tyrannical Powers effected the second partition on the ground that the Constitution of the 3rd of May, by strengthening the kingly power, tended to the introduction of despotism. It is true that when they had consummated their crime, they accused the Poles of "Jacobinism"—as at intervals, even now, they charge the principal nobles of Poland with being "demagogues." In reality it was because the Poles had found the safe path between the two extremes, and had succeeded in reconstituting their State on the firm basis of rational and progressive liberty, that their country was invaded in 1792. The Allies feared that what was left of Poland would escape them altogether, and that the diminished kingdom would, in time, regain the provinces which had been torn from it.

The fall of Poland may, no doubt, be traced to the abuse of the "aristocratic" principle, if by that be meant that all power was vested in the hands of the so-called "nobility," to the enfeeblement of the Central Government. But the same result might have been produced had Poland been a pure democracy. Indeed, it was by weakening so much of the aristocratic principle as did exist in Poland, and by taking the right of electing the king out of the hands of the Senate and entrusting it to the whole body of freeholders and descendants of freeholders (otherwise called nobles), that the ruin of Poland was prepared. Most of the electors were about as "aristocratic" as our forty-shillings voters in counties; many of them were even less so, for they were only children of freeholders, who had inherited scarcely a patch of land. No doubt they had a sentiment of their own importance. But the leaders of the nobility delighted to compare the whole mass to the Roman *plebs*. And the transfer of power from the Polish Senate to the Polish "nobility" was really equivalent to an elevation of the "*populus*"* above the "*senatus*." From that moment the *populus* were everything in the State, and soon afterwards the State began to fall. As if the usurpation of the right to elect the king was not sufficient, the nuncios, *i. e.* the members of the Lower House, the representatives of the *populus*, went to Stephen Batory, the first-elected king,† and by their en-

* The Poles also (and more generally) called the noble class the "*ordo equestris*"; but it included equestrians by tens of thousands who could not afford to keep their own horses.

† Without counting Henry of Valois, who took flight immediately after his coronation.

treaties secured his consent to a new arrangement, by which, on all important occasions, the votes of the Chamber of Nuncios and those of the Senate were to be counted together. This amounted in practice to depriving the Senate of all legislative power. There was now nothing to counterbalance the influence of the *populus*. Its will became supreme.

Nobility, peerage, and aristocracy are constantly confounded. In most countries nobility is an affair of good birth, while peerage is an affair of political rights, aristocracy an affair of social position. In France, at democratic periods, every one is considered more or less an aristocrat who wears a coat instead of a *blouse*, or a hat instead of a cap. A political song used to be sung in Paris in 1848, and for some years afterwards, of which each verse ended with these remarkable lines:—

> "Car moi, j'ai payé ma casquette,
> Et toi, tu n'as pas payé ton chapeau."

The man who wore a hat (and who had not paid for it) was an aristocrat.

In England we mean by a "nobleman" a peer, or, by courtesy, a son of a peer; and we have no notion of a class corresponding to the *noblesse* of ancient France—*noblesse de sang, noblesse de robe, noblesse d'epée*—with its privileges and exemptions;

nor that of Russia, where all State functionaries of a certain rank become nobles by favour of the Czar; nor that of Poland, where nobility was conferred by the representatives of "the people," as we should say in England—meaning thereby the electoral body—and where every freeholder and descendant of a freeholder was born a noble and an elector. In Poland, the court was nothing, and, consequently, there was no court aristocracy; and, though there were great patrician families, they were not distinguished by titles, and possessed no privileges. The only titles legally recognized in Poland were those of seven Lithuanian princes,* descendants of Rurik or of Gedeymin, who, at the legislative union of Lithuania with Poland in 1569, could not be prevailed upon to abandon these tokens of their high descent, though they gave them no political advantages whatever over other nobles. Probably it was the admission of these titled Lithuanians to all the franchises of the Polish nobility that caused John Zamoyski to assert, immediately afterwards, the principle of the complete equality of all nobles in the Polish State. The really aristocratic names in Polish history are

* Only three of these families have now living representatives, the Czartoryskis, the Sanguszkos, and the Radziwills. All other titles borne by Poles are of foreign origin. Some of them are of disgraceful origin, having been conferred by Russia, Austria, or Prussia after the partition of Poland.

those of men who distinguished themselves in the Diet or the army, and the only great Pole ever rewarded with a title was John Sobieski—who from a private gentleman became king.

I will endeavour, in another chapter,* to point out all the causes of a political nature which contributed to produce the fall of Poland; and, in the meanwhile will only observe, that however bad the Polish system (dating from the end of the Jagellon line, and the change in the mode of electing the king) may have been, it was not bad because it was too aristocratic; for under a more aristocratic system, penniless nobles would not have been allowed to remain on a precise equality with the heads of the great patrician families.

Can any one imagine a more dangerous, a more bribable class of electors than must have been formed by a mass of hereditary nobles, having no property but the sabre they carried at their side, legally condemned by their birth to abstain from labour and commerce, under pain of losing their nobility, and brought up in those very habits of dependence which must always render the existence of such a class worse than useless in a State? The indigent nobles of Poland were courtiers at the houses of the rich magnates, just as the nobles, indigent or not, of France were courtiers

* Chapter XV., *How Poland fell*, p 233.

in the palaces of the later French kings. As long as the king was elected by the Senate, the elective sovereignty was no source of danger to the country. Each monarch was succeeded, as a matter of course, by his son, or by the nearest heir. No one thought of attempting to corrupt the Senate, and the Senate and the whole country wished the crown to remain in the family of the Jagellons. When, however, the Jagellon dynasty became extinct in 1574, John Zamoyski ("*eques Polonus omnibus par,*" as he described himself at the end of a treaty signed by various foreign princes and dukes,) came forward as a leader of the *populus*, as a sort of noble demagogue, and declared that all nobles in Poland were equal, and possessed equal privileges. It was thereupon formally acknowledged that a noble, even if he were nothing more than a servant at some great house, was on a political level with nobles possessing incomes greater than belonged to some European princes— proprietors of whole provinces, who lived like sovereigns, kept up courts of more than regal splendour, and could take their five, six, eight, or as many as ten thousand men into the field of battle, or on to the plain of Wola where the king was elected.

It will be said that the democratic principle introduced by John Zamoyski had, after all, the effect of strengthening in an undue manner the territorial aristocracy. That, indeed, must always be the tendency of democratic institutions in a country where there are a certain number of influential families, powerful by their wealth and by their vast landed possessions. Under a monarchy, with an immense administrative machine working at its orders, democracy produces despotism; under a closely-limited monarchy, where a few great families possess abundant means of influencing the masses, it leads inevitably to oligarchy. Some four or five families in Poland could command among them from twenty to thirty thousand votes. Prince Radziwill alone had ten thousand at his disposition. Thus ten thousand small independent proprietors voting as one man could only just have counterbalanced the influence of a single rich magnate. Every Polish and Lithuanian noble was "*omnibus par*," but somehow the " vote and interest " of a Radziwill, a Czartoryski, or a Sapieha, was worth more than that of one of Radziwill's, Czartoryski's, or Sapieha's followers. Lelewel, the great Polish historian (in whose pages, however, instead of the large, truly liberal views of Miçkievicz, we sometimes find narrow ultra-democratic squints),*

---

* Here, for instance, is a curious view of English monarchy:—
" In the Middle Ages the infallibility and responsibility of the Emperor were transmitted to the Pope, so that he was looked upon as an infallible and inviolable monarch. Some Christian

tells, with evident satisfaction, in his *History of Lithuania and Ruthenia*, how, when the last* union between Poland and Lithuania was being prepared, the powerful Lithuanian princes regretted the loss of their political privileges, and took their departure from Lublin in the night, "*non salutato hospite.*" Afterwards, finding that the king remained, they went back and signed the act by which they sacrificed all their feudal rights, and placed themselves on an equality with their former vassals, and

States doubted this infallibility, and after breaking off all connection with Rome, refused to regard the Pope as chief of the Church. At this epoch, the King of England declared himself chief of the Anglican religion, and infallibility and inviolability became from that moment one of his attributes. It is thus that, in accordance with the example of England, the political fiction which renders a king infallible and inviolable, and pretends that his ministers alone are fallible and answerable, has been introduced into all constitutions." (*Analysis and Parallel of the Three Polish Constitutions*, by Lelewel.) "In Poland, as elsewhere, the cause of the people was in opposition with that of the aristocrats" (that is to say, the richest of the nobles). "The Czartoryskis, seeking to render the crown hereditary" (a project, of which it is sufficient to observe that Catherine and Frederic were its sworn opposers), "wished to establish monarchy on the ruins of the republic." Ministers under a constitutional monarchy of the English pattern are "the king's valets." The king and the people "have distinct and opposite interests."—*Analysis and Parallel, &c.*

* The first union, placing Poland and Lithuania under one crown, was signed at Horodlo in 1389; the last, which established a common Diet for the two countries, at Lublin, in 1569.

with the nobles, great and small, of republican Poland, where feudalism had never existed. This step was "democratic" enough, but it would not be difficult to show that it was the first step towards the destruction of Poland. The powerful feudal chiefs of Lithuania, though they lost their special political privileges, retained their vast domains. They were no longer hereditary senators by law, but their influence at the elections for the Diet in their own districts was all-powerful. It would have been far better for the liberties of the nation had all these magnates been kept together in one Chamber, shut out from the Diet and the Dietines —the meetings of electors, at which members for the Diet were chosen; but the democratic feeling of the small proprietors of Poland would not have been gratified had not the great Lithuanian princes been brought down to their level. The Lithuanian princes—the Radziwills, the Czartoryskis, the Sanguszkis, the Sapiehas, &c.,—had their revenge, and brought that natural influence which boundless wealth and well-established social position gave them, to bear in the elections for the Diet, and above all, in the election for the throne. Democracy will never prosper, will never even attain the end which it proposes to itself, unless it adopts communism as its ally. It is all very well to declare a duke with half a million a-year, the equal of a man who can just contrive not to die of starvation. To put the two on some sort of level, it would be necessary, in the first instance, to give the poor man half the duke's income. So it was easy enough to declare all the Polish nobles equal: the mere fact of the political equality of men who had nothing with men of vast possessions made the former the slaves of the latter. Between the two, that estimable class of voters, the small proprietors, too independent to be influenced by the magnates, and not caring, or, perhaps, not rich enough to be surrounded by parasites of their own, a class which produced John Zamoyski in the sixteenth century and Pulaski and Kosciuszko in the eighteenth, were nearly swamped. One understands democracy when it is established in a new State by a number of men of tolerably equal means; but in Poland, after the reduction of the really powerful Lithuanian magnates to the nominal position of Polish nobles, it was as sure to lead to abuses as it would in England were the House of Peers abolished, and dukes and earls declared on an exact political equality with all electors. Such a measure would certainly be democratic in form, but it would evidently lead to oligarchic and factious results; and proportionately with the extension of the suffrage, the power and influence of the great proprietors deprived of their peerage would increase. Lelewel and the democratic party among the Poles, say that the partition of Poland would never have been effected, had the peasants possessed a political interest in the affairs of the country, as if patriotism and the right of voting came and went together—a doubtful theory; and as if the Russians, who possess no political rights, were not always ready, from the prince to the peasant, to defend their territory inviolate—an indisputable fact. If the peasants had possessed votes, they would have had to give them to the great landed proprietors. The Poles would have had theoretical democracy and practical oligarchy on a larger scale. As it was, theoretically speaking and as far as the law could bring it about, there was as much democracy in Poland from 1574 until its fall, as there is now in the Southern States of America. All things considered, there was even more, for in the Southern States of America a large slaveholder has votes in proportion to the number of his slaves; whereas property, legally speaking, counted for nothing in Poland. Nor does each American freeman vote individually at the election of President; whereas, from the year 1574, every Pole of the freeholder class had a direct voice in choosing the king. In a word, the right of participating in the affairs of the State was not entrusted to too few, but to too many; and it may be seen that this was felt to be the case when the great work of reform was undertaken which terminated in the adoption of the Constitution of 1791.

"The equestrian order," says the protest against the adoption of this constitution, signed by thirteen influential nobles,* "felt and appreciated the advantage of liberty; accordingly the aim was to weaken it, and this was attained by depriving *gentlemen without incomes* of their privileges of nobility, while rich lords were called 'aristocrats,' though they, politically, were only on an equality with the former." To state the plain truth in simple language, the reform of 1791 was just and wise; but if it be absolutely necessary to characterize it in political terms, it was not a change from an aristocratic to a more or less democratic system, but from a nobiliary democratic system to an aristocratic system on a broad basis, in which the claims of birth, wealth, and personal merit were all fully recognized. Political privileges were not thrown at the feet of the people; but they were placed within the reach of all deserving persons who might think them worth striving for. The Poles did not say, "We will have no more nobles," but, "We will enable members of all classes to acquire nobiliary privileges or franchises, either by the purchase of land (which everyone was to be allowed to buy), or by distinction in commerce or the arts, or by gallantry in the field of battle, or by so many years' State service of any kind."

* Constitutional Act of the Confederation of Targowiça.— *D'Angeberg*, p. 262.

Such improvements as some of our demagogues would introduce in England had already been tried in Poland. Thus Poland, immediately before the first partition, did not need the services of a Peace Society, for she had scarcely any standing army. How could she want one, when her neighbours were always assuring her of their peaceful intentions, and when Russia had repeatedly declared that she could not view without uneasiness any augmentation of her military force? Nor could her national expenditure have been reduced much in other respects. Her navy had gradually but totally disappeared; Dantzig was a commercial, not a military port, and who was likely to attack it? The great offices of state were filled by men who would have disdained to accept salaries, and who, according to the Byronic sarcasm, "ruined Poland gratis." There was no diplomatic service; and if an ambassador was sent abroad on some special mission, he went at his own expense. Poland took so little interest in the affairs of foreign countries that she did not even care to be represented at the Congress which settled the affairs of Europe after the Thirty Years' War. To apply Mr. Bright's description of a model State,* a description which applies far more forcibly to the Polish than to the North-American Republic, "It was not a costly monarchy; it was not an aristocracy,

* Mr. Bright, at Birmingham, Dec., 1862.

creating and living on patronage; it did not support a very burdensome foreign policy; it had no great army, no great navy." Nevertheless, it became divided against itself; it was treacherously invaded in time of peace by three Powers who *did* support great armies; and when by a common union of its citizens it proceeded to strengthen itself as a monarchy, to create new ministries, and to increase its permanent military force, it was already too late; the "costly monarchies," with their great armies, fell upon it and destroyed it.

After this, the reader will perhaps think it hard that the Poles should have found in Mr. Cobden the bitterest enemy they have ever had in England, except, perhaps, Mr. Carlyle. Mr. Cobden and Voltaire, M. Proudhon and Mr. Carlyle—that is to say, a utilitarian democrat, a heartless scoffer,* a revolutionary cynic, and a philosophical despotist— these are the great haters of the Poles in the two countries where the fate of Poland has excited the greatest sympathy. If countries, like persons, are to be known by their friends, we may also form some opinion of them by their enemies. As for Mr. Cobden,† he misrepresents Polish history,

* Voltaire actually wrote a burlesque poem on the sufferings of the Confederates of Bar—thirty thousand warriors, who defended themselves for four years (1768–72) against the armies of the three invading Powers! Any species of martyrdom sufficed to amuse the author of *La Pucelle*.

† See his *Russia, by a Manchester Manufacturer*.

misunderstands the Polish system of government, gives no account of the simple and satisfactory manner in which that government was reformed in 1791, and, irritated, no doubt, by finding that all the legislative power was in the hands of the "nobles," falls foul of the unfortunate country as though it had possessed an aristocratic ministry, an expensive standing army, and a really efficient diplomatic service. Mr. Cobden's instinct, however, has not deceived him, though the word "noble" *has*. The Poles recognized no political aristocracy, but their best men were always very popular among them, even when they were of illustrious descent; and although they had no great standing army, they preserved a high military spirit until they fell into the state of demoralization in which the first hostile advances of the Empress Catherine found them. It was not until they became demoralized that they grew really careless about the national defences and the national honour, and gave themselves up to mere pleasure—of which the debauchery of the Saxon kings is one form, and the passion for money-making another.

That Voltaire, the friend of Frederic and Catherine, the despiser of popular liberties (as M. Louis Blanc has well shown in the first volume of his *History of the French Revolution*), should hate the Poles is not to be wondered at ; that Mr.

Carlyle should look upon Poland with the eyes of his hero is to be expected, however much it may be regretted; that Proudhon, the author of *La Proprieté c'est le Vol*, and *Dieu c'est le Mal*, should declare that if Poland had not been partitioned it would be necessary to partition it, is perfectly natural; but there is something inconsistent and ungrateful in Mr. Cobden's cool condemnation of a country which perished by the very system under which he would have England and Belgium * endeavour to live.

"Call it an aristocracy or call it a democracy, it was nevertheless through her nobility that Poland fell," it may be said. Undoubtedly; for the nobility was Poland. Thus, if the nobility had quitted Poland at the time of the partition, as the *noblesse* quitted France at the time of the Revolution, there would have been nothing left in the former country but a lifeless body. So, when the nobility became corrupt the whole life of the country was poisoned. But it owes all its glory, as well as all its misfortunes, to the nobility; and if the chiefs of the nobility allowed the country to

* Mr. Cobden recently advised the Belgians to pursue (virtually) the same policy, or want of policy, which brought Poland to destruction. A Belgian diplomatist has published a witty and spirited reply to Mr. Cobden's recommendation, under the title of *Richard Cobden, Roi des Belges.*

fall into a bad way, it was also they who made the greatest exertions to save it when what had always been regarded as an impossible coalition* had been formed for its destruction. Unfortunately they were divided against one another. Some were for fighting and maintaining the ancient system; others were for diplomatizing and changing the ancient system. In the meanwhile, however, we read in a despatch addressed by the French envoy at Warsaw to the Duke de Choiseul in March, 1768 (four years before the first partition, and four after the elevation of Stanislaus Augustus to the throne), that Russia "has increased her party by the favours which she has obliged the King to confer on an infinity of people of no position, who only owe their existence to the degradation of their country, to which they have contributed by showing an unbounded devotion to the slightest wishes of the Russian ambassador. She has lowered, as much as she could, the principal families whose credit and consideration could counterbalance her influence; and has caused the vacant offices to be filled by persons without honesty and without merit, but of whose attach-

---

* The Poles never believed that Austria and Prussia or Prussia and Russia would form an alliance; and nothing seemed more improbable than that Austria should join in destroying the barrier which existed between herself and Russia.

ment she is sure, and whom her ambassador treats already as his subjects."

Sixty-four years afterwards, the great families are all of one mind, all in one camp, all fighting against Russia for the independence of Poland. For two generations they had suffered immensely. Some had gone round by way of Italy, St. Domingo, and Spain, in the hope of reaching Poland at last under the auspices of Napoleon. Others had put their trust in Alexander. At last they were all together; and after their defeat, when some had been sentenced to death, some banished to Siberia, and when all the immense estates in the Lithuanian and Polish provinces of Russia had been confiscated, we find Lord Heytesbury writing to Lord Palmerston, from St. Petersburg, to explain that the true reason why the Polish Constitution will not be restored is because, "in the first place, it is believed that no measures of conciliation or favour would ever reconcile the higher classes in Poland to Russian dominion."*

Whether this belief be well founded or not, it is easy to understand why these classes are looked upon in Poland with a respect and confidence which they could not obtain in many other countries; not in France, for instance, where the nobility represent either a system which was abhorred, or

* *Correspondence with the Government of Russia, &c.*, p. 10.

nothing; nor in Austria or Prussia, where they represent the existing Government and the principle of class-privileges. Thousands and tens of thousands of Poles have given all they had for their country, but some have been able to do more than others; and it is natural that those should be considered the greatest who have made the greatest sacrifices.

The Poles, moreover, have always been an aristocratic people in another manner; they have been an aristocratic people with a democratic government. The chiefs of the great families often organized and commanded important expeditions against Turks, Tartars, and Muscovites; they always loved to distinguish themselves in the Diet, and, seeking for the applause of their countrymen, and possessing brilliant talents, naturally became popular. If Poland had not been a highly-democratic State, the great orators of the country would have had no commensurate field for their ambition; the interests to influence in the Diet would not have been sufficiently important, and there would have been no echo to their eloquence from outside. As it was, the political reputation of some of the most illustrious Poles extended throughout the country. Men of high birth, when they began their political life, were no doubt listened to with more attention than others; but if they commenced with a certain *prestige* they often knew how to keep it. Finally, the nobility, in the best days of the Republic, was not only a numerous, but also an accessible and constantly-increasing order; and meritorious citizens were ennobled at every Diet on the recommendation of the nuncio of their district.

CHAPTER X.

PROPRIETORS AND PEASANTS.

THE Poles in general, but especially those of the modern democratic party, lay great stress on the fact of the Polish nobility not having been of feudal origin. They seem to think that it was somehow advantageous to Poland to have escaped the feudal system, and to have had no division between classes except one which in time became impassable. We have seen, however, that feudalism *did* exist in Lithuania,* and have a right to suppose that some harm was done by suddenly reducing the great feudal chiefs to the same level as their vassals, sub-vassals, and freemen of all kinds, and letting them all loose together, weak and powerful, poor and rich, paupers and territorial princes, on the wide, fenceless common of an equal electoral system.

The Lithuanian nobles are either of Lithuanian

* For an account of the relations between the Grand-duke and the feudal proprietors of various degrees, see *Histoire de la Lithuanie et de la Ruthénie*, par Lelewel, p. 211.

or ancient Russian origin, the chief families being descended either from Gedeymin, the great Lithuanian prince and warrior, or from Rurik, the great Russo-Norman chief, or his companions. As the descendants of the companions of Rollo are found both in England and in France, and have become English and French, so the descendants of the companions of Rurik are found both in Russia and in Lithuania, and have become Russian and Polish. Russia, in the present day, asserts a right to all territory inhabited by the descendants of Rurik—including Lithuania, which, thanks to the partition of Poland, she possesses, and Eastern Galicia, which, owing to the same operation, is held by Austria. France might as well claim England as having been conquered and ruled by Norman dukes, or England Normandy as an ancient possession of her Norman kings.

The origin of the Polish nobility is disputed. There are at least three theories on the subject. The Polish democrats, from hatred of the great Polish families, maintain that it is some sort of Tartar race, and that it has always oppressed the Slavonian peasantry in Poland, with which it has nothing in common except language, religion, national customs and traditions, history, and a residence in the same country for upwards of a thousand years. Russian, Prussian, and Austrian writers have taken advantage of this theory, and I possess one very remarkable pamphlet,* written evidently either by a Russian or a German, in which the reader is assured that Poland is inhabited by two races, the Lechites, or descendants of the companions of Lech, and the Poles, or people of the plain (*pola*); that the Lechites are short, thin, dark-complexioned, black-haired, bright-eyed, hook-nosed, fiery men, and the Poles—their slaves—tall, fair, blue-eyed, snub-nosed, rather watery men. The author who made these observations had good eyes, or, more probably, had never been in Poland, and wrote from imagination.

It may be said that there are "two nations" in Poland, just as, according to M. Thierry, there are two nations in England and in France; but it is not easy to make the division according to physical characteristics; and what Hallam says of Thierry's argument—that it cannot be maintained "without a blind sacrifice of undeniable facts at the altar of plebeian malignity," may also be said of the Polish democratic theory, so ingeniously handled and perfidiously extended by the enemies of Poland in general. The nation in Poland was divided into a class possessing political rights, and a class without political rights; and between these two classes the line became more strongly marked as Poland degenerated, until at last the catastrophe

* *Appel à la Presse Libérale.* Dentu, Paris. (One of several of the same kind.)

arrived. Then the spirit of the country was awakened, and the barrier between nobles and non-nobles thrown down. If the Polish nobility had come in a body from beyond the Caucasus, and had maintained themselves ever since as a separate caste, like the Magyars of Hungary, we should, doubtless, find two types in Poland,—one among the nobility, or, speaking generally, the educated class, the other among the people, or, speaking generally, the peasantry. That a well-descended, well-educated proprietor in Poland has, generally, not the same aspect as one of his peasants, is true enough; but this difference is found between well-bred and ill-bred classes in all countries.

Szaichova, the Polish historian, considers the Polish nobility to be of Norman origin, founding his argument, partly on etymological grounds, and on the presumed derivation of certain significant words in the Polish language from the Gothic. It would, indeed, be strange if the Normans, who established themselves as an aristocracy in Russia, Lithuania, and various parts of Germany, to say nothing of France, England, and Southern Europe, never landed on the Polish coast. Whether from Scandinavia or direct from the Caucasus (as most of the modern Polish historians hold), it appears certain that the race which established itself as an aristocracy in so many other European States became also dominant in Poland. Judging from the identical principles* introduced by the nobility in Poland and in Hungary, one cannot but think that they must have been of the same race in both countries. It is certain that these principles are not of Finnish origin, like the Hungarian language; and that, in their essence, they belong to that Caucasian race which is supposed to have led the Finnish tribes into "Pannonia," and to have afterwards adopted their tongue.

The generally-accepted theory in the eighteenth century appears to have been that the Poles were an Asiatic race, and no attempt was made to show that the nobility and peasantry were of different origin. "The Poles, in their features, look, customs, dress, and general appearance," says Cox, "resemble Asiatics, rather than Europeans; and they are, unquestionably, descended from Tartar ancestors. A German historian,† well-versed in the antiquity of nations, remarks that the "manner in which the Poles wear their hair is, perhaps, one of the most ancient tokens of their origin. So early as the fifth century, some nations who

---

* Such as elective sovereignty, equality of all nobles, exercise of legislative power by an assembly of representatives possessing strictly *delegative* functions, absolute independence of every proprietor, great or small, on his own land, &c.

† Mascow.

THE UNIVERSITY OF CRACOW

were comprehended under the name of Scythians had the same custom; for Priscus Rhœtor, who accompanied Maximus in his embassy from Theodorus II. to the court of Attila, describes a Scythian lord, whose head was shaved in a circular form, a mode perfectly analogous to the present fashion in Poland."

Apparently, the shaving of the head was a "fashion," and nothing more, among the Poles; for in the library in the University of Cracow, I saw a collection of engravings, exemplifying Polish costume in various centuries, from which it was evident that the mode of wearing the hair had changed from time to time in Poland, as in the countries of Western Europe. Unfortunately, until quite lately, artists and writers have not thought it worth while to study the manners of the people; but Cox, towards the end of the eighteenth century, tells us that "men of all ranks in Poland" shaved their heads in the "Scythian" style, and though ethnology was clearly not his *forte*, he could use his eyes, and was much struck by the different manners in which the Polish and Russian peasants wore their hair, the former shaving it all off with the exception of one long tuft at the top; the latter wearing it all, but cutting it short, as in the present day, over the forehead. In a well-known picture, representing the meeting of the Diet, on the 3rd of May, 1791, by far the greatest day in the constitutional and in what may be called the moral history of Poland, all the members are represented with shaven heads. We see, however, by authentic portraits of the time, that John Zamoyski, at the end of the sixteenth century and Chodkievicz, the great general, in the middle of the seventeenth century, wore their hair as it would be worn in the present day, and also wore beards. The Swedish kings, Sigismund III. and Ladislas IV. may have set the fashion in both these respects; but if we go back to the fourteenth century, we find Kasimir the Great with the *chevelure* of a Merovingian king.

It may not seem very important to any but hairdressers to know how the early kings of Poland did their hair, but it is very interesting to know whether the Polish nobility were ever, until the production of recent democratic theories, thought to form a different race from the Polish people. There seems to have been no suspicion of such a thing until after the publication of M. Thierry's theory of the "two nations" living together side by side, or rather, one above the other, in England and France. Mickievicz, speaking of this theory in his lectures, says, "It has lately been *discovered*," &c., assumes it to be true of England and France, but does not think of applying it to Poland. Indeed, we find the Poles describing themselves as Sarmatians, Slavonians, and Poles, and foreigners speaking of them as Scythians; but these terms are always applied to the whole nation.

Thorough Slavonians, men so full of Slavonianism that they will, whether or not, find a Slavonian origin for everything in their country except the Russians (whom they stigmatize as Fins, Tartars, Mongols, Ouralians, and generally as a mixed race of Turanian origin), deny that any, even the slightest, trace of conquest is to be found in the early history of Poland. Whoever the ancient Sarmatians may have been, wherever Lech and his brothers came from, they all became Slavonianized at some almost pre-historic period. If all the Poles are not of the purest Slavonian race, the immigrants from the Caucasus who settled in Poland some time before the eighth century, established themselves there quietly without fighting, and soon mingled with the Slavonian population. Like the Norman invaders of Russia, they became absorbed, and afterwards received Christianity with the mass of the inhabitants of their adopted country. In spite of the real importance of Lech to the Poles, who derive the name of their order of nobility *Slachta* (*s-lech*, "with Lech," "the fraternity of Lech"), and also (among other derivations) the name of their countrymen in general (*po-Lech*, whence our old English, Shakspearian "Polack"—"by the side of Lech") from him; in spite of Lech's national importance, an inhuman German of the last century proved him to be a fabulous personage. While Schlötzer was engaged in this tragic work, Prince Jablonowski is said to have called upon him, and, from pure patriotism, to have offered him his own terms if he would allow the hero of so many Polish traditions to live.

But whatever the conquering, or superior, race may have been, there is no evidence to show that it constituted, in early ages, a separate body, or that it assumed that exclusive right of holding land, which the Polish nobility (with a few exceptions in favour of certain towns *) afterwards possessed until it was formally rejected by the Constitution of 1791. Feudalism was never introduced, and the enslavement of the peasantry appears to have been the result of an abuse of power, and to have been brought about by a series of encroachments on the part of the proprietors, not justified in the first instance by any law.† Every Pole who could equip himself

---

* Cracow, Wilna, and Dantzic.

† In Russia, too, the peasants were only affixed to the soil at the end of the sixteenth century, and were scarcely looked upon as the property of the landholders until the reign of Peter.

and a horse for battle was styled *eques*, and when he was under arms for the defence of the country, it was but fair that his land should be cultivated for him. Thus, land was cultivated by communes of peasants for the benefit of *equites* who were away fighting, the peasants at the same time cultivating land for themselves. Gradually, however, the knight or noble seems to have assumed that he could not only claim a portion of the peasants' labour in consideration of services rendered by him to the country, but that the peasants themselves, and the land cultivated by them for their own subsistence, also belonged to him. Yet it has been shown from written contracts of the thirteenth and fourteenth centuries, that peasants were, at that time, invited by the knights to settle on their estates, guaranteed a portion of land in perpetuity, and assured of protection, on condition of giving so many days' labour in the week; and in earlier times it is said that the peasant was free to pass from one estate to another as he pleased—much to the injury of the general agriculture of the country.

The peasant, however, in Poland never became a slave. He could not be sold by auction, staked on a card, or exchanged for a dog, as happened in Russia, at least as late as the reign of Alexander I.*

* Sales of slaves used to be advertised openly at St. Petersburg. When Alexander I. came to the throne, he forbade

It is folly, too, to pretend that he derived no advantage, unfortunate serf as he was, from living under a free Government, and that it is not better to be the slave of a freeman than the slave of a slave. In ancient Poland, at the end of the sixteenth century, there were a million* freeholders, all electors and eligible as members of the Diet, all on an equality, and of whom not one would have been allowed by the rest to suffer in his political rights. If liberty does not degrade but elevates man, these Polish nobles must have been more generous masters than the nobles of Russia, whose lives and fortunes were at the absolute mercy of the Czar, and who were free only to oppress their inferiors. There was a public opinion, too, in Poland. The most perfect liberty of speaking, writing, and printing, existed, such as has never yet been known in Russia. This must often have had a salutary effect in checking acts of injustice not specially prohibited by law. It must be remembered that the Polish nobility were far too numerous to form anything resembling a clique or a corporation. A million freemen, accustomed to criticise one another's actions at the Dietines or in

---

these advertisements, and the sales were afterwards announced by means of handbills circulated from house to house. See *La Régénération Sociale de la Russie*, par V. Porochin.

* The number given by Miçkievicz.

the Diet itself, could not well have entered into a general understanding to overlook all acts of tyranny committed against the peasants.

If we look to Polish authors we find them often dwelling on the unfortunate position of the peasantry. This proves, at least, that there were persons who interested themselves in their position and wished to benefit them. In England more is written than in any other country about the condition of the working classes, the state of the poor, &c. Is it to be supposed that there is no suffering in those countries where suffering passes unrecorded, and comparatively unnoticed? The Polish historians and chroniclers attack all sorts of abuses in the political and social system of Poland, with a vigour which might mislead foreigners in general but ought not to mislead Englishmen.

Nevertheless, the travellers of the eighteenth century do indeed describe the state of the Polish peasantry as very wretched. What principally strikes them is not their misery in a material point of view, but the abject spectacle they present in their general bearing as compared with that of their gay, careless, and slightly-haughty masters. In Switzerland, says one writer, the peasants are open, frank, rough, but ready to serve you; they nod their heads, or slightly pull off their hats, as they pass by, but expect a return of civility: they are roused by the least rudeness, and are not to be insulted with impunity. "On the contrary, the Polish peasants are cringing and servile in their expressions of respect; they bowed down to the ground, took off their hats or caps and held them in their hands till we were out of sight; stopped their carts on the first glimpse of our carriage; in short, their whole behaviour gave evident symptoms of the abject servitude under which they groaned."*

Another English author † who visited Poland about the same period is equally impressed by the degraded condition of the peasants, but accepts the explanation given by some of his Polish friends.

"The condition of the Polish peasants," he says, " is unquestionably very calamitous: yet many intelligent, humane, and impartial persons with whom I have conversed here assure me that it is not in fact so deplorable as we are led to conceive from appearances. Every peasant, even the meanest, is provided by his lord with two oxen, two horses, and a cottage. In case of fire, the house is rebuilt; and if they die, the beasts are replaced by their owner. A certain fixed portion of

* Cox. *Travels into Poland* (1784), vol. i. p. 279.
† Wraxall. *Memoirs of the Courts of Berlin, Warsaw, &c.*, p. 133.

their time and labour is appropriated to their lords, and the remainder they are at liberty to convert to their own profit or purposes. The number of days destined for their masters varies in different provinces and on different estates; but in none is the proportion so severe or exorbitant as not to leave them time sufficient to cultivate their own little land. In some parts of Poland, the peasants often become rich, or, at least, perfectly easy in their circumstances. Their poverty and wretchedness are not, therefore, say these persons, the inevitable and necessary result of their condition. It arises more from their national and characteristic indolence, drunkenness, and want of industry or exertion."

Another explanation to have been given was, that though the patriarchal system might have been unobjectionable in a simpler age, the adoption of foreign and luxurious habits by the proprietor had so separated him from the peasant that it had now become high time to make this separation complete.

Abuses, too, had no doubt crept into the system. Thus, when the serf first agreed to do so much work for the right of holding so much land, it is not likely that he also agreed to receive so many blows with a stick in case the master, through his overseer, thought he was not working hard enough.

The intelligent and benevolent statesmen of Poland saw that the system ought to cease, and, first among them all, the Great Chancellor Zamoyski resolved to try the experiment of emancipation in six of his villages. Wiebitski, in a volume called *Patriotic Letters* (addressed to the Great Chancellor) brought the subject before the public, and the example of Zamoyski was afterwards followed by several other "aristocrats," whose interests, according to Lelewel, are "everywhere opposed to those of the people." On signing the deed of enfranchisement, Zamoyski cautioned the inhabitants against making a bad use of their liberty, to which they are said to have replied with considerable *naïveté*, "When we had no other property than the stick we carry in our hands, there was nothing to encourage us to good conduct. If we have acted wildly and foolishly, we felt that we had nothing to lose; but when our houses, our lands, and our cattle are our own, the fear of forfeiting them will restrain us."* In fact, while they were in a state of serfdom, Zamoyski was occasionally obliged to pay fines for the outbreaks of his subjects ("*pro incontinentiâ subditorum*") who, while drunk, would attack, and sometimes kill passers-by. "Since

---

* Cox; quoting from Wiebitski and from the accounts of various proprietors who had imitated Zamoyski's example. (*Travels into Poland*, vol. i. p. 160.) See also on this subject Miçkievicz's Lectures (*Les Slaves, &c.*).

their freedom," we are told, "he has *seldom* received any complaints of this sort against them." On the whole, Zamoyski was so pleased with the thriving state of his six villages, and with the general success of his experiment, that he freed the peasants on all his estates. He also published full particulars of the benefits which he as well as the peasants derived from the change in their mutual position. *He* found the advantage of employing hired labourers instead of serfs; *they* were delighted to pay a small quit-rent instead of performing task-work. In the first ten years of freedom, as compared with the last ten years of slavery, the number of births in the six villages had increased about fifty per cent. The peasants were happy and prosperous, had comfortable houses and plenty of cattle; and altogether the estate produced nearly three times what it had yielded before.

Prince Czartoryski, Chreptowicz, the Vice-chancellor of Lithuania, Prince Stanislas Poniatowski, the King's nephew, the Abbé Brzostowski, and other large proprietors, now liberated their peasants, and with excellent results. The Abbé's peasants on his estates near Wilna, could be at once recognized by "their happy countenance and comfortable air, which made them appear a different race of men from the wretched tenants of the neighbouring villages." * Penetrated with a sense of their

* Cox.

master's kindness, they "erected, at their own expense, a pillar with an inscription expressive of their gratitude and affection."* Some proprietors, in their ardour for reform, established little commonwealths, and allowed their peasants to administer justice among themselves, to levy taxes, and even to form their own police. One proprietor wished to bring his peasants back to a primitive patriarchal state. He bought a virgin forest for them, and proposed that they should dwell there in peace and meditation. "What they were to meditate about is not very clear," says Miçkievicz. However, Rousseau was invited to come and live in the forest, as a model. He did not accept the invitation.

By the side of all this effervescence very serious reforms were being prepared. Zamoyski had drawn up a code of laws on the subject of serf emancipation to present to the Diet; and it is doubtless to the influence of his advice, and above all, of his example, that Kollontay's and Potoçki's clauses in favour of the peasantry in the Constitution of 1791 are to be attributed.

A dozen years after Zamoyski had commenced his experiments in emancipation, the first partition was effected. Then the *Patriotic Letters* appeared, calling the attention of the Poles to the necessity of all sorts of reforms, which they had frequently

* Cox.

endeavoured in vain to introduce, but which it seemed now absolutely necessary to adopt, unless the country was to perish from its own internal weakness.

The Constitution of May 3, 1791, provided for the gradual emancipation of the peasantry, but its adoption was the sign for the second partition. The second partition was followed by Kosciuszko's insurrection, and Kosciuszko's insurrection by the destruction of Poland.

Under the three partitioning Powers serfdom was everywhere maintained. In the eighteenth century, neither Prussia, Austria, nor Russia had even conceived the idea of serf emancipation. In Samogitia (Lithuania), where serfdom had never existed, it was introduced by the Empress Catherine, as it had previously been introduced by the same sovereign in the Ukraine.

In 1807, Napoleon, in forming the Duchy of Warsaw, found the peasant "attached to the soil," and in a certain manner "liberated" him. That is to say, he gave him leave to move about wherever he pleased, and to make the best terms he could with the proprietors of land. If the peasant did not like the proprietor, all he had to do was to leave him.

And his house, and his land, which he and his ancestors had cultivated for centuries? These also he would and must leave if he had any intention of trying to better his position. Altogether, this was a very bad prospect for the peasant; and it was contrary to all right, and to all custom in such cases since the existence and abolition of serfdom, to deprive him of his heritage under pretence of emancipating him. What the poor serf needed was, that his burdens should be lightened, not that he should have the barren choice given him between bearing them and going elsewhere.

However, in the Duchy of Warsaw, the peasants, though not in so good a position as the liberated serfs of the Zamoyskis and Chreptowiczs under the ancient system, were nevertheless free. They kept the land, and paid a fixed price for it in task-work—so many days' labour in the week, according to contract. If they neglected or avoided their work, the only way to keep them to it was by the old plan of beating them. This was by no means a satisfactory solution of "the peasant question."

When the Duchy of Warsaw, considerably diminished, became, in 1815, the Kingdom of Poland, the relations between peasants and proprietors were not changed. No one seems to have proposed any alteration during the constitutional period, which was a mistake if nothing worse; and when the insurrection broke out in 1830, it was considered inopportune and dangerous to entertain the question, though a plan was laid before the Diet for liberating the peasants from task-work, and endowing them with their portions of land.

Soon after the accession of the Emperor Alexander II., and by his permission, the Agricultural Society of the Kingdom of Poland was formed, under the auspices of Count Andrew Zamoyski, the great-grandson of the Chancellor Zamoyski, who had set the first example of serf emancipation in Poland a hundred years before. This Association included some four thousand landed proprietors of the Kingdom; its meetings were attended by delegates from Posen, Cracow, and Leopol (Lemberg); and when it was dissolved, in the midst of the disturbances which led to the massacre of the 8th of April, 1861, it had just voted a project for relieving the peasantry from task-work, and making over to them their portions of land. The value of the task-work due was estimated in money: the proprietors proposed to sacrifice one-fifth of the amount, and, for the remaining four-fifths, to take bank bills bearing interest.

The project of the Association was not adopted, and the Government has now put in action a plan of its own. The peasants pay rent instead of performing task-work; and their portions of land are declared inalienable, and redeemable by extra payments extending over a period of forty years.

Under the Prussian and Austrian Governments, the peasants have been more fortunate. They were made proprietors of their land in Posen when that portion of the Duchy of Warsaw was recovered by Prussia in 1815. The proprietors had to sacrifice two-thirds of the estimated money value of the *corvée;* for the remaining one-third they had to look to the Government, which, after a liberal deduction for office expenses, &c., paid the redemption money in State bills bearing interest. The peasants have to pay one-third of the value of the *corvée* to the Government for a period of years, after which they are freeholders.

The Galician peasants received their land in freehold in 1848, the proprietors being partially indemnified by the Austrian Government. The Galician Diet had petitioned for permission to alter their relations towards the peasants and to abolish the *corvée* in 1845, but their prayer was not granted; and in Galicia, as in every part of Poland, the peasantry have been made to feel that they owe their liberty not to the Polish proprietors but to one of the three Governments under all of which the proprietors have long been powerless.

In the Kingdom of Poland, then (as also in the Russo-Polish provinces), the peasantry are now in the same position as in Russia Proper, and under existing arrangements must either pay rent for their land, or may purchase it by instalments extending over a long period. But the Revolutionary party in Poland, as represented by the central committee at Warsaw, propose to draw the peasants into their movement by making them a present of their portions of land freehold as soon as this utterly hopeless movement has succeeded; the proprietors to be indemnified out of the National Treasury.

The peasants of the Kingdom should no doubt have been liberated when the Poles had an opportunity of liberating them peacefully, that is to say, some time between the years 1815 and 1830. It is proposed now to enfranchize them for a revolutionary purpose, and an appeal is made not to their patriotism but to their cupidity. But, if the Government likes to play with the same weapons, it can paralyze this movement at any time. If, instead of only promising the land, it actually gives it to the peasants, and taxes the whole kingdom for the indemnity payable to the proprietors, the only motive which (according to the democrats of Russia and Poland) can cause the peasantry to take up arms will have ceased to exist.

In the meanwhile, the peasantry would seem to form the most important class in the Kingdom, and to run the risk of being as unduly raised up, as they were in the old days unduly kept down.

The proprietors do not press them for rent, overlook their little shortcomings of all kinds, and give them from time to time a conciliatory banquet at the best hotel in Warsaw. The Government will not take them for recruits—would not disturb them in the midst of their useful agricultural pursuits on any account! Finally, nothing will satisfy the democrats but to make them a present of all their land in freehold.

The Polish serf of former days is indeed avenged. In this state of things, however, the Slavennophils of Poland ought to indulge no more in their empty boast that their country escaped the feudal system. At least, under the feudal system peasants easily became proprietors; and if the feudal system, with its variety of tenures and its numerous social gradations, had existed in Poland, it would not be so easy as it is now to divide the country into two great classes, and to paralyze all national action by raising up the lower, in the name of communism, against the upper, whenever it may venture to move in the name of patriotism. In Austria this was done in 1846, and caused the Galician massacres, which, though they were at the last moment directed and paid for by the Austrian police, had, to a certain extent, been unwittingly provoked by the propagandists of socialism. All the evils, moreover, of feudalism (such as servitude of the peasants, territorial jurisdiction of the proprietors, right of proprietors to maintain an unlimited number of domestic troops, inalienability of land from the noble class, legal inferiority of persons engaged in trade, &c.), existed in Poland up to the moment of the first partition, though it is quite true that the superior men of the country were making earnest efforts to abolish them; and this in spite of the nobiliary democracy, who would hear of no change, and who preferred that Poland should die rather than that the monarchy should be strengthened— as the democrats of the present day would rather it should not revive than that it should live again through the influence of " aristocrats."

CHAPTER XI.

THE LAST CONQUEST OF POLAND.

No injustice is done to Russia when it is said that she governs Poland as a conquered country. The Russians of the last reign were proud of having subdued it, and seem, for the most part, to have looked upon slavery as the natural lot of a vanquished people. I have already mentioned that a bunch of flags captured from the insurgent Poles by the troops of their sovereign is displayed as a trophy in the Treasury of the Kremlin, with a bunch of Russian flags opposite to it, and the Polish Constitution on the ground between the two. The whole affair says, as plainly as flags and boxes with portable Constitutions in them can speak : " Judgment in the case of Poland *v*. Russia, *in re* the Polish Constitution." For upwards of a quarter of a century Poland has been governed through the formidable citadel erected just outside Warsaw, *vice* the said Constitution captured, and forwarded in a cart to Moscow. Count Nesselrode, in a letter to the

British Government on this very subject, argues that the Constitution was nullified by the rising of the Poles against their sovereign; that they declared themselves independent, and being afterwards conquered, were placed once more in the position they had occupied before the Constitution was granted to them; that is to say, at Russia's mercy.* The Kremlin argument, though somewhat crude, somewhat savage, is much simpler and quite as fair as Count Nesselrode's. "The Poles cannot have their Constitution, because we have taken it from them, and locked it up in a box, and put it away in the Treasury at Moscow, where we mean to keep it."

Nevertheless, some of the Poles hope to get this Constitution back again; others seem to care but little about it, and think themselves entitled to a better one—one of wider application and not confined merely to the present Kingdom of Poland. At least they are of opinion that anything less than a Constitution for all the provinces of Poland now in the hands of Russia ought, if accepted at all, to be regarded only as payment in part of a debt ultimately to be acquitted in full. It appears strange that Poles should think of pro-

* Despatch addressed to Prince Lieven, Russian ambassador at London, to be communicated to Lord Palmerston (*D'Angeberg*, 904). Lord Palmerston replied by a protest, which has often been repeated, and which still holds good.

posing conditions and terms to Russia, but so it is; and as Russia has tried everything to "pacify them," except exterminating them on the one hand, and doing justice to them on the other, it is possible that their proposals may be listened to and considered, if not directly acted upon. But the reader ought to be able to form some idea of what the position of the Poles under the Russian government has been for the last thirty years. I will therefore give a short account, exclusively from Russian official documents, of the measures of persecution taken against them since the suppression of the insurrection of 1830.

A number of causes, direct and indirect, immediate and more or less remote, contributed to produce this movement, which, as it is so easy to see after the event, had scarcely a chance of success, and which had the effect of enraging and even terrifying the Russian Emperor to such an extent, that he never forgave the Poles, and only knew them afterwards as "those whom he hated and those whom he despised." The insurrection of 1830 was conducted by Poles of the former class, and no one can say that it was unjustifiable, unless prepared to maintain that insurrection is unjustifiable under all possible circumstances. Whether or not it was prudent is a different question, and, doubtless, M. Guizot takes a wise view of the matter when (in the second volume of his *Memoirs*) he points out that the true policy of the Poles was to regard the Constitution of 1815 as their sheet-anchor, and hold to it through all possible trials, so that, at least, Russia might have no pretext for formally withdrawing it. But the Poles suffered every kind of injustice, cruelty, and insult before they rose, and when the rising had taken place, and when they had permitted Constantine, with the Russian troops under his command, to leave Warsaw, the Government was still carried on in the name of the Emperor Nicholas. All that General Chlopiçki, the provisional dictator, demanded in the first instance, was that the Constitution, so frequently violated, should be faithfully observed, and that, in accordance with the spirit of the Treaty of Vienna, and with the right expressly stipulated for and secured by the Emperor Alexander, the Polish provinces annexed to Russia at the first, second, and third partitions should be united to the Kingdom of Poland. This project was entertained by the Emperor Alexander to the last day of his reign. He always spoke of it as "his favourite project," and it was not until after the accession of the Emperor Nicholas that the Poles despaired of seeing it executed. Probably, neither this great disappointment, nor the repeated violation of the Constitution, would in themselves have led to an appeal to arms. The rising seems to have been directly brought about by the barbarous treatment to which the officers and cadets of the Polish army were subjected by the Grand-duke Constantine; by the excitement caused by the French Revolution (which was felt, not in Poland alone, but throughout Europe); by the struggles of Greece and Belgium for national independence, and by the favour shown to these Powers by France and England, on whose support the Poles thought they also might rely; by the knowledge that the Russian army was about to march upon Paris, and that the Polish troops were to lead the van; and, finally, by the fact that numbers of Polish officers and students had been already arrested, and that more arrests were hourly expected.

A few cadets commenced the insurrection by an attack on the Palace of the Belvidere, where the Grand-duke Constantine resided. Several sentinels were killed, but the Grand-duke escaped, and was afterwards allowed to retire unmolested with a small body of Russian troops, all the Polish troops who had until that time remained with him being ordered to return to Warsaw, where they at once joined their comrades. The morning after the outbreak of the 29th of November, the President of the Administrative Council formed by the Emperor Nicholas, with some new members attached to it, issued a proclamation, in which the events of the preceding evening were described as being "as sad as they were unexpected," and in which the Poles were adjured to remain quiet, inasmuch as "their own moderation could alone save them from the abyss over which they were placed." *

"Think of the future of this country, which has passed through so many misfortunes! Keep away from it all that may endanger its existence! As for us, our duty will be to watch over the general safety, the execution of the laws and the constitutional liberties which are guaranteed to us." Thus ended the first Polish proclamation, issued after the Revolution of the 29th November. It was signed by Count Sobolewski, Prince Czartoryski, Prince Lubeçki, Prince Radziwill, Kochanowski, Count Paç, and Niemcewicz, and is a proof that the influential men in Poland, even at the last moment, were opposed to violent measures, though they considered that the time had now arrived for demanding the fulfilment of the Imperial promises, if their fulfilment was to be demanded at all. Representations on the subject had repeatedly been made, but quite in vain. Nevertheless, the Poles had suffered patiently, resolved to do nothing that might compromise the position of their country.

Officers, for the slightest offence against disci-

---

* *D'Angeberg* (*Recueil des Traités, &c.*), p. 768.

pline, had been grossly insulted, and subjected to the most degrading punishments, by the Grand-duke Constantine, whose utter unfitness to govern had been fully recognized in despotic Russia, but who appears to have been thought quite good enough for constitutional Poland. Many of them, stung to madness by these outrages, and unable to reply to them, committed suicide. Lelewel, the historian, has written an account of the cruelties inflicted upon the students of the University of Wilna, where he was professor, and has named those who, on suspicion of belonging to secret societies, were imprisoned, beaten, and tortured.[*] These atrocities must not be disbelieved because they appear incredible, for they are only too well authenticated. I do not cite them as a reproach to the existing Russian Government, but simply to show that the Polish insurrection of November 29, 1830, was not (as the enemies of the Poles assert) a wanton, thoughtless movement got up in imitation of the French Revolution of June, but that it was morally inevitable from the persecutions which preceded it.

It think it will seem to every Englishman, who looks calmly at the question, that the Poles bore about as much as they ought to have borne—as much, perhaps, as they could possibly bear, with-

[*] *Guerre aux Enfants, &c., à Wilna.*

out forfeiting their self-respect. Had they not protested, their position must gradually have become that of a nation of slaves. As it was, they lost everything "*fors l'honneur*," but, at least, they have never ceased to feel that they are free men, held temporarily in captivity; and when they regain their rights, they will be as able to profit by them as though they had never lost them. We know the value of liberty to a tame bird. The best thing that can happen to it, is to be caught again as soon as possible—like the eagle of the Boulogne expedition, which, after the capture of its untameable master, led a glorious life in the court-yard of the Boulogne slaughter-house, feeding plentifully on the freshest carnage. The Polish eagle, however, has never been tamed. Its wings have been cut, and it has received some terrible wounds in beating its breast against the iron wires of its cage; but its nature is as free now as when it took its last great flight, more than thirty years ago. We cannot, positively, predict its fate; but the spirit of the bird is unquenchable, and we know that the cage cannot endure for ever.

Inevitable as was the crisis of 1830, some of the most important men in Poland endeavoured to avert it, and when at length it arrived, did their best to mitigate its dangerous character. After the proclamation of the 30th of November, calling upon the people to remain quiet, the Administrative Council issued a second proclamation, on the 3rd December, informing them that the Grandduke Constantine was retiring with his *corps* of Russian troops, and that he must not be molested in his retreat.* What could be more chivalrous than to issue such an order, when the Poles had Constantine entirely in their power? But he had appealed to their generosity, and they wished to prove that it was not from a feeling of vengeance that the nation had risen—though, doubtless, vengeance had prompted the attack made by the cadets on the Palace of the Belvidere. For my part, I also cannot help thinking that some sort of compunction must have been felt by the Polish leaders. If Constantine had really behaved like a fiend, as he is said to have done, would the Poles have allowed him to retire in this manner in peace?

However, the die had now been cast, and it was utterly impossible that the Emperor of Russia could treat with his insurgent subjects as from Power to Power. First, there was the attack on the Grand-duke to be atoned for. Then, it was not to

* "The Grand-duke does us justice in 'hoping, from the loyalty of the Poles, that he will not be disturbed in his retreat.' The Council calls upon the people to insure all facilities to His Imperial Highness for executing this movement."—*Order of the Administrative Council*, Warsaw, Dec. 3, 1830.

be expected that the most despotic sovereign in Europe would lower himself in the eyes of his own subjects, by granting to the Poles in arms what he had refused to them when making their representations peaceably. General Chlopiçki, appointed dictator, despatched a letter to Nicholas, in which he assured him that although the Poles were prepared to sacrifice everything for their national independence, yet they had no thought of breaking the bond which united them to the Russian crown; that all they desired was to see the Polish provinces of Russia united to the Kingdom of Poland, and the Polish constitution —extended to all that portion of the Poland of 1772 which was under the sceptre of Russia— faithfully observed.*

Nicholas replied that he had heard, with horror, of the crimes perpetrated at Warsaw, and of the attempt made upon his brother's life; that he would not confound the innocent with the guilty, but that the Poles must lay down their arms and trust to his magnanimity. "If," the proclamation ended, "they have dared, in taking up arms, to flatter themselves that they will obtain concessions as a reward for their crimes, their hope is vain. They have betrayed their country. The misfor-

* Precisely what the Polish nobility asked last autumn, in the address which Count Andrew Zamoyski was not allowed to present to the Grand-duke Constantine.

tunes they are preparing for it must be on their heads."

Two days after the appearance of this proclamation Colonel Wylezynski, one of General Chlopiçki's envoys, had an interview with the Emperor Nicholas at St. Petersburgh, at the conclusion of which General Benkendorf said to him, "Your Revolution, at least, has not the merit of being well-timed. You have risen just when all the forces of the Empire were marching towards your frontiers. You must be aware that such an unequal struggle cannot last long."

Colonel Wylezynski observed, that "Poland was strong enough to stem the torrent of the north until the other Powers should be in a position to keep off the danger which threatened all of them."

Thereupon Marshal Diebitsch is said to have pronounced these remarkable words,* "Well: what will the result be for you? We intended to make a campaign on the Rhine; we shall now make it on the Elbe, or even on the Oder, after crushing you. If, however, you could come to an arrangement, the Emperor assures you that he would forgive everything. You must feel that the word of a sovereign is something; of a sovereign, above all, who will keep it towards and against everyone, as he is resolved to keep his word to Charles X."

* *Archives of Poland.—D'Angeberg*, 770.

The Poles attach great importance to the speeches of two Generals who were known to be in the secret of the Imperial policy. But it is impossible to admit that they opposed the Russian forces simply with the view of "stemming the torrent of the north." There is General Chlopiçki's letter to prove (to the credit of the Poles) that after the first outburst, which the national Polish Government deprecated the morning afterwards, all the Poles demanded was, that the Emperor should respect the Constitution, and extend it to the Polish provinces incorporated with Russia. Surely Chlopiçki's envoys, when they saw the Emperor Nicholas, did not tell him that the object of the Poles in rising was to "stem the torrent of the north"? In that case they need not have left Warsaw; nor ought they to have allowed the Grandduke Constantine to leave, with some thousands of northern troops, to swell this "torrent." The Emperor Nicholas felt himself called upon to maintain a certain state of things, in France perhaps, in Holland certainly, for there he was bound by very precise treaty obligations. It was his duty to be prepared for war, more especially as it was notorious that France, in 1830, wanted to fight for the mere sake of fighting. No one knew what the result of the French Revolution of 1830, republican in its origin, might be; and the notion that the Poles had a right to rise against their sovereign because he thought fit to place his army on a war-footing, is most preposterous. One would think that they might, at least, have waited for the order to march before assuming that Europe was threatened with an invasion of barbarians, which, if terms had been made with them, they had no intention of averting. It must be remembered that the advance of a Russian army is always an "invasion of barbarians" in the eyes of the Poles, whether the object be to drive the French out of Italy, or even to expel them from Russia itself, so effectually as to diminish considerably the chances of their returning there. On the other hand, the progress of a French army, plunder and massacre as it may, is always that of a liberating host intent on planting the Tricolor of Freedom in whatever countries it may happen to desolate.

That the Russians meditated a march to the south is certain enough; and it also cannot be denied that the Polish campaign rendered their projects, whatever they were, impossible to execute. But the Poles do themselves an injustice in saying that their prime motive in rising was to frustrate these projects, the particulars of which were not known to them when the rising took place.

Under these circumstances, however, it was natural that the Poles should look for assistance to those whom they had saved from a possible invasion. They appealed, moreover, to France, and also to England, as having signed the Treaty of

Vienna, and both these Powers have been much blamed for not coming to their aid by making a joint representation to the Russian Government, if by no other means. Indeed, this course was actually proposed by France and rejected by England, and as the French have taken care to make it known, England would appear to have behaved in a most unfriendly manner, in 1831, to the nation whose fate had inspired her with so warm an interest in 1815. French writers have not always told the whole story, and the Poles have been led to believe, that if France did nothing for them in 1831, that was owing, in a great measure, to the refusal of England to co-operate. Undoubtedly, England received and rejected a proposition to that effect, and did so on the ground that the presentation of joint remonstrances would lead to nothing (or, worse still, would increase the irritation of Russia against the Poles) unless it was intended to support it by force of arms. This, England was not prepared to do, and she was therefore determined not to put herself in a position which, in the end, would have left her no becoming alternative but to declare war.

Lord Palmerston had already been assured by Lord Heytesbury, the British ambassador at St. Petersburg, that "any proposal to mediate, whether from France or from any other Power, would be received with high indignation, and lead to no beneficial result;" and Lord Durham, Lord Heytesbury's successor, declared that if, after the formal protest against the abolition of the Polish Constitution had been entered, England still continued to interfere by presenting diplomatic notes, he feared "the publicity of an interference would oblige the Emperor to take steps of additional severity in order to prove to his Russian subjects that he was not controlled, in what they consider the administration of their internal affairs, by a foreign Power."

Here is an important extract from one of the earliest of Lord Palmerston's diplomatic notes, addressed to Lord Heytesbury, at St. Petersburg:—

"By Article I. of the Treaty of Vienna, it is stipulated that the Poles, subjects respectively of Russia, Austria, and Prussia, shall obtain a national representation, and institutions regulated according to the kind of political existence which each of the Governments to which they belong shall think it useful and fitting to grant them.

"It is understood that although this stipulation has been executed by Austria and Prussia, it has hitherto been entirely unfulfilled by the Russian Government. His Majesty's Government has been informed by the French Ambassador at this Court, that instructions have been sent to the Duke de Mortemart to draw the attention of the

Russian Government to this matter, and the French Government have expressed a wish that your Lordship might be instructed to support the Duke in his representations on this subject.

"Your Lordship will, of course, be careful not to take any step in this business which could lead to any unfriendly discussions with the Russian Government, with whom His Majesty's Government are, under present circumstances, more than ever desirous of keeping up the closest relations of friendship.

"But if the question should be agitated, your Lordship is instructed to state, that as far as His Majesty's Government are informed of the facts of the case, it does not appear to them that the provisions of the Treaty of Vienna applicable to the Polish provinces of Russia have been hitherto carried into execution."

Now let us see Lord Heytesbury's answer :—

"With respect to the want of institutions in the ancient Polish provinces of Russia," he writes to Lord Palmerston, "a question upon which I was instructed to support any observations that might be made by the Duc de Mortemart, Count Nesselrode informed me that the Duc de Mortemart had held vague language to the Emperor, but had not given any official character to his conversation.

"Upon my opening myself to the Duc de

Mortemart upon the subject, and expressing my readiness to co-operate with him to a certain extent, His Excellency confirmed what had already been stated to me by Count Nesselrode, namely, that he had not as yet considered himself bound to do more than to recall to the recollection of the Emperor, as well as to that of Count Nesselrode, the engagements taken at Vienna; and to express the hope of his Government that they would not be violated. His instructions, he said, were not very precise, and were applicable rather to the moment of victory (which he did not think by any means arrived), when it might be attempted to give a good direction to the well-known magnanimity of the Emperor, than to the present state of things, when all was uncertainty and doubt."

There was evidently no possibility of co-operating with the Duke de Mortemart at this period, for his policy consisted in doing and saying nothing. What are we to think, too, of the French Government informing the English Government that it had sent instructions to its ambassador, which this ambassador declares he never received, and in getting England to support an alleged representation from France, which France had never made?

Perhaps, however, France was sincere in proposing a joint representation some time afterwards? Perhaps so; but it would have been necessary to follow it up with a declaration of war, and this would not have suited England, who was sufficiently occupied with the Reform-bill agitation at home, and with the settlement of the Greek and Belgian questions abroad. It might have suited France, whose Government desired a foreign war, in order to escape domestic revolution; but France could not by herself fight a Power like Russia, simply for the sake of a little healthy exercise, and as England refused her co-operation (instead of pretending she had given instructions to her ambassador to co-operate, while, in fact, giving no such instructions at all), the plan of a joint representation fell to the ground.

France, however, may have been sincere in making the proposition. On the other hand, she may not. M. Guizot, in his very valuable *Memoirs*, tells us that soon after the Revolution of 1830 it was thought absolutely necessary to get up a foreign war in order to carry off the dangerous humours with which France was troubled. Some thought one country would be the best to attack, some another. M. Guizot quotes the words of a friend of his, the Prefect of a department, who did not think much of a war on behalf of the Belgians, and declares the cause of Poland to be "more dramatic," and therefore more likely to strike the French imagination. Whatever the Poles may say about the matter, the French, at least, have no right to complain that we did not show any disposition to join them in a war for an idea—and a " dramatic idea" above all—of which part of the realization would, no doubt, have been the establishment of the French on the left bank of the Rhine.

The Poles, however, without troubling themselves about the Rhine frontier, and the possibility that the French might have left us in the lurch had the opportunity been offered them, complain that, as it was, *they* were abandoned; that they had a right to claim the assistance of the Western Powers, and that they were deserted in their direst need. The fact appears to have been, that as the partition of 1815 had been partly arranged so as to suit the views of the two German Powers, everyone imagined Austria and Prussia would be glad to maintain that arrangement, and to join England and France at any time to prevent Russia from absorbing the Kingdom of Poland. Who could have thought that Prussia and Austria would willingly allow Russia to come nearer and nearer to Berlin and Vienna? As it was, when Lord Palmerston represented to Russia that in destroying the character of Poland as a constitutional kingdom, having its own national army, she took a step which was very alarming for the independence of Prussia and Austria, Count Nesselrode simply replied that he " could not understand why England and France should object to this, if the two Powers who might be supposed to be more immediately interested approved of the measure." Indeed, Prussia and Austria will always agree with Russia when Russia wishes to persecute the Poles, and will never fear her as long as she keeps her Polish subjects in a state of discontent. But let Russia once give all her Polish subjects free institutions and a national Government, and from that moment Prussia and Austria will tremble, and with reason, for Posen and Galicia.

Again, apart from the question of what we could or ought to have done by reason of the treaties of 1815, the Poles say that both England and France actually promised them assistance, and that they would have acted with more vigour, and given the insurrection a wider field, had not both countries cautioned them to keep within bounds, and to confine their action to the "Kingdom" of Poland. Count Andrew Zamoyski, Prince Leon Sapieha, the Marquis Wielopolski, and other Poles of high position, were sent as ambassadors to various Courts. Now, one of the emissaries, who came to London, told me himself that when he saw Lord Grey, that minister assured him from the first that the condition of our foreign relations, and, above all, the state of France, which seemed quite ripe for a revolutionary war, would prevent England from giving any military aid to the Poles. "Then," Lord Grey was asked, "you think the sooner we make terms with Russia the better?" His Lordship intimated that that was his opinion.

As to any promises of help on the part of France, M. Guizot declares positively that none were given. According to M. Guizot the Poles, or at least a party among them, counted on the French democracy forcing the Government to send them aid. The Duke de Mortemart, in passing through Poland, on his way to St. Petersburg, met a party of Poles in a wood. He stopped his carriage, conversed with them for some time about their prospects, and his instructions, and this strange interview was brought to a close by the ambassador assuring the insurgents that he was only empowered to make representations on the subject of the "Kingdom" of Poland. The Poles said that was not sufficient, that they had taken up arms not for the rights of the kingdom alone, but for those of all the Russo-Polish provinces, that popular feeling in France would force the Government to interfere, whether it liked it or not, and, finally, that they meant to have all or nothing.

"Then," said the Duke de Mortemart, "it will be nothing."*

The great step in the insurrection, after which it was impossible to go back, was the declaration of the Diet that the Emperor Nicholas had ceased

* See *Guizot's Memoirs*, vol. ii.

to reign in Poland, and that the throne was vacant. Before that it had been proposed to carry on the contest in the style of feudal barons levying war against their feudal king, not with the view of dethroning him, but simply of bringing him to terms, and keeping him to his compact. It was even said that affairs ought to be so arranged that Nicholas, the Constitutional King of Poland, should seem to be fighting Nicholas, the Emperor of Russia; but this was a distinction which Nicholas, Emperor and King together, was not at all likely to appreciate. Besides, there was no clause in the Polish Constitution which gave the Diet the right of distressing the sovereign under any circumstances. The Czar Nicholas would not accept the part of mediæval king. Indeed, he was far more inclined to come out in the style of a Mongol chief, as the following manifesto sufficiently shows :—

Manifesto of the Emperor Nicholas on hearing that the throne of Poland had been proclaimed vacant by the Diet; issued January 25th (February 26th), 1837.*

(Extract.)—This audacious forgetfulness of all laws and all oaths; this indescribable madness has filled the measure of their crimes to overflowing.

* *Archives of Russia. D'Angeberg (Recueil des Traités, &c.),* p. 798.

The moment has arrived for us to put forth all our strength; and, having invoked the Supreme Judge of kings and nations, we now order our faithful soldiers to march against the rebels and exterminate them. Russians! At this decisive moment my paternal heart is grieved, but my tranquillity as a monarch is untouched: I shall fulfil my duty to the end. You are about to draw the sword of vengeance to maintain the honour and integrity of our Empire. You will unite your fervent prayers to ours, that God may bless our arms, and that He may grant His mercy to the rebels when they are brought to reason. *Know that God has destined us to establish order among all nations:* but, first of all, you must restore Poland, torn from us, for a moment, by revolution. You must replace it on firm foundations conformable to the interests of our Empire, and cut short, once and for ever, the insane projects of those who would separate it from Russia."

Everyone knows how admirably the Poles fought, and how lamentably their insurrection ended. But every one does not know how the Emperor Nicholas, after his soldiers had restored Poland to his crown, proceeded to place it on "firm foundations conformable to the interests of the Empire." The reader will get some notion of what these "firm foundations" were, and are, from the next chapter.

CHAPTER XII.

FIRM FOUNDATIONS.

October 30th (November 11th), 1831.— Oukaz, abolishing all national Judicial Forms in the Lithuanian and Ruthenian provinces of Poland.*

(Extract.)—" WE have, therefore [in consequence of the insurrection in these provinces], commanded and now command, in virtue of the oukazes of Her Majesty the Empress Catherine II., of glorious memory, and in order to extirpate all vestiges of Polonism, that in future, the Russian denominations made use of in the provinces of Great Russia be applied in all the western provinces. The administrative and judicial authorities will be entirely changed," &c., &c.

April 3rd (15th), 1832.—Order from the Emperor Nicholas, communicated to Marshal Paskievitch,

* Archives of Russia. D'Angeberg (Recueil des Traités, &c.), p. 887.

by General *Tchernyscheff*, *confiscating the library and medals belonging to the University of Warsaw.**

(Extract.)—" In communicating to your Highness this supreme decision, I have the honour to inform you, that it has pleased His Majesty to command that the debts, for which the University of Warsaw is liable, and which amount to fifty-one thousand florins, as well as those of the cabinet of medals, which amount to a hundred and fifty thousand florins, be paid out of the revenues of the kingdom, inasmuch as the Russian troops having taken Warsaw by force of arms, all these objects [*i. e.* books and medals] belong to Russia by right of war."

April 6th (18*th*), 1832.—*Order, signed by Bloudoff, Minister of the Interior, in reference to a previous order for the Transportation of* 5000 *families of the Polish nobility to the Caucasus.*†

" In the month of October, last year, a supreme order appeared concerning the transportation from Podolia to the Caucasus of five thousand families

* *Archives of Russia.* D'*Angeberg* (*Recueil des Traités, &c.*), p. 928. The Universities of Warsaw and Wilna, and the Lyceum of Kaminieç-Podolsk, were now suppressed.

† *Archives of Russia.* D'*Angeberg* (*Recueil des Traités, &c.*), p. 933.

of Polish gentlemen, formerly so-called, henceforth to bear the name of freedmen and citizens. The committee entrusted with the affairs of the provinces reconquered from Poland,* to be reunited to Russia, has ordered, by a rescript confirmed by His Majesty, that all persons be transported who desire it, and moreover, 1. Those who having taken part in the last insurrection returned at the appointed time to testify their repentance, as well as those who were included in the third class of offenders, and obtained the grace and pardon of His Majesty. 2. Those persons whose mode of life, in the opinion of the local authorities, is not such as to entitle them to the confidence of the Government, but may be regarded as suspicious. The rules presented for carrying out this order have received His Majesty's sanction. His Majesty in confirming them deigned to add with his own hand : (these rules are to serve not only for the province of Podolia, but also for all the other western provinces ; Wilna, Grodno, Witebsk, Mohilew, Bialystok, Minsk, Volhynia, and Kieff; *which will make altogether forty-five thousand families.*) His Majesty has moreover ordered, 1. That in no case shall the

---

* That is to say, the provinces seized by Catherine at the first, second, and third partitions, and which are now said to have belonged in the fourteenth century to " Russia," which, in the fourteenth century, had no existence as a State.

Government be responsible for the debts of the persons transported. Nevertheless, the persons to be transported are not to be warned beforehand; their creditors will act according to law, but this must not prevent the transportation taking place. 2. In the first instance men capable of working are to be transported; their families to be sent on afterwards. 3. Gentlemen, formerly so-called, who are not landed proprietors, who have no fixed incomes or occupations, who leave their places of residence, or who remain without employment, are to be transported to the line of the Caucasus, among the Cossacks and to be enrolled among them; and as in future they will form a part of the Cossack troops, their colony must have no communication with the colonies of the other Polish gentlemen, formerly so-called."

*May 3rd (15th), 1832.—Order signed by General Rautenstrauch, Military Governor of Warsaw, addressed to the Municipality of the City, in reference to the Incorporation of Polish children in Russian Battalions.**

"His Imperial Majesty has deigned to order that the male children of from seven to sixteen years of age who are without a home in the king-

---

* *Archives of the Administration of the Kingdom of Poland. D'Angeberg (Recueil des Traités),* p. 937.

dom be incorporated in the battalion of soldiers' children. In consequence, I order the munincipality to issue to the proper authorities the following regulations:—1. All vagabond, orphan, and homeless male children of the above-mentioned age, wherever found, are to be collected and transferred to the Alexander Barracks, under the inspection, and in exchange for the receipt of ex-captain Szaiewski. 2. In the number are to be included the male children of soldiers if their parents have declared themselves unable to support them. 3. As the said children immediately after their collection are to be forwarded to Minsk, chief town of the province of that name, and from there to the battalions for which they may be destined by the staff, they must have with them a paper, setting forth in due form the day and place of their birth, their names, those of their parents, and the occupation of the latter. The Municipality will supply the funds necessary for the maintenance of these children during the short time which will elapse until the moment of their delivery into the hands of ex-captain Szaiewski. It is the wish of His Highness the Prince Lieutenant of the Kingdom, that in case of illness the said children be sent to the nearest military hospitals. I inform the municipality of this, and order it to make the proper arrangements for carrying out the said orders."

June 4th (16th), 1832.—Order from Prince Dolgorouki, Military Governor of Wilna, directing the Russian officials to act as spies towards their subordinates and towards the Poles.*

"His Excellency, the General Governor of Wilna, having decided that all persons who render themselves dangerous by promulgating news and opinions of an injurious character must be prosecuted and exiled, has ordered me, under date of June 4th (16th), 1832, No. 1460, to announce to all the authorities that it is their most essential duty to watch all the functionaries subordinate to them, not only in respect to their public and private conduct, but also as regards their family connections and acquaintances. The presidents of all the departments, in their reports, based on their own suppositions, must, for my guidance, set forth their opinions and observations, so that according to the culpability of the persons accused they may be suspended or deprived of their functions; brought to trial or merely placed under the surveillance of the police; arrested and imprisoned in the fortresses, or exiled to the extremities of Russia, or to Siberia.

"If His Excellency, the General Governor, should happen to hear, in a direct manner, of any ill-will, or of rash opinions pronounced on political subjects,

---

* *Archives of Russia.* D'*Angeberg*, p. 939.

or of suspicious conduct on the part of a citizen or functionary—in such a case the superiors of the accused and the presidents of their respective departments will be examined most severely as to the causes which led them to keep silence on the subject; they will be discharged as incapable of occupying their posts, and will afterwards be subjected to an exemplary punishment in proportion to the extent of their culpability. The same rules are to be observed in respect to the conduct of Polish citizens and nobles."

These cruel, tyrannical, and illegal measures did not escape the notice of the English Government. On the 3rd of July, Lord Palmerston wrote a despatch to Lord Durham, who had just been appointed Ambassador at St. Petersburg, reminding him that England had protested and continued to protest against the abolition of the Constitution guaranteed to the Poles by the treaty of Vienna.

"The treaties of 1815," continued his Lordship, "to which Russia was a party (not only the general act of the Congress of Vienna, but the separate treaty between Russia and Prussia), clearly stipulate that the nationality of the Poles shall be preserved. But statements have reached His Majesty's Government which, if true, tend to show a deliberate intention on the part of the Russian Government to break down the nationality of Poland, and to deprive it of everything which, either in outward form or in real substance, gives to its people the character of a separate nation.

"The abolition of the Polish colours; the introduction of the Russian language into public Acts; the removal to Russia of the National Library and public collections containing bequests made by individuals upon specific condition that they never should be taken out of the Kingdom of Poland; the suppression of schools and other establishments for public instruction; the removal of a great number of children to Russia on the pretence of educating them at the public expense; the transportation of whole families to the interior of Russia; the extent and severity of the military conscription; the large introduction of Russians into the public employments in Poland; the interference with the National Church;—all these appear to be symptoms of a deliberate intention to obliterate the political nationality of Poland, and gradually to convert it into a Russian province.

"It is evident, upon the slightest reflection, that such a project could not be accomplished. To change 4,000,000* of Poles so entirely as to impart to them the character of Russians is an attempt for the success of which it would be difficult to assign a limit, either of time or perseverance. But

---

* Or rather, 12,000,000, for these measures were not taken against the Poles of the Kingdom alone, but against those of the Polish provinces also.

the endeavour would lead to a severe and continued exertion of arbitrary power which would create a strong and general feeling against Russia, and must be regarded as a decided violation of the engagements contracted by Russia at Vienna in 1815.

" Your Lordship will endeavour to obtain accurate information as to what is true on these points, and if you should find that the reports which have reached His Majesty's Government are well founded, you will take every favourable opportunity of urging the Russian Government, on the part of His Majesty, with the earnestness, and at the same time with the freedom, of a sincere friend, to adopt a milder and juster system; founding yourself upon the treaty of Vienna, as the basis upon which rests the right of His Majesty to interpose this expression of his feelings on the affairs of Poland."

To this Lord Durham replied that he had informed Count Nesselrode how completely the English Government adhered to its first opinion as to the right claimed by Russia to abrogate the Polish constitution. " I also told him,"* continues Lord Durham, " that the accounts which had reached England of the severities which had been practised towards the Poles had produced the most unfavourable impression on the public mind, of

* Despatch dated St. Petersburg, 22nd of August, 1832.

which acts no contradiction had ever appeared; that when I mentioned this to Prince Lieven, he denied the truth of the statements in the strongest terms, but said it was beneath the dignity of the Emperor to notice such calumnies." Count Nesselrode "used the same expressions nearly as Prince Lieven, with reference to the charges brought against them in the public papers, denied their truth, and told me that, before my departure, I should be put in possession of such details as would convince me how much the Russian Government had been calumniated."

I will now continue my extracts from Russian official documents, and will, first of all, print an order signed by the Russian Minister of the Interior, issued four days after Lord Durham's despatch was written, and which does not, precisely, confirm Prince Lieven's and Count Nesselrode's statement that the Russian Government had been "calumniated" in the reports communicated to Lord Palmerston.

*August 14th (26th). Order from Bloudoff, Russian Minister of the Interior, to Loubianoffsky, Civil Governor of Podolia, as to the transportation of Polish noblemen to the Caucasus.**

"In your report of the 27th July, you desire

* *Archives of Russia. D'Angeberg (Recueil des Traités),* p 917.

that your doubts may be cleared up as to the transportation to the Caucasus of the Polish gentlemen, formerly so-called, now citizens and freedmen. As all your steps to induce these people to give their consent to the measure have been in vain, you wish to know whether, without reference to their unwillingness, you are to cause them to be transported, in accordance with the oukaz of the Senate of the 3rd of May, 1832, and according to the rules confirmed by His Majesty on the 25th of May, 1832. The committee has decided that only those gentlemen who are landed proprietors, and who belong to the first two classes* are to be transported . . . . If the Polish gentlemen do not wish to be transported, you are authorized to take them by force."

September, 1832.—Circular to the Russian police authorities from the Civil Governor of Podolia, stating how many families are to be transported from each district in the province.†

"Take from Kamieniec one hundred and fifty families; from Proskurow fifty; from Latychew

---

* That is, 1. Insurgents who had received the Emperor's pardon, and, 2. Persons whose mode of life was "not such as to merit the confidence of the Government."

† *Archives of Russia. D'Angeberg (Recueil des Traités)*, p. 947.

one hundred;" and so on for eleven districts.
..... "Choose those gentlemen who have families, and who are proprietors, farmers, or inhabitants of towns; commencing with those who took part in the revolt, or whose mode of life is suspicious."

September 7th (19*th*), 1832.—*Address from the Assembly of the Nobility of Podolia to the Emperor Nicholas, begging him to preserve the Polish language and the Catholic religion in the Polish provinces, and not to transport Poles to the Caucasus.**

(Extract.)—"We, like other Slavonian nations, have our own language, rich in memories, and which we have used for many centuries. Common to millions of your subjects, it was left to us by your predecessors, and we cannot dispense with it in our social relations, all our contracts, agreements and other documents being drawn up in this language. . . . Leave us this language, Sire, that we may be able to pray to God for you and your family in it . . . Sire, you have thought proper to suppress the convents and confiscate their property: but from those convents came priests and preachers, the want of whom is now keenly felt. Deprived of the succour of religion, the morality of our people, with every-

* *Augsburg Gazette*, May 22, 1833. *Kubalski* (*Memoirs of*), p. 125. *D'Angeberg* (*Recueil des Traités, &c.*), p. 948.

thing overturned, would be exposed to great dangers. We beg, then, that you will be pleased to remedy the evil which threatens us. We also beg, Sire, that you will be pleased to order that no one be transported to distant regions. The poorest man that exists loves that corner of the earth where he has first seen the light. The universality of this attachment, attested by the tears of numerous families, encourages us to make an appeal to the feelings of His Majesty himself."—(*Signed by the marshals of districts.*)

Let us allow a period of six years to elapse. The following ludicrously tyrannical order then appears:—

August, 1838.—*Order signed by General Schipoff, Director of the Interior in the Kingdom of Poland, as to the abolition of the Polish costume.**

"1. The inhabitants of Polish villages and towns are not in future to wear the national costumes of Warsaw and Cracow. In consequence, it is forbidden to wear square crimson caps, peacock's feathers, belts studded with metal ornaments, or to dress in blue, crimson, or white; this last colour, however, may be used for shirts, handkerchiefs, and drawers. 2. The Russian costume, brown in colour, is to be adopted in future; women, however, can

* *Archives of Russia. Lescœur (L' Eglise Catholique sous la Russie)*, p. 120. *D'Angeberg (Recueil des Traités, &c.)*, p. 998.

wear green or red. 3. The Russian costume being much more economical, the central administration will cause shops to be opened in stated towns and villages in which Russian dresses will be sold to indigent persons at reduced prices. 4. A reward of one rouble will be given to those who hasten to obey this order; those who delay will be flogged, and their punishment doubled in case of persistence."

This last order would have a comic effect in a pantomime or a burlesque, but can scarcely have been a laughing matter to the poor Polish peasants, who no more like to be dressed up as Russians than our peasants would like to be dressed up as Frenchmen or Chinese. Whether it was found impossible to execute the order I cannot say; but even if every Russian official had been made an inspector of costume, it would have been difficult to carry it out, and certainly, at the present time, the peasants in the Kingdom of Poland wear the dress which they have been accustomed to for centuries. I saw, however, last year, on the walls of Kovno, a proclamation quite in the style of General Schipoff's, and which expressly forbade the Lithuanian peasants to wear Polish costumes.

The notion that a Lithuanian or Pole has only to put on Russian clothes in order to become a Russian seems to be deeply rooted in the Russian official mind.

The history of conquered countries must always be more or less the same. There are certain recognized forms of oppression which have been known for centuries, and which are still practised. But the Poles have suffered more in this respect than other vanquished nations, because they have never accepted their fallen position, and still persist in proclaiming themselves unconquerable, which, in a moral sense, they certainly are. No subjugated people, in modern times, has ever risen against the yoke in so resolute a manner as the Poles, and in the exact proportion to the heroic and indomitable spirit which they have shown has been the severity of the three Powers in beating them down.

The German University of Strasburg, the university where Goethe studied, was allowed to continue its existence, and the German language continued to be used in public proceedings throughout Alsace until the French revolution came and swept away provincial distinctions of all kinds.

Austria never destroyed the important municipal institutions of her Italian subjects in Lombardy and Venetia. She never abolished their universities, or merely tolerated them on condition that all the lectures should be delivered in the German language. She never ordered that at the Scala and Fenice theatres only German companies should be engaged, and that all Italian operas should be played in the German language. Yet, in the province of Galicia, with a Polish population of only four millions,* Austria endeavoured to destroy all traces of national institutions, made German the language of the law courts,† public offices, gymnasiums, and universities, and even committed the absurdity of establishing in Polish towns German newspapers, which no one reads, and German theatres which no one enters.

Prussia has been more systematic still in her plan for denationalizing the Poles of Posen, a plan which she pursues now as rigorously as ever. Russia does the same in the Polish provinces incorporated with the Empire, which she affects to regard as having nothing whatever to do with Poland.

But I was saying that the history of conquered countries must always be more or less the same, and some curious points of analogy may be shown between the position of the Poles in the present day in Russian Poland, and that of the Saxons in Norman England eight centuries ago. The conquest of Poland by Russia is generally looked upon only as a political conquest, and therefore as something quite different from that of England by

---

* Even now, by the last census, the population of Galicia is only five millions, out of which 2,800,000 are returned as Russians or Ruthenians.

† The custom of pleading in Latin was maintained in the law-courts of Galicia until the Austrian Revolution of 1848. The Polish advocates and judges preferred any language to the German.

the Normans, which was also a territorial conquest,. and from that of Russia by the Tartars, or of Hungary by the Turks, which last were conquests with a view to tribute. The Tartars, however, with all their cruelties, never did the harm to Russia that the Russians would have done to Poland, had they succeeded in their endeavours to disorganize it, and to set up class against class so as to render the whole country powerless. The Tartars did not meddle with the internal affairs of Russia, but left the people to govern themselves much as they pleased. They never systematically interfered with them in the exercise of their religion, nor endeavoured to force upon them an alien creed.

On the other hand, the Russians have made no systematic attempt to dispossess the Polish proprietors, though after the insurrection of 1830–1 the Emperor Nicholas confiscated a mass of estates in the Russo-Polish provinces, and even in the kingdom made a faint endeavour to some extent to replace the ancient Polish by a newly-created Russian aristocracy. The reader is aware that, in a political sense, there was no aristocracy in ancient Poland; but, though all nobles possessed equal political rights, of course a major influence was exercised by the chiefs of certain wealthy and illustrious families.

The Emperor thought this influence could be

secured for Russians, and that he had only to endow some of his generals with vast landed possessions, entailed after the English mode, in order to lay the basis of a powerful Russian hereditary aristocracy in Poland. The lands on which the experiment was tried were for the most part crown lands (the ancient *starosties*), and it was made a condition that the proprietors should reside on their estates. The peasants, instead of performing taskwork, were to pay rent, which the Russian generals preferred to spend in Paris, or at the German watering-places, instead of remaining in Poland to play the part of territorial aristocrats. These half-measures are of no use. The Russian Government should either have dispossessed the whole of the Polish proprietors, and made them farmers or cultivators on their own estates in the old style; or it should have governed them justly and given them such liberties as they were entitled to demand.

Besides the seizure of the crown lands, the Russian Government confiscated* a few private estates in the Kingdom, from which the income now derived amounts to about 36,000 roubles *per*

---

* A special clause in the Constitution of 1815 declares the punishment of confiscation illegal in Poland. Another declares that no Pole shall be sent to Siberia. It is rather remarkable that it should have been thought necessary to insert these clauses at all.

THE VAULTS OF THE CATHEDRAL OF CRACOW, BURIAL-PLACE OF KOSCIUSZKO, SOBIESKI, & PONIATOWSKI

annum. The country was charged with 22,000,000 roubles for the expenses of the war, and with the cost of erecting fortresses at Warsaw, Modlin, Zamosc, Demblin, and Brest. The Polish army having been suppressed, the annual sum of 3,150,000 roubles which had been paid for its maintenance, was fixed as the Polish contribution towards the support of the army of the Empire.

Thirty years afterwards I found the inhabitants of Warsaw obliged, not to put their lights out at eight o'clock, but to carry lanterns if they appeared in the streets after nine. I found them praying in the churches for Kosciuszko, and wearing his portrait in rings and brooches, as though he were a saint, which, in the eyes of the Poles, he is, just as Waltheof was one in the eyes of the Anglo-Saxons. I found them looking back to their Constitution of the 3rd of May as the English looked back to the laws of Edward the Confessor. I found their conquerors forbidding them to wear their national dress, and forcing the Lithuano-Polish peasants to disguise themselves as Russians, as the Normans ordered the English when they were expecting assistance from the Danes to assume Norman attire, Norman weapons, and to shave their beards in the Norman fashion. Historians express their surprise at the singularity of this order. They would scarcely do so if they had examined the history of the Russian rule in Poland for the last thirty years.

Finally, I found the Poles singing their national hymn and their patriotic litanies in spite of peremptory commands to abstain from doing so, just as the Anglo-Saxons persisted, through hatred of the Normans, in singing the Gregorian chant. I will here quote a passage from Thierry, and the reader will see whether it reminds him of anything that occurred in Warsaw, not eight centuries ago, but only last year, on the anniversary of Kosciuszko's death.

"They received repeated injunctions to renounce it (the chant), as well as many other ancient usages; but they resisted, and at length declared, in full chapter, their resolution not to change it. The Normans arose in a fury, went out, and immediately returned at the head of a body of soldiers, fully armed. At this sight the monks fled towards the church, and took refuge in the choir, the door of which they had time to shut. The soldiers attempted to force it, and meanwhile some of them climbed the pillars, and, placing themselves on the rafters at the top of the choir, assailed the monks below with discharges of arrows. The latter, retreating to the high altar, glided behind the shrines or reliquaries, which, serving them as ramparts, received the arrows charged against them. The great crucifix of the altar soon bristled with these missiles. By-and-by, the door of the choir yielded to the efforts of the soldiers, and the Saxons, forced in their retreat, were attacked with swords and lances; they defended themselves as best they could with the wooden benches and the metal candlesticks; they even wounded some of the soldiers, but the arms were too unequal; eighteen monks were killed, or mortally wounded," &c.

Of course, nothing like an exact parallel can be established between the conquest of Poland by Russia, and that of England by the Normans. But the Poles, like the Saxons, had to resist a combined invasion. Like them, they were always ready to fight, and often fought quite recklessly, and without the least chance of success. Harold attacked an army four times as great as his own at Hastings; Kosciuszko never did battle at such odds as these. The Poles have not struggled with more energy for their national existence than did the Anglo-Saxons in their hopeless insurrections against the Normans during the first three-quarters of a century after the conquest of England. But the Saxons had been deprived of everything at one blow, and the Normans were among them, living in their houses, on their lands, and making those whom they had dispossessed, labour as their slaves. It is no use asking whether Poland had done anything to deserve the partition. What had the

English done to deserve a simultaneous invasion on the one side from the Danes, on the other from the Normans? At least, they had not invited the Normans to England, as the Poles invited the Russians to Poland, allowing them to remain in their country for eight years before the first partition, and twenty years after it, without once rising as a nation to attack them. Neither would it be to the point here to consider the relative merits of Saxon and Norman civilization. But the Saxons, at the time of the invasion, possessed some of the virtues (such as love of liberty and patriotism) for which the Poles have been celebrated throughout their history, and also some of the faults (such as turbulence and excessive love of conviviality) for which the Poles were notorious during the reigns of *their* Saxon kings. It is quite certain, too, that the English regarded the Normans as unmitigated barbarians, or rather as degraded savages; treacherous, cruel, and abominably vicious. The Poles of Warsaw give the Russians no better character in the present day; and, indeed, much of the scum of the Russian Empire finds its way to Poland, as much of the scum of all the continent of Europe was brought over by the Norman chiefs to England. The Russians in Poland have not acted quite so barbarously as either our Normans, or their own, but on the whole, it may be said that

DIFFICULTIES OF CONQUEST. 205

they have behaved like the modern representatives of Normans who never went to the Crusades. And it is just because they are modern, and because there is a kind of conquest which in modern times is impossible, that they will never conquer Poland. They cannot hold the land without entirely subjugating those to whom it now belongs and depriving them of the means of resistance in the future as well as in the present. With all their confiscations they have not gained possession of so many estates (in proportion to the amount of territory held in a political sense) as the Prussians have in Posen by their system of forced sales, followed by loans without interest, to German purchasers. Moreover, the very Russians to whom estates have been given in Poland have either absented themselves systematically from the country, or, if they have remained, have, as a rule, acquired Polish sympathies. It is a hopeless case for Russia: she must either do justice to the Poles, or adopt measures of confiscation as extensive and as cruel as that measure of conscription which has just roused the indignation of all Europe, to such an extent that the Russian Government has found itself compelled to make an attempt to explain it away. A middle course between justice and the most terrible fear-inspiring injustice is not at all safe. Poland has had two periods of profound peace during the last half-century. The first was immediately after the promulgation of the Constitution of 1815, the coronation of Alexander I., and the announcement of his intention to extend the Constitution, already given to the Kingdom, to the Polish provinces incorporated with the Russian Empire. The second was a few years after the suppression of the insurrection of 1830, when the Emperor Nicholas, having caused the citadel to be erected outside Warsaw, informed the municipality of the city that he would not listen to a word they had to say, but that at the first sign of tumult he would lay the place in ashes. Experience, then, has shown that there are two ways of maintaining order in Warsaw. Alexander II. has hitherto endeavoured to steer between the two—with what success need not be said. If he does not like to try the mode which the Emperor Nicholas favoured, and which, to be permanently effective, ought to be carried out further than even the Emperor Nicholas ever dreamed of, why not try the system introduced by Alexander I., and gradually give it the development which that monarch certainly intended it should receive?

CHAPTER XIII.

EFFECT OF PERSECUTION ON THE POLES.

Lord Heytesbury appears to have been misinformed as to the effect of the representations made to the Russian Government on behalf of the Poles of the Kingdom. Instead of only twenty persons in the Kingdom of Poland being proceeded against, upwards of two hundred were actually sentenced to death, though their punishment was afterwards commuted by the Emperor to perpetual exile to Siberia. Then it must be remembered that thousands of insurgents, including most of the members of the Diet, many of the soldiers, and nearly all the officers of the army, had left the country, and were not to be enticed back by promises of a pardon, which some did not choose to solicit, and which others knew, if they did solicit, they would only obtain in form. Lord Heytesbury justly remarked that "in the Russo-Polish provinces incorporated with the Empire, confiscation of property, exile, or deportation to Siberia were the general lot. Not an individual has been suffered to escape who took any active part in the Revolution." He was convinced, too, that the merciless severity practised towards the Poles, after their entire submission, was chiefly due to the anger and indignation of the Russian nation, the Emperor himself being inclined, by his naturally soft heart, to deal tenderly with his erring Polish subjects now that they had returned once more to the right path.

"If" (Lord Heytesbury wrote to Lord Palmerston) " after all the blood that has been spilt, and the treasure that has been expended, in the recovery of Poland, everything is placed again upon the ancient footing, and if no punishment is inflicted on the authors of the cold-blooded assassinations* which took place in Warsaw on the first breaking-out of the insurrection, I do not believe that, irritated and exasperated as this nation is, the exercise of such magnanimity will be unattended with danger. The cry of the nation may become too powerful for even the sovereign to resist, and, in despite of himself he may, perhaps, be forced into measures which his own nobler feelings, his own unbiassed judgment, would probably induce him, under other circumstances, to reject."

* What were these " cold-blooded assassinations "? People who have suffered insults and persecution for years do not suddenly rise *in cold blood*. The generals who were killed in Warsaw on the night of the 29th November were struck down because they were endeavouring to prevent their troops from joining the national movement.

It is now known, however, that the Emperor Nicholas hated the Poles with a hatred sufficient for his whole Empire; that he added cruelty to cruelty, and with his own hand wrote directions for aggravating the punishments already decreed against them by his not too lenient ministers and judges. The reader has already seen * that when the order for transporting five thousand families from Podolia to the Caucasus was submitted to the Emperor by the Minister of the Interior he " deigned to add," with his own hand—" These rules are to serve, not only for the province of Podolia, but also for all the other western provinces; Wilna, Grodno, Witebsk, Mohilew, Bialystok, Minsk, Volhynia, and Kieff; *which will make altogether forty-five thousand families.*" The officials hesitated to carry out this inhuman order, asked for further instructions, and interposed various delays. Ultimately they removed a certain number of families by force from Podolia; but this first step caused so much indignation that it was thought advisable not to repeat it.† The Russians were either ashamed or afraid to drive some two hundred thousand Poles to the last pitch of despair, and this gigantic scheme of expatriation was abandoned. Frederic the Great had transported whole colonies from Saxony into his Prussian dominions, and

* See page 185.
† Forster, *La Pologne.*

after the Hussite war thirty thousand Bohemians were driven from their native land by Austria. But, as the immense Frederic remarks in one of his letters, "These vain and intriguing Poles cry out about everything." * They are, indeed, very like the inhabitants of certain isles who have been described as "so ferocious that when they are attacked they defend themselves."

But perhaps the blackest and most cowardly action committed by Nicholas in his persecution of the Poles, and certainly one of the most cruel actions ever committed by a ruler in the history of Europe, was his condemnation of the young Prince Sanguszko as a felon. I have seen Russians and Poles who had been confined in fortresses, sent to the east of Russia, exiled even to Siberia (one cannot know many subjects of the Russian Empire without being acquainted with a few who have felt individually the hand of despotism pressing upon them), and have always heard them say that what they had to complain of was, that they had been imprisoned or exiled, and not of any positive ill-treatment beyond that. These, however, must have been fortunate men who had not seriously provoked the Government. Very different was the fate of Prince Roman Sanguszko. Until I went to Poland, I

* Correspondence of Frederick II. in *Frédéric II., Catherine, et le Partage de la Pologne.*

could scarcely believe the story of his having been sent to Siberia on foot with a gang of robbers and assassins; I thought there must be some exaggeration (a fault from which Polish writers are, of course, not entirely free), or perhaps some mistake. Since then, however, I have met near relations and intimate friends of this unhappy man, and there can be no doubt as to his having been subjected to the vilest punishment, and that by the express order of the Emperor. The crime committed by the Prince was that of having fought for his country. He was well acquainted with some of the members of the Imperial family, had been in the habit of meeting the Empress at Berlin when he was a student and when she was still a Prussian Princess, and had often danced with her at her father's court. She was horrified, as any woman of the least heart must naturally have been, at the thought of this young man of twenty-four being sent for life to Siberia to work in the mines, and entreated the Emperor to pardon him, or, at least, to mitigate his punishment. The Empress herself and all the sisters of the young Prince went down on their knees and begged the Emperor to spare him. These prayers were not without their effect on the tyrant. He sent for the order condemning the Prince to hard labour in the mines, and "deigned to add" with his own hand, "*To be conducted to his destination on foot.*"

Did the Emperor Nicholas really feel touched by the prayers addressed to him? Was he afraid of showing that he was not absolutely inflexible, and was it to prove the contrary that, with the obstinacy of a savage, he increased a punishment already atrociously severe, simply because he had been implored to diminish it? Or was he enraged that any member of his family should dare to take an interest in the fate of a Polish insurgent and determined to punish such audacity by making that fate still worse? However this may have been, Prince Roman Sanguszko, dressed as a felon, and chained, wrist by wrist, to a murderer, was compelled to make his terrible march to Siberia in the convict gang.

A picture has been painted of Prince Sanguszko working in the mines; but this, however truthful, is still the offspring of an artist's imagination. I was much more impressed by seeing a little black cross in Siberian wood, which he had cut out himself, and marked with his initials in Siberian stones, picked up in his own mine. He had sent this memento, this palpable cry *de profundis*, to a friend in Galicia, at whose house I also saw a model he had made of his half-subterranean hut, and a portrait he had painted of himself, in the loose grey coat of a Russian soldier—for after a certain period of probation under ground, he had been promoted to be a private in some regiment of the line, where his great misfortunes did not save him from being struck on those numerous occasions when a recruit who is being drilled is tolerably sure to come in for hard blows. It is to be hoped, and I think, may be supposed, that his officers were ignorant as to who and what he was.

Formerly, when a Pole took leave of his friends, to go to Siberia, his parting salutation was "Goodbye, may we never meet again!" for there was no chance of his returning. Prince Roman Sanguszko, however, has come back totally deaf, but not dumb. Indeed, the present Emperor, soon after his accession, recalled all the Polish exiles who were suffering for political offences in Siberia.

The worst of the Poles is, that they come back from exile, if possible, greater patriots than when they went there; calmer, perhaps, and more resigned, but certainly not less determined. There are many of these returned exiles in Warsaw now, and they even form an important element in the population of that unhappy city. They are the living witnesses of the indestructibility of the Polish national spirit; and the sight of these brave, indomitable men, who have come back from the mines with the loss, perhaps, of their health, and their gaiety, but with no loss of faith in the future of their country, is an encouragement to those who have yet to make that terrible journey, the recognized "grand tour" of the Polish patriot.

The anguish caused in the mind of a Pole by the thought of the fate that awaits the noblest children of Poland, unless the history of their country and of its former glory, is kept from them like a forbidden book, has found vent in an admirable poem by Miçkievicz, addressed "To a Polish mother." I give the best translation of it that I can make, and am sorry that it is not more worthy of the original :*—

1.

O Polish mother! when thy son's bright eyes
Flash with the light of genius; when he flies
The games of his young playmates, and aspires
To hear the story of his noble sires,

2.

Whose glories cast a halo round his brow;
—O Polish mother, pray for mercy now!
Down on thy knees, before the Virgin kneel:
The sword which pierced her heart *thy* heart shall feel!

* A very beautiful translation of another of Miçkievicz's poems, in quite a different style, will be found in the Appendix (No. 3).

3.

Though peace may smile benignant o'er the world,
The cannons silent and the banners furled;
No peace for him, nor e'en a glorious strife:
A martyr without hope he ends his life.

4.

Send him to breathe the air of some damp cave,
To ponder o'er his fate, his early grave;
There on a little straw thy son should crouch,
Sharing with reptiles his uncleanly couch.

5.

There let him learn to check all manly pride,
All natural joys, all natural rage to hide;
There let him seek his vengeance to control;
There let its poison eat into his soul.

6.

Teach him to clothe his thoughts in mean disguise,
To speak each word as though the walls were spies;
Until by dint of study he can make
Himself as cold and crawling as a snake.

7.

The Infant Jesus, as the legends say,
Played with the cross at Nazareth, one day:
O Polish mother! this thy lesson be:
Thy child must learn to feel his destiny.

8.

Before the tumbril he must not grow pale,
Nor redden at the hangman's rope, nor quail
Before the axe, nor dread a felon's brand:
To manacles accustom his young hand.

9.

Think not because his ancestors could boast
Of having routed many a Moslem host,
Of having fought in freedom's glorious name,
That *he* can ever earn a warrior's fame.

10.

His fate is not in open field to die;
His one acknowledged foe will be—a spy!
Vanquished, his only monument will be
The warning figure of the gallows-tree;

11.

His immortality a passing tear
Shed by some foolish girl upon his bier;
While other youths—a sympathetic crowd—
Whisper the fate they dare not tell aloud.

CHAPTER XIV.

EFFECT OF PERSECUTION (CONTINUED).—"THE MARTYRS."

THE sort of impression which the tyranny of the Russians makes upon a number of innocent, enthusiastic young men is set forth in a drama by Miçkievicz; a drama in which every scene, every personage is real, and in which the author himself played a part. A portion of the action takes place in the prison of Wilna, where the poet was confined with Sobolewski, Joseph Kavalewski, Felix Kolakowski, the Abbé Lwowicz, Freiend, Jegota, and others, for the most part members of the Wilna University, on a charge of belonging to an association having for its object "the maintenance and propagation of the insane Polish nationality." * Sobolewski has just returned from the police-office, where he has been undergoing an examination. On the principal

---

* By Article I. of the Treaty of Vienna it is stipulated that the Poles, subjects respectively of Russia, Austria, and Prussia, shall obtain "a national representation and institutions!"

square, between the Town Hall and the Church of St. Kasimir, he has seen twenty *kibitkas*,—

("A cursed sort of carriage without springs,
Which on rough roads leaves scarcely a whole bone,"

is Byron's description of a *kibitka* in *Don Juan*,) full of young men and even children, about to be sent into exile. The square is filled with a dense crowd, and the congregation rushes out of the church to see what fresh horror is being enacted, leaving the priest at the altar to continue the mass by himself. Sobolewski and the corporal who has him in charge, stop for a moment under the church porch.

"The *kibitkas* advanced," says Sobolewski in narrating what he has seen to his companions, "and the prisoners were thrown into them one by one. I looked at the compact crowd of spectators and soldiers. All their faces were as pale as death, and in this immense assemblage there reigned such a silence that I could hear every footstep and the rattling of every chain. The people, the army, were all moved, but all were silent, for all dreaded the Tsar. At length, the last prisoner was brought out. He seemed to resist; but the fact was he could scarcely drag himself along, poor boy, and tottered as he moved. They made him walk slowly down the steps; but he had hardly put his foot on the second when he rolled over, and fell to the ground. It was Wassilewski, our neighbour in captivity. He had received so many blows at the interrogatory two days before that his face was as pale as death. A soldier came and raised the motionless body. With one arm he carried it to the *kibitka*, while with the other he wiped away the tears he could not restrain. It was an awful sight. Wassilewski had not fainted, but he had become stiff with the fall: he was as straight as a beam, and his arms were stretched out above the soldier's neck as if he had died on the cross. His eyes were staring lifeless and wide open; and the crowd also opened its eyes and its lips; and from a thousand breasts an immense sigh burst forth, a deep hollow sigh, as though all the tombs in the vaults beneath the church had given out one general groan. The commander stifled it beneath the rolling of his drums, and the order "To arms, quick march!" put the column in motion. All the *kibitkas* went off like lightning down the street. One only seemed to be empty. It contained a prisoner whose body could not be seen, but whose hand, all numb and dead, hung out stretched towards the people, and trembled and shook as if to say farewell. This *kibitka* disappeared with the rest. Before the driver could whip his way through the crowd, he was obliged to stop before the church, and just as the corpse was passing, I heard the altar bell. The nave was now deserted. I saw the hand of the priest raising to heaven the body and blood of the Saviour, and exclaimed, "Lord, Thou who didst shed Thy innocent blood for the salvation of the world, Thou who wast condemned by Pilate, receive this young victim condemned by the Tsar! He is less holy, for he is not divine, like Thou, but he is not less innocent!'" (*A long silence.*)

JOSEPH.

I have read the histories of certain wars in primitive and barbarous ages. It is written that in those days the enemy did not spare the trees of the forest, and that he set woods and harvests on fire. But the Tsar is more ingenious; the bloody wounds he inflicts on Poland are deeper and more cruel. He carries away and buries even the seeds; and Satan himself has taught him the secret of destruction.

FELIX.

And Satan himself will give his pupil a prize. (*Silence.*)

* * * *

JEGOTA.

Joseph was speaking just now of seeds . . . If the Tsar wishes to carry away and bury all the seeds of our garden in his own land, wheat may become dear, but there need be no fear of famine. Anthony has already given us a treatise on this kind of rural economy.

A PRISONER.

What Anthony?

JEGOTA.

Do you know the fable of Gorecki,* or rather do you know the truth?

SEVERAL PRISONERS.

Let us hear it.

JEGOTA.

When God banished the first sinner from the garden of Paradise, He did not wish the man to die of hunger, and caused the angels to spread along the road all the seeds of the earth. Adam came by, and, not knowing the use of them, went on. But the Devil, being a *savant*, came at dusk, looked at them, and said to himself, " It cannot be without reason that God has strewed these handfuls of wheat about : there must be some secret virtue in the grains ; let me put them out of sight before the man knows their value." He then dug a furrow in the ground with his horns, filled it with wheat, inundated it with saliva, covered it up, and beat

---

* Colonel Antony Gorecki, one of the heroes of the national war of 1830. Amongst his comrades was another great fabulist, General Theodore Morawski. " We are waiting for you with open arms," said a Russian general to the latter during a conference. " Yes, that you may stifle us," replied Morawski.

down the earth with his feet and nails. Proud and joyful at having frustrated the designs of God, he burst into a roar of laughter, and disappeared. But He lost nothing by waiting. The spring brought forth the corn, grass ear, and grain, to the utter stupefaction of the Devil.

O you who rule the world by favour of night, who call craft genius and atrocity power; know that those who find faith and liberty, and, thinking to deceive God, bury them in the earth, make no dupes but themselves!

JANKOWSKI.

But look at Lwowicz. I declare he is praying. Stop; I will sing him a Litany.*

N'attendez pas que je m'écrie,
Jesus-Marie!
Pour que je croie et que je prie,
Jesus-Marie!
Il faut avant qu'elle châtie,
Jesus-Marie!
Le Tsar qui souille ma patrie,
Jesus-Marie!

Tant que le Tsar est plein de vie,
Jesus-Marie!
Que Novosiltzoff communie,
Jesus-Marie!
Tant que je crains la Sibérie,
Jesus-Marie!
N'attendez pas que je m'écrie,
Jesus-Marie!

* This translation is by M. Christian Ostrowski.

The above scene (which the reader must remember is simply a fine poetical painting of a scene in real life) shows perfectly how persecution will affect persons of different temperaments, dispositions, and power of resistance. It fortifies some minds, perverts others, and others again destroys altogether.

Some of the Poles issue from the Russian furnace stronger and purer than ever, with the original iron of their nature tempered into the finest steel. Others are rendered more or less malleable, and it is sad to think that those of baser metal must sometimes be reduced by the trial to the merest dross. It is a trial that any man, however confident in himself, may well pray to be spared; but, as a rule, the baser Poles can contrive to avoid it, and it is only the best and bravest among them who have to suffer. Accordingly, persecution, on the whole, has had a really elevating and ennobling effect on the character of the Poles; and if in former times they were too gay, too careless and thoughtless in the midst of their liberty, God knows that the shade of seriousness, said to have been wanting, has now been added in sufficiently deep tints!

But does not persecution turn some of them into assassins?

Here I may give another fragment from

Miçkievicz's drama. To quote instances, to repeat anecdotes in a case like this, would be of no avail. But Miçkievicz has felt everything that a Pole can feel, and he writes out of his own heart as if out of the heart of Poland. He can sympathize with the ardent, impulsive Pole who, maddened by repeated acts of oppression, would strike a fatal, hopeless blow in a moment of despair; with the calmer Pole (or Russian) who is ready to strike but at the proper moment and not in vain; and, finally and above all, with the religious Pole who would not strike at all, but leave the punishment of his country's oppressors to Heaven. The scene has changed to a ball-room in the Governor's palace. Novosiltzoff, the instigator of the prosecutions directed against the students, is passing to and fro. The mother of a dying prisoner has forced her way into the room, followed by a priest who seeks permission to attend the victim in his last moments. Among the functionaries, military and civil, who crowd the room, are one or two officers, members of the secret society for the liberation of Russia and Poland, directed by Ryleieff and Pestel. Bestoujeff* is speaking to Justin Pol, one

---

* Bestoujeff was the plenipotentiary in Poland of the Russian Revolutionists of 1825. " He used to reproach our patriots," says M. Ostrowski, in one of the notes to his translation of Miçkievicz, " with their attachment to the monarchical form, and their repugnance to shedding the

of the associates of Miçkievicz, Sobolewski, and the other inmates of the prison of Wilna. The dialogue is supposed to be recited to music—that of the minuet in the ball-scene of *Don Juan*. At the end, the orchestra make a mistake, and pass on to the trombone music of the *Commendatore*.

> JUSTIN POL. (*as* NOVOSILTZOFF *approaches*). Oh,
>   let me stab him to the heart!
> If not, I slap the villain's face.
>   BESTOUJEFF. Be pleased to play no foolish part:
> You do not understand the case.
> Put up your dagger! what's the use
> Of this one miscreant to dispose?
> You'll only give them an excuse
> The University to close.
>   JUST. But will he not in torments die,
> Both in thy country's name and mine?
>   BEST. Not yet: the day is drawing nigh;
> And then my arm shall follow thine!
>   JUST. My hand is itching for the blow.
>   BEST. In Poland's name, your vengeance stay!

blood of sovereigns. Let the Russians proceed. When they once begin their revolution, they will go further than the Poles. Their despotism is after the Tartar model, and their liberty will be of the Scandinavian pattern." (The Poles affect a great contempt for Scandinavians, probably because the principal men in Russian history have been of Scandinavian descent.)

JUST. I do but strike my country's foe.
BEST. And all your countrymen betray.
JUST. Tyrants, oppressors, filthy spies!
BEST. (*leading him towards the door*)—As well
our homeward path we trod.
JUST. Unless to-night this monster dies,
Who shall avenge my country?
THE PRIEST. God!
(*Music changes.*)

SEVERAL GUESTS. What means this music?
(*A clap of thunder is heard, &c., &c.*)*

In spite, however, of the hatred of the Russians nurtured in every Polish breast, and which is kept up not only by the recollection but by the constant repetition of acts of cruel persecution, the fate of all Poland seems to be linked indissolubly (at least for a time) with that of Russia. Putting aside the question of community of race (which a Pole will assert or deny, according to his political feelings, without any reference to strict ethnology), the Poles certainly feel that the Russians have a greater respect for them than the Germans, and

* Early one morning, in the finest possible weather (according to the tradition), Dr. Bécu, Novosiltzoff's confidential friend and agent, was struck by lightning. General Baikoff, another of Novosiltzoff's agents, died of apoplexy after a night's debauch. The Mozart-like termination to Miçkievicz's drama is quite in accordance with facts.

that they do not, cannot, like the Germans, affect to look upon the civilization of the Poles as inferior to their own.

"I do not pretend to like either Russians, Austrians, or Prussians," a Pole said to me one day who had lived upwards of twenty years in Russia. But at least the Russians do not despise us; they take an interest in our ideas, they study our literature, they respect the heroism of our soldiers, though it has been exhibited against themselves. Then, they are not pedants; they are a young people, and there is more to be hoped from them than from any of the Germans, so strong in their own conceit. If the Russians find a Pole among them, they will often show him an amount of attention which he never could expect or in any way desire from Prussians or Austrians."

Any Polish reader will guess that this gentleman was a native of Posen. But I have heard Poles from all parts of Poland say the same thing in other words, though, as a rule, one must not expect the Poles of the Kingdom to be so well inclined towards the Russians as those who have suffered for some time under a German Government. Doubtless, it is only out of despair that the Poles turn to the Russians at all; but, nevertheless, and in spite of occasional massacres at Warsaw, they do turn to them, as a nation, more and more every day; and you may often hear Poseners and Galicians say, "Why, even the Russians, with all their ferocity, are better than these mean, pettily-persecuting Germans!"

On the other hand, did anyone ever know a Pole of Russian Poland who thought his countrymen could under any circumstances form an alliance with Prussia or Austria? I think not. I could mention several instances of Poles leaving Posen to live in the Kingdom of Poland, or in Russia Proper, but not one of a Pole leaving the Kingdom of Poland (unless driven out) to live in Posen or Galicia. This does not, of course, prove that the Germans rule the Poles more harshly than the Russians. It only shows that the Poles do not dislike the Russians, as a nation, so much as they dislike the Germans.

One thing which quite convinces me that the Poles will ultimately form a union with the Russians (whether for a long time or not is another question) is that, attack them as they may, they attack the Germans quite as much; while they often attribute a superiority to the Russians over the Germans and over other nations, which it is certain that the Russians do not possess; admire them for qualities in which, as a nation, they are deficient; and see in them virtues which one would like to see, but which are really far more visible to the Slavo-Polish than to any other foreign eye. With the Germans they will have nothing whatever to do, but they have already a *nec sine te nec cum te* sort of feeling towards Russia; and in the same volume you may find a Polish author representing the Russians as a nation of sanguinary, degraded, superstitious savages, and as a strong, truthful, simple-minded, religious people, with a glorious future before them. He will perhaps establish a distinction between the Slavonian Mongolized and the Slavonian pure and uncorrupted as he has been, and as he may be again; he will say that the bad qualities of the Russians are attributable to the manner in which they have been governed, and that their good qualities are natural to them; finally, he will separate the Government from the people, and will tell us that the demoralization caused by the action of the Government is all on the surface of society, and that beneath this crust there is a mass of goodness, which will either throw off the crust or absorb it and transmute it.

This, it may be said, is very like revolution. It certainly has that disadvantage; and, no doubt, many of the Poles look to a revolution in Russia as a necessary step towards their liberation; though there are others who think the Russian Government will, before long, find it to its interest to carry out the programme of Alexander I. in 1815, and unite all the Polish provinces under the Russian sceptre into one constitutional kingdom; and others again (namely, the Marquis Wielopolski, with a few friends and agents) who would have the Poles at once cease all agitation, trust implicitly to the generosity of the Emperor, and sacrifice for the present all legitimate demands, so that they may gain in time even more than they are entitled by treaties to ask for; so that by the aid of Russia they may reconquer Posen and Galicia from the Germans. There is, however, one revolutionary party among the Russians who, at this moment, would gladly join the Poles in an attempt to subvert the existing Imperial Government, with the view of forming a free Slavonian confederation, in which Poland would be one of the principal States.

I do not say that at present there exists much sympathy between Poles and Russians. The Poles have had and still have a far greater sympathy for other nations; but other nations do not respond to it, or respond to it by diplomatic despatches, speeches, and newspaper articles, whereas the Russians, it is thought, would, at the proper moment, be ready to fight on behalf of a united Poland under the Russian Crown—which, for the Poles, is the next best thing possible to a Poland united and independent. France and England have been appealed to, over and over again, to assist Poland against the partitioning Powers. Who is to complain if, having no other course open to her, she shall some day, in her despair, accept the aid of the strongest and most enterprising of those Powers against the two weaker ones?

CHAPTER XV.

HOW POLAND FELL.

FROM the first to the third partition of Poland, scarcely a word was said about Polish affairs in the British House of Commons, though, shortly before the second partition, there were numerous debates on the war between Russia and Turkey. England viewed the partition of Poland with complete indifference. The King made a vague allusion to the first partition in a speech from the throne of the same year, but only spoke of it as a political change which did not endanger the peace of Europe.

The seizure of the fortress of Oczakow was considered a far more alarming event, and it was formally proposed to declare war against Russia unless the Empress Catherine surrendered it. In one of the debates on the Oczakow question,[*] Burke defended Russia very vigorously, saying that Russia was a barrier against the Turks and against the Tartars of the Crimea, who, but for it, might easily penetrate through Poland into the heart of

---

[*] 1791. See *Parliamentary History*.

Europe, "carrying with them devastation and plague." Poland, therefore, must have been regarded, some years after the first partition, as a lost country, unable to defend its own frontiers; and, doubtless, this opinion was entertained of it before the partition took place. We are often told in the present day that Poland was "the natural barrier against Russian aggression"; but in the early part of the eighteenth century it had already ceased to be a barrier against aggression of any kind, more especially against that of Russia. Prussians, Austrians, and Russians violated Polish territory just as they pleased, and the Russians marched through the Ukraine to attack the Turks, as though the Ukraine were already one of their possessions.

Prussia, in the Seven Years' War, had been able to resist with success the arms of Sweden, Saxony, Russia, Austria, and France; and Poland would not have succumbed beneath the threats of Russia, Austria, and Prussia, had not the country been thoroughly disorganized at the time. The partition really brought the country to life again by reviving the national spirit of the Poles, and stimulating them to make enormous sacrifices, which some day will bear their fruit.

Fox said nothing about Poland during the debates on the Russo-Turkish war; but he complimented the Empress Catherine on her great abilities, upon which Pitt remarked that the bust of Fox figured at the Hermitage, between those of Cicero and Demosthenes. Fox replied that if great potentates liked to do him honour, it was not for him to complain.

In 1791, two years before the second partition, there were several debates on the subject of the Prussian alliance, in the course of which Prussia was represented as being greatly alarmed at the progress of Russia. She was justly taunted by Lord Fitzwilliam (debate of April 1) with having been a party to the very act by which Russia had rendered herself formidable to her; but the partition seems still to have been reprobated more as a political than as a moral iniquity.

It is remarkable, too, that in Boswell's *Johnson* there is not a word about Poland, though the first partition took place within the period over which the conversations extend. Catherine, however, is mentioned, and we are told that one of Johnson's reasons for wishing to make his projected Baltic tour was that he might see an Empress "whose abilities, information, and *magnanimity* astonish the world;" and that when he heard the *Rambler* was to be translated into Russian he was much delighted, and exclaimed, "I shall now be read on the banks of the Volga. Horace was only read on the banks of the Rhine," &c.

Thanks to the Russian reviews, all our best historians, novelists, and essayists of the present day are read on the banks of the Amoor, and wherever the Russian language penetrates.

The bust of Fox was, no doubt, placed between those of Cicero and Demosthenes that Fox might feel disposed to speak favourably of the Empress in the House of Commons. The *Rambler* may have been translated into Russian for similar reasons, the Empress being well aware that Johnson was the greatest talker and one of the greatest writers of his day. So Catherine invited the French encyclopædists to continue their work in Russia after it had been stopped in France, that she might win the good opinion of them and all their friends, a design in which she fully succeeded.

But I was remarking, that whereas now scarcely a session passes without a debate on the affairs of Poland, not a word was said in Parliament when the first partition was taking place—in spite of a direct appeal from Stanislas Augustus to George III., which must have passed through the hands of the Ministry. "That is no honour to the English Parliament," said a Pole, a member of the Galician Diet, to whom I was speaking one day of this remarkable silence. Such is also my opinion, but I also think it was no honour to Poland that her misfortunes should have excited so little sympathy in an assembly where Pitt, Burke, and Fox were sitting, and which, on other subjects, showed itself ready to listen to every generous call. How energetically the natives of India were defended against the oppression of our own administration! Even the Turks had their champions at a time when it was even more difficult than it is now to say anything in their favour. But at least the Turks were a living people, whereas Poland seemed to have fallen into a state of atrophy. There was a much stronger anti-Russian party in the House of Commons then than there is at present—if any such party now exists at all. Burke, opposed as he was to the destruction of Poland, was almost the only man who was not alarmed by the success of the Russian arms in Turkey, and said, ninety years ago, what is now beginning to be generally understood—that if Russia extends her territory much further to the south, the Russian Empire must break up, and that St. Petersburg and Constantinople can never belong to the same Power. The "House of Brandenburg" had also numerous enemies in the English Parliament, where the swindling policy of Frederic, the great utterer of false money in Poland, kidnapper of men, women, and children in Saxony, and violator of his word everywhere, was often appreciated at its just value. We may be sure that Poland would have had her friends had she deserved them, and she *did* have them when she reformed her institutions and went into the field to fight for them;

but it was then too late to save her. We know that Kosciuszko, before marching against the enemy, took an oath at Cracow, in presence of his troops, to drive the three invaders from his native land, or perish in the attempt; but Lelewel has told us that Kosciuszko's companions knew the insurrection to be hopeless, and that they fought from a sense of duty and from despair.* In 1772, it was from her own sons that Poland would have had to be rescued. Some were traitors in the pay of Russia. Many were blindly attached to the ancient state of things, and violently opposed to the most necessary reforms. The Czartoryskis, who knew well the defects of the Polish Constitution and were earnestly bent on remedying them, relied on Catherine to enable them to introduce the necessary changes. The King was not by any means a willing tool in Russian hands; but, after being told by the King of England that " God alone could help him," and receiving no answer to his prayer for assistance from the King of France, to whom was he to appeal? Without money, without troops, without allies, he had no choice but to submit. Had he resisted—had he, for instance, joined the Confederates of Bar (which, as Miçkievicz tells us, he was often in moments of despair on the point of doing), it may be considered certain

* Lelewel's speech on the first anniversary of the insurrection of 1830.

that the existence of Poland as an independent State would have been terminated in 1772. As it was, Poland had time to make her political will before the last blow was struck.

The Constitution of 1791 is an admirable memorial. It tells us what Poland died for, and by what right she claims to live again. It was put in action, too, at the proper moment, though human foresight had nothing to do with this. The Poles, when the Great Diet met for the purpose of reforming the laws of the State in 1788, could not tell that the French Revolution was at hand. But it was precisely this Revolution, and the war to which it led, that enabled them to take an active part in the affairs of Europe immediately after the third partition of their country,* and so to distinguish themselves in their national legions as to encourage Napoleon to form the Duchy of Warsaw.

Why, however, it may be asked, were the necessary reforms delayed so long? Why, above all, were they not introduced long before the fatal year of 1772?—for the partition ought certainly to have taken no one by surprise.

Sobieski, on his death-bed (1695), spoke of the state of Poland as hopeless, and refused to make

* 1795.

his will, on the ground that such a proceeding was ridiculous in a country where corruption universally prevailed, and where any legal decision could be obtained for money. "*O medici mediam contundite venam!*" he exclaimed to Bishop Zaluski, and asked him whether he was delirious, to talk of will-making in Poland, and whether he imagined that a king, whose orders had not been executed during his lifetime, would be obeyed when dead? *

Twenty-seven years before, John Casimir, in his speech to the Diet on the occasion of his abdication, had foretold the ultimate fate of the Republic, in precise terms, mentioning the very portions of territory which would be seized, and which, a century afterwards, *were* seized by the surrounding Powers.†

Augustus II. did more than this. He himself arranged a plan of dismemberment—keeping, of course, for himself a considerable share. Russia was to have taken Lithuania and the Ukraine; Austria, the province of Zips; Prussia, the province now called West Preussen; while the "Man of Sin," the "Physically Strong," was to have become real hereditary King of a Poland, not

* *Zaluski, Epistolæ*, vol. iii. pp. 5—14.
† *Zaluski, Epistolæ*, vol. i. p. 57—quoted in every history of Poland.

much larger than the Kingdom of Poland of 1815, and of the present day, with Galicia and Posen added. This plan was about to be put into execution when Augustus died.*

But the most striking prediction of the downfall of the country was uttered in the beginning of the seventeenth century, during the reign of Sigismund III., by the priest Skarga, in a sermon which breathes such lofty indignation against the tyranny of the Polish nobles, and such sublime tenderness for Poland, that, in reading it, one is reminded of the love of the Hebrew prophets for Jerusalem, and of their terrible denunciations against their own countrymen. Skarga is full of the most exalted patriotism, and it can be seen that he loves the men on whom he is pronouncing a kind of malediction. Even the worst of them could not have been thoroughly bad, or they would not have listened to him. He is preaching before the Diet.

"Trustees of the governing power, guardians of the public liberties," he commences, "do not forget that you are here in presence of God, accompanied and mysteriously surrounded by the souls of the nations you represent. The people of Lithuania, Russia,† Samogitia, Prussia, and Samo-

* *Carlyle, History of Friedrich II.*, book ix. chap. 6.
† *i.e.* the Polish Province of that name, known also as

gitia, watch you, and adjure you by my mouth. Our safety is in your hands; save us from internal discord and from foreign invasion. This Diet is our mother and our nurse: we hunger, we thirst; it is for you to feed us with justice and with mercy. In the Diet resides the wisdom of the nation. We need your enlightenment; you are our chiefs, our fathers; we are your soldiers, your children. Brought up in honour and dignity, you are those mountains spoken of by the prophet which the Lord commanded to receive from heaven the dew of peace, and to shower upon the plains the rain of justice. Have pity on us. May God inspire you with the love of your country, with love as vast as the country itself. Let us love this country, my brethren, this Jerusalem. Let us say with the prophet, 'If I forget thee, may my right hand forget its cunning! May my tongue cleave to the roof of my mouth, if I forget thee, O my country!'"

The men he was addressing often interrupted him with murmurs.* With one exception all the senators were Protestants. They stood before the altar, lifting up their heads, and moving them about so as to make the diamond clasps in their caps

---

*" Red Russia," or " Ruthenia," and which, since the partitions, has been included in the Austrian Empire under the name of Eastern Galicia.

* Miçkievicz, Cours de Littérature Slave, vol. ii. p. 264.

glisten the more. When the host was elevated, the King alone went down on his knees.

Skarga had not much sympathy to expect from his congregation. He was addressing the most powerful men in Poland. Their soldiers were encamped in thousands round the church, and their lawlessness was precisely one of the things he had to reproach them with.

"When I see you all here before me, I can tell what your habits and general conduct are," he continues; "I perceive the great evil of the country in all its fulness." After speaking of the ambition of political parties, the power usurped by the nobility, the little respect paid to the authority of the King, he bursts into the following indignant appeal on behalf of the peasants:—

"And the sweat, the blood of our peasants, which flow incessantly, and moisten and redden the whole earth — what a terrible future they are preparing for this kingdom! I know of no country in Christendom where the peasants are so treated. And you cry out against absolute power, which no one either wishes or is able to impose upon you. Hypocrites and declaimers! 'You have destroyed my vine,' saith the Lord; 'why crush ye thus my people, crushing it as the millstone crusheth the corn?' By what right do you obstinately refuse to change this infamous law? These peasants are your neighbours. They are Poles like you. They speak the same language and are children of the same country. Formerly the Christians gave liberty to their slaves when they baptized them, and they became their brothers in Jesus Christ; but you, you dare to keep Christians, who are your fellow-countrymen, in bondage. I know that you do not all act in this manner; but those who commit such crimes, how do they not blush in the face of Christendom, which beholds them, and of which they call themselves members?"

"Skarga plunges his dagger," says Miçkievicz, "into the heart of the national conscience, and turns it round and round."

He then predicts all the terrible calamities which a century and a half afterwards fell upon the Polish nation; not in symbols or metaphors, but in the clearest and most precise manner. There were no external signs of Poland's breaking-up, nor signs of any kind that would have been visible to a man of less insight than Skarga. The Poles, during the reign of Sigismund III., gained numerous victories over the Swedes, the Muscovites, and the Tartars. A Polish army took Moscow, and Ladislas, Sigismund's son, had the throne of Muscovy offered to him by the boyards, and, but for the refusal of Sigismund to give guarantees for the maintenance of the Russian national religion, would have been crowned king. Nevertheless, Skarga addressed the principal nobles of Sigismund's reign as follows :—

"The foreign enemy who is seeking to crush you will advance towards you, and, seizing you by your weak side, laying his hand on your dissensions, will cry out, 'Now that their hearts are no longer of one accord they are lost.' And he will profit by this moment so fatal to you, and so favourable to his tyranny. . . . . . On the traces of your discords foreign despotism will advance and swallow up all your liberties. These liberties, of which you are so proud, will become the fable of posterity, and the laughing-stock of the world. For your children will perish, with their families and all that belongs to them. They will die in misery in the hands of their enemies. . . . . . .

"Your language, the only one among the Slavonian tongues chosen and adopted by liberty, you will see destroyed. You will see your race degenerate, and what remains of it will be dispersed through the world. And you will be condemned to undergo a horrible metamorphosis; to assume the manners and habits of a people who hate and despise you.

"You will no longer have a King of your nation, you will no longer be permitted to choose any King. Poor, miserable, vagabond exiles, you will be driven out of those very countries which now court your alliance."

In the midst of his sermon Skarga was interrupted by the arrival of a courier, who brought the news of a great victory gained by Chodkiewicz over the Swedes. All the members of the Diet, senators and nuncios together, fell on their knees, the *Te Deum* was sung, and Skarga then continued as follows:—

"How can this unhappy nation be saved? I ought to go, like Isaiah, barefooted, and covered with rags, crying out, 'Hardhearted sinners, rebels against the law of God, thus shall you be stripped, thus shall you be seen in your misery.' Your wickedness, like a high wall, in which the cracks can even now be seen, will fall upon you when you least expect it, and crush you. I ought, like Jeremiah, to appear before you with my feet in irons, and with a chain round my neck, and cry out, 'Thus will your chiefs be bound and carried into slavery!'

"I ought to come before you with my coat in tatters and eaten by worms, and shaking it, show you, when it falls into dust, how your glory and grandeur will also pass away. Finally, taking a vessel of clay, and throwing it with all my force against the wall, I ought to cry out with the prophet, 'Thus will I break you, saith the Lord, like this vessel, that cannot be made whole again.'" . . . .

Then stopping suddenly, and as if struck by a vision, he exclaimed:—

"Who will give me enough tears to weep day and night, the misfortunes of the children of my country? So thou art bereft, beautiful land! mother of so many children. I see thee in captivity, O proud kingdom! and thou bewailest thy sons, and there is no one to console thee. Thy former friends betray thee, and drive thee out. Thy leaders, thy warriors, are driven like a flock; they traverse the earth without stopping, and without finding a refuge. Our churches and our altars are given up to the enemy. A drawn sword is before us; misery awaits us abroad: and still the Lord says unto us, 'Go on! go on!'

"But whither shall we go, O Lord?

"'Go and die, those that are to die; go and suffer, those that are to suffer.'"

Afterwards Skarga, quoting the prophet Hosea, says:—

"God himself, after two days, will revive you; and in the third He will raise you up."

"The first day," says Miçkievicz, in his *Book of the Polish Pilgrims*, thinking, perhaps, of this last prophecy of Skarga's,—"the first day ended when Souvaroff took Warsaw, and the second when Paskievitch took Warsaw; and the third has not yet risen, and it will have no end."

Skarga's prophetic sermon (published under the title of *A Call to Repentance*) was, as I have mentioned, preached in the reign of Sigismund III.;

and as so much has been said of the bigotry and intolerance of that reign, we must not forget that Skarga, a Catholic priest, was addressing a congregation in which all the principal men were Protestants. Indeed, the Protestants were at that time in such force in Poland that, probably, if there had been any persecution at all, not they, but the Catholics, would have been the victims. Nevertheless, when Henri de Valois arrived in Cracow to be crowned, two years after the Massacre of St. Bartholemew, Catholics and Protestants united in compelling him to swear an oath to respect religious freedom in Poland; and in Skarga's time, though the King was a Catholic, his subjects, in virtue of their general liberties, were free to adopt or reject Protestantism as they pleased. The Poles, as a nation, have never been given to persecution; and when, towards the close of their history as a republic, the quarrels about the "dissidents" began, the "dissidents'" demands were chiefly resisted because Russia and Prussia supported them; just as we should have objected, more than ever, to grant equal political rights to the Catholics, had we, at any time, been recommended to do so in a threatening tone by France and Austria. The influence of the Jesuits increased greatly under Sigismund III., but until their power became supreme, persecution in Poland Proper was simply out of the question. A gentleman was a gentleman, and had a right to believe what he liked. Unfortunately, the Cossacks were not looked upon as gentlemen; they were not allowed to vote at the election of the King, their Russo-Greek bishops were not treated with respect, and their religion was despised. In the country of the Cossacks the Jesuits established in Poland really became persecutors; and although Poles and Russians do not at all agree as to the extent to which persecution was carried, it had the effect, in the middle of the seventeenth century, of forcing the Cossacks of the Ukraine to take refuge under the protection (soon converted into dominion) of Russia. When the Cossacks found that they had only exchanged Polish whips for Russian scorpions, they endeavoured to liberate themselves; but Poland had neither the political sagacity nor the power to help them, and they were ultimately subdued at Pultava—the Poles fighting some on one side, some on the other!

The Russians do not seem to have shown any remarkable ability in gaining possession of the Ukraine and the line of the Dnieper; but the Poles showed an utter absence of wisdom, prudence, and, in a certain sense, of patriotism, in laying their eastern frontier, almost of their own free-will, at the mercy of Russia. In ceding Kieff to Peter the Great's father, in time of peace, Sobieski deliberately placed the keys of his house in the hands of his most determined enemy. The battle of Vienna was, no doubt, a magnificent fight, and Sobieski an admirable warrior. He certainly saved the House of Austria; and all Christendom, if all Christendom was really in danger—which is less certain. But he did his best to ruin Poland. The modern Russian historians say calmly that the Polish game was irrecoverably lost when the Poles drove the Cossacks to seek Russian protection; the ultimate effect of which was to establish Russia firmly on the Dnieper. One more fatal false step, however, was taken when Poland gave up the city of Kieff, and thus brought Russia across the river.

The fall of Poland, and the triumph of Russia, were fully prepared, from the outside, before the end of the seventeenth century. The internal causes of its destruction had already shown themselves, in germ, at the end of the sixteenth; the two principal ones being the *veto* and the right of every Polish gentleman to vote at the election of the Sovereign. But although the principle of the *veto* was asserted as a right by John Zamoyski at the end of the sixteenth century—probably with the view of enabling the Poles to defy, if necessary, the power of the rich magnates of Lithuania, then just united to Poland—the right was never exercised until the middle of the seventeenth; when in the year

1652, while the Diet of Warsaw was deliberating on a matter of the greatest importance, Sicinski, the nuncio of Upita, in Lithuania, suddenly forbad the continuance of the proceedings, and broke up the assembly.

At first sight it seems absurd that the right of *veto* should ever have been tolerated at all. The *veto*, however, was not a Polish invention, and the principle was recognized in the early communal life of all the Slavonian nations. It existed in Russia and Bohemia, where, in the deliberations of the village communes, unanimity was necessary for every decision. Up to a certain point, this secured individual liberty; beyond that point, any peasant who held out too obstinately was forced into acquiescence by the clamour of the majority, by threats, and, if necessary, by blows. At present the Russian peasants in their communal meetings take the opinion of the majority; and even in trial by jury, which it is now proposed to introduce into Russia, the verdict of the majority is to be binding. Our English jury system still recognizes the *veto*, for if one juryman disagrees permanently with all his fellows the jury must be dismissed.

In Poland, as long as every member of the Diet was animated by a patriotic spirit, there was at least the appearance of unanimity in all its resolutions. Those who differed from the majority yielded at last; as in our House of Commons, on questions of great national moment, such as a declaration of war, members who do not altogether agree with the majority will, nevertheless, either vote with it or abstain from voting, so that if the country is to speak at all to the foreigner, it may speak with one voice.

The Reform Bill is known to have been passed in the House of Lords by a similar sacrifice. It was passed by a minority, a sufficient number of peers stopping away on the night of the division, to ensure the adoption of a measure believed by the House of Commons and the King, but not by themselves personally, to be for the good of the country.

When, therefore, it is said that among other causes which led to the ruin of Poland was the *Liberum Veto*, it would be really more correct to assert that the country was destroyed by the immorality of men who were prevailed upon to exercise, for a base purpose, a privilege which, until the corruption of the Republic, had always been held in reserve.

What is far more extraordinary than that the *veto* should have existed as a principle is the fact that when it had been put into practice, and when all the best men in the country were scandalized at seeing such a right abused, it should yet have been found impossible to abolish it. The bad effects of the *veto* were so soon felt by the nation that eighteen years after its first exercise, when it had already broken up several Diets, all the members of the Diet of 1670 bound themselves by an oath not to make use of it, and even proceeded to pass a resolution declaring the utterance of the fatal word to be without effect as regarded that Assembly. This very resolution, however, was negatived by the single vote of one Zabokrziski, the nuncio of Bratlau.

Under the reign of John Sobieski, seven Diets, and under Augustus II. and Augustus III. as many as thirty, were dissolved by the operation of the *veto*. For half a century it may be said that there were no Diets at all; they were broken up as soon as they met. Finally, when Stanislaus Augustus, the last King of Poland, came to the throne, the Diet, by a general agreement, resolved itself into a "confederation," a form of assembly in which questions were decided by majorities, but which the Diet had no legal right to assume except during an interregnum, or upon foreign invasion, or in defence of the King's person.

But for the partitioning Powers the Poles would now have formally abolished the *veto;* instead of which it was formally imposed upon them, as a burden they must bear, by one of the articles of the Constitution of 1768. The publication of this

Constitution, which perpetuated the right of *veto* and the elective sovereignty, was understood by the Poles to be little less than a declaration of war. The Empress Catherine was the author of the two fatal clauses, the provisions of which both she and Frederic had bound themselves mutually to enforce.

Of course the right of *veto* availed nothing in the Diet summoned by the partitioning Powers for the purpose of giving its formal sanction to the ruin of the country. This Diet, called the " Burial Diet," deliberated in the midst of foreign troops, and with cannons pointed at the doors. It was not until nineteen years afterwards that the *veto* was finally abolished by the celebrated Constitution of the 3rd of May. But this was the signal for the destruction of Poland. In 1792 came the second invasion of the partitioning Powers; in 1793, the second partition; in 1794, the great insurrection of Kosciuszko; in 1795, the division of all Polish territory between Russia, Prussia, and Austria.

The memory of Sicinski, the nuncio of Upita, who first pronounced the *veto* at the Diet of 1652, is accursed throughout Poland. When he uttered the fatal word the Diet broke up in consternation, and on going home he was struck by lightning. His house was burned to the ground, his family was destroyed, but he himself is said to have been preserved in a sort of parched-up, mummified condition. On the anniversary of the ill-omened day, and on other days as well, the thunder-blasted frame of Sicinski used to be carried round the town of Upita in the style of our Guy Fawkes. He, indeed, deserves his shameful celebrity far more than Guy Fawkes, who only intended to blow up the members of one particular English Parliament. Sicinski did really blow up the Polish Diet as an institution, and with it the whole of Poland.

Under the title of *The Inn of Upita, a Travelling Sketch*, Miçkievicz has written a poem on the subject of Sicinski, his life, his death, his durability, and the impossibility of burying him. For the earth vomits him forth whenever he is placed under ground, and the worms have always known better than to touch so venomous a carcase. Various persons are sitting in the inn, and various legends are told of Sicinski, and his unpardonable crime. One man says that, under pretence of inviting the electors of Upita to dinner, he gave them a kind of wine which drove them all mad; another, that on some important occasion he tied the King's hands, and left him at the mercy of his enemies; a third, that he caused an inundation which brought ruin upon the whole country.

While the conversation is going on the dried-up skeleton of Sicinski is brought in.

"The squalid smoke of death," says Miçkievicz, "has dried up his cheeks. Here and there a tooth may be seen glistening in his withered mouth. Otherwise all his body has preserved very much the appearance of life. His head has kept its strange expression; and as an old picture, through the coating of centuries, still leaves the features of the original model perceptible, so, although the light of life has departed, the figure would enable anyone who had known Sicinski living to recognize Sicinski dead. One sees, at the first glance, that there is something in it which cannot be expressed by words. The savage contortions of a face over which crime has passed seem still to give a look of menace to the features of the carcase. A perfidious delight contracts them into a frightful smile. There is the fury of an assassin on the forehead, the pride of a devil in the curve of the eyebrow. The head is stuck into a pair of shoulders which are bent, as though the weight of his ignominy was crushing him to the ground, or as if, dragged up by force from hell, he wished to force his way back again.

"If a cavern which has been the abode of crime, when men have demolished it, or the thunderbolt has struck it, enables us to guess, from its wild situation and its horrid aspect, that brigands have dwelt there; if the serpent can be recognized by his skin; then the life of Sicinski may be told from his carcase!

"'My friends!' I exclaimed, 'I can make your stories agree. He was not guilty of one crime alone, but of all possible crimes. It was through him that Poland, intoxicated by the poison he had prepared, went mad; it was through him that the King's hands were tied; it was through him that the country was inundated with calamities.'

"I then reflected and said to myself, 'What are popular legends? Ashes concealing just a spark of truth; hieroglyphics engraved on a stone eaten over with moss; an inscription in a lost language; an echo borne across the ocean of time, which breaks upon new facts, and strikes and resounds again upon fictions worthy only of the smile of a sage. But before he smiles let the sage tell us what all other histories are worth.'"

CHAPTER XVI.

HOW POLAND FELL (CONTINUED).—THE ELECTIVE SOVEREIGNTY.

When I meet with an author who speaks of Poland as of a chaste Susanna betrayed and ruined by three political elders, I conclude, if he is a foreigner, that he has not studied his subject. If he is a Pole I excuse him and perhaps like him for his patriotism, but do not agree with him on this particular point.

The atrocious perfidy of the elders cannot be denied, and we must admit the beauty and original virtue of Susanna, but not her unimpeachable purity in 1772. Besides much perfidy and half-a-million bayonets, there were Prince Repnin's drafts on the house of Clifford and Co., Amsterdam.* It was a shameful thing, no doubt,

---

* "Make use of all the money you have in your hands, and the 100,000 roubles besides, for which you have an order on Clifford and Co., Amsterdam, so as to increase the number of the chiefs and adherents of our party," &c. (*Letter from Catherine to her Ambassadors at Warsaw*, found in the archives of the Russian Embassy during the insurrection of 1794; quoted by D'Angeberg, page 3.)

to buy from Poland her honour and independence, but "if they were purchased it was because they were for sale."* Sievers used also to draw on Clifford and Co., and, in his *Memoirs*, tells what he gave to this noble and what to the other, and how they took it.

Nor can I look upon Poland as a thoroughly-honest, simple-minded man defrauded by three swindlers, or knocked down by three robbers—though the swindling and the robbery certainly took place. When the partitioning Powers seek to justify their conduct, I think of three garotters who were brought a few months ago before a London magistrate, accused of assaulting a gentleman in the streets.

"He had no business to be out so late," said garotter No. 1. "What was he doing in the streets till three in the morning?"

"He was drunk," said garotter No. 2; "he could scarcely stand, and we had to hold him up."

"Besides, we didn't hurt him, after all," said garotter No. 3; "and he has lost nothing."

---

* The words of a Polish Bishop, accused of purchasing ecclesiastical honours, to Queen Bona, of whom it was written—

"Ut Parcæ parcent, ut luci lumine lucent;
Ut bellum bellum, sic bona Bona fuit."

All kinds of false charges are brought against Poland, which, even if they were true, would not lessen the guilt of those who attacked her—for at least Poland was not injuring *them*. Compared with what she ought to have been, and had been, Poland, at the end of the eighteenth century, was very corrupt. The society of Warsaw was dissolute; but not more so than that of most other capitals at the end of the eighteenth century. On the other hand, a certain number of the Poles, including those who were seeking earnestly to save the country by means of political reforms, and some of the leaders of the Confederates of Bar, were superior, as men, to any ministers or generals to be found in Russia, Prussia, or Austria.*

Nevertheless, the Poles, as a nation, were far less estimable and far less national in 1772 than they are now. Curiously enough, just after the first partition, the dress of the West of Europe was in high fashion among the Poles, and at that time ten thousand Russian soldiers held Poland in subjection, though she had still twenty thousand soldiers of her own.

Now the national costume is the rage in Poland. Warsaw and the whole country are crowded with Russian soldiers (there were a hundred thousand in

* See Cox, *Travels, &c.*; and Wraxall, *Memoirs, &c.*

the "Kingdom" alone during the Crimean war), and not a Pole is allowed to carry arms.

At the period of the first partition, and for some years afterwards, the Poles gave themselves up in the most reckless and shameful manner to luxury and dissipation of every kind. "Neither St. Petersburg nor Naples can surpass Warsaw in these respects," we are told by Wraxall.* "It is not, in fact, gallantry, but licentiousness that here reigns without control." . . . "The Russian Ambassador's Hotel resembles at noon-day, as I have seen, rather a club of gamesters than the residence of a great public minister charged with the administration and Government of Poland. Similar scenes are enacted in the houses of the first nobility, who, after having sold their country, often lose in an evening the fruit of their venality or their dishonour."

At present, and for the last two years, there has been an end to all kinds of entertainment in Poland; mourning is worn everywhere; the hatred of Russia, Austria, and Prussia, is universal; and the Poles, chastened and purified by long suffering, love their country with one accord.

However, there was a strong Russian party in Warsaw just before the fatal year of 1772; and

* *Memoirs of the Courts of Berlin, &c.*, vol. ii. p. 168.

Poles of high position were not ashamed to declare that they had Russian, Austrian, or Prussian sympathies. Some were in the pay of the partitioning Powers; others inclined to Russia from motives of policy, thinking to defeat her ultimately with her own weapons, and to baffle her schemes by a superior power of intrigue; others, again, had already risen in the name of their country's independence, and been defeated.

There were three great parties: the party of scoundrels sold to Russia, Austria, or Prussia, or to all three; the political patriotic party, directed by the Czartoryskis, Oginskis, and Zamoyskis, which prepared the mind of the country for the admirable reforms of 1791; and the brave, headlong, non-reforming, patriotic party of the Confederates, which, in opposition to the King and to the political party, attacked the Russians in the field, and sought, before everything else, to clear Poland from the disgrace of a foreign occupation. Prince Radziwill, at the head of his own private troops, and those of a few confederates, engaged a greatly superior Russian force as early as 1764. On this occasion his sister and his wife, a girl of seventeen, fought by his side. The Princess rode up and down the line, pistol in hand, encouraging the soldiers; and, when they were defeated, effected her escape by swimming across the Niemen. The

Polish ladies, then, were not all given up to frivolity in the hour of Poland's danger. "In Poland," says Frederic the Great, in one of his letters, "the women attend to politics while the men are drunk." "An accusation," remarks Professor Raumer, in his *Fall of Poland*,* "which in itself disproves a great deal that has been said against the Poles." Indeed, if there were so many women in Poland who interested themselves in matters which inferior women always despise, the country could not, after all, have been in such a hopeless state of corruption as its enemies pretend.

After the first partition had been consummated the brave and beautiful Princess Radziwill lost her senses, and was confined for many years in a castle in Lithuania. The Marchioness Wielopolska, in a fit of despair, committed suicide. The present representative of the Wielopolski family seems anxious to imitate this action, in a political sense, and to make the whole country do the same.

It is difficult to decide whether the temporizing policy represented by the Czartoryskis, or the policy of direct resistance represented first by Prince Radziwill and afterwards by Krasinski, Pulaski, and the Confederates of Bar, was the best. The former appears to have been the wisest, and without it one can scarcely believe that Poland would have lived to proclaim the Constitution of

* Raumer's *Untergang des Polen.*

1791, and to fight the great battles of 1794 under Kosciuszko. Had there been a general resistance—had there been enough unity of feeling at the last moment to render such a resistance possible—it may still be assumed that Poland would have been destroyed by the overpowering forces marshalled against her in 1772, and had she perished then she would have left a questionable reputation behind.

On the other hand, the policy of the Radziwills and Pulaskis, if policy it can be called, seems at first sight to have been the noblest. The Czartoryskis, in bringing the Russian troops into Poland and leaning upon Russia to enable them to introduce reforms of the most vital necessity, did evil that good might come; and good *did* come of it, though it was immediately afterwards destroyed. They looked to Russia much as Piedmont looked for a time to France, hoping that their powerful friend and enemy would at least keep all other enemies off while they were occupied in reforming the institutions of their country and strengthening their Government in every possible manner. But if the Czartoryskis acted in the spirit of Victor Emanuel and Cavour, the leaders of the Confederates had more of Garibaldi's spirit. They took no note of obstacles, and would hear of no policy which was based on the expediency of allowing foreign troops to remain on Polish soil.

The Czartoryski party, who had been working with indefatigable earnestness at their reforms ever since, and even before, the accession of Stanislaus Augustus, their own candidate, complained that but for the commotion and tumult caused by the Confederates, they would have been able to introduce these reforms without trouble. The Confederates were also accused "of having caused the ruin of the Republic, by using and consuming the forces which Poland needed to resist a Power of superior force."

"We ask, in our turn," says the admirable manifesto in which this charge was taken up,* " why these same forces were not employed before we employed them, and at the first infringement of the rights of the Republic? We have been only too patient, and we should now have nothing to fear it what we have attempted in vain—in spite of all our efforts and all our sacrifices—had been done at once . . . If the weakness and cupidity of some had not fettered the valour of others; if the entire nation had displayed its force; if it had shown that warlike spirit which has so often rendered it victorious, we should now be on the eve of recovering our liberty and of terminating our period of misfortune."

The Confederates apparently did not know that

* Last protest of the Confederates of Bar, dated November 16, 1773. *Loyko Felix*, vol. ii. p. 369. *D'Angeberg*, p. 149.

their ruin had been deliberately planned in 1762, when Frederic II. of Prussia and Peter III. signed a secret treaty (renewed in 1764 by Frederic II. and Catherine II.) binding them mutually to maintain "freedom of election" in Poland, and not, under any circumstances, to allow the Crown to be made hereditary;* and that in 1763 Catherine had given secret instructions to her ambassadors, Count Keyserling and Prince Repnin, to take care "that the actual form of the Polish Government be maintained in its integrity, that the law of unanimity in the Diets be not changed, and that the army be not augmented."†

It has been said that the Czartoryskis had not faith enough in the ancient Constitution of their country. But the worst of it was the great faith Catherine and Frederic reposed in it! The Czartoryskis were seeking to introduce the very changes which Catherine had secretly declared she would not permit, and we may be sure that Frederic, Catherine, and the Czartoryskis all knew what they were about.

The history of this struggle between the Polish

* *D'Angeberg*, p. 1.
† *D'Angeberg*, p. 5.—These instructions were found in the archives of the Russian Embassy at Warsaw during Kosciuszko's insurrection in 1794.

reformers, who had sworn to save their country and the Russian and Prussian Conservatives, who had sworn to keep it in a state of fever and exhaustion until it perished, is as exciting as the history of any life and death struggle must be, and it derives a peculiar dramatic interest from the fact that it was carried on as if in the dark, each side feigning ignorance as to the intentions of the other.

"The Czartoryski family," says Miçkievicz, "which, during the last days of Poland, was known simply as the 'family,' is the only private family in Europe which has its own political history." Its history is also intimately connected with that of modern Polish literature, as all the most remarkable works published in Poland from the accession of Stanislaus Augustus in 1764 until the insurrection of 1830, were either dedicated to them, or brought out under their patronage and printed at their expense. Since the last emigration, the Czartoryskis have been at the head of what is called the aristocratic party of the emigration. Many members of this party, however, are only aristocrats in the style of M. Jules Favre, who lately offended the democrats of Imperial France by maintaining that people, before they are allowed to vote, ought to be able to read and write. As far as I have been able to discover, every one is looked upon as an " aristocrat" by the democrats of Poland and

Russia, who does not believe in universal suffrage, and the absolute wisdom of the most numerous and ignorant class of the community.

In Poland itself it never occurred to me that there were two parties among the Poles. Perhaps it is that there they feel themselves in face of the enemy. The Russian bullets did not look out for aristocratic or democratic Poles in the crowd of the 8th of April, and workmen and princes were sent to Siberia, without distinction of rank, by the Emperor Nicholas. The impossibility of getting up any discussion in the journals as to whether the future Poland is to be governed on aristocratic or democratic principles, may also have something to do with this seeming absence of party spirit—so that, for some things, even the censorship is good. In the grandest days of modern Poland, in 1794, when the national troops were fighting against the armies of Russia, Austria, and Prussia, and the Poles were distinguishing themselves as they had not distinguished themselves before since the days of Sobieski, there were no aristocrats and democrats. The generalissimo, the immortal Kosciuszko, was a noble or freeman, but of no aristocratic means or position. He was a man of the simplest tastes and habits, and a true friend of the suffering people. His first proclamation in the name of the Polish nation prescribed a considerable diminution in the peasant's task-work, while his last letter to the Emperor Alexander (1814), contained a prayer that he would abolish it altogether.*

Prince Poniatowski did not ask whether Kosciuszko was an aristocrat or a democrat, and, though superior to him in military rank as well as in social position, was proud to serve under him in 1794 as a volunteer.

Again : even Kilinski, the shoemaker, who sat in the council at Warsaw with the heads of the most influential families in Poland, and who led the insurrection inside the city—certainly neither he nor those who were glad to have him for a colleague can be styled " aristocrats," in the odious sense in which the word is used by the Polish and Russian democratic party.

The Marquis Wielopolski, who perhaps *is* an aristocrat, but who does not appear to have any followers out of his own chancelleries, has called modern Polish democracy " the corruption engendered by the festering of the Polish wound"; and he is right in so far, that the notion of saving Poland by swamping the best class of Poles was first conceived by a few unhappy men in the torments of exile, and among foreign revolutionists.

The democratic party first showed itself in Poland during the insurrection of 1830-31, under the leadership of Lelewel, the historian. Had this

* See page 321.

party, however, been really numerous and well-organized, it could not have accepted Lelewel as its chief, for he was by no means a democrat in the ordinary acceptation of the word.

"Lelewel," said a friend of his to me, one day, "was a regular democrat. He wore a *blouse* when he was in Paris, and looked like a workman." Kosciuszko, however, wore the dress of the Polish peasant, and lived in the most simple and austere style, and certainly was not a democrat in the universal suffrage sense of the word. Kosciuszko had the greatest admiration for Prince Adam Czartoryski, and, as the reader will afterwards see, entertained the same political views as the Prince. Lelewel, on the other hand, after the failure of the insurrection of 1830, as if determined to blame some one for a result which was simply inevitable, persuaded himself that but for the "aristocratic" policy of the Czartoryskis and their adherents, the great majority of the representatives of the Polish nation, it might have been successful. In his preface to his pamphlet on the *Three Constitutions of Poland*, which was written abroad—and not in the work itself, which was printed in Warsaw during the Revolution—Lelewel accuses the Czartoryskis of having caused the ruin of Poland by introducing aristocratic ideas into the country; and by seeking to make the crown hereditary, and to strengthen the central power. He also charges them with

LELEWEL, THE POLISH HISTORIAN

Hanhart lith

having brought uniforms and court-dresses into fashion; an innovation which, however undesirable, could scarcely, in itself, have led to the dissolution of a great republic. And we must not forget that Frederic the Great and Catherine the Great both objected, in the most violent manner, to the abolition of the elective sovereignty and the formation of a powerful government in Poland. In short, Lelewel was a thorough republican, and he maintained—what was, no doubt, true, and is true, of the fall of all countries—that Poland perished, not because her system of government was bad, but because all sorts of abuses had crept into it. The fact, however, remains the same, that the arch-enemies of Poland approved of the system, as one into which abuses could be more easily introduced than into any other.

Lelewel, however, republican as he was, was far from being a democrat of the extreme modern Continental type. He was a republican, because, looking back through the history of his country, he saw that as a republic, it had done many glorious things; that the elective sovereignty for centuries was no source of weakness to the country, and that even after the right of choosing the King had been taken from the Diet and placed in the hands of the entire body of nobles or freemen, it gave Poland many excellent monarchs, and that it was no more a cause of civil war than the disputes which, from time to time arise for succession under a hereditary system. It is an article of popular historical belief in most countries, that a regal election in Poland was usually followed by a civil war, and that the election itself was a frightful scene of turbulence and riot. It is also too frequently asserted that bribery played an important part at these elections, whereas the fact is, taking the accusations altogether, they can only be proved as regards the elections of the last sixty-nine years of the Republic, after an existence of more than four centuries. The last King of Poland was imposed by Russia in conjunction with Prussia, and accepted, it is true, without immediate resistance. The last King but one was placed on the throne by a Russian army after the rival and national candidate, Stanislas Lesczinski, had been chosen by an overwhelming majority. There were plenty of intrigues, no doubt, at the election of Augustus II., and it is the description of this one election which is usually quoted by writers who wish to give as unfavourable an idea as possible of Polish history in general.

What, however, can any one say against the choice of the Poles having fallen on Sobieski in 1673, or on any one of his predecessors? The reader is aware that until the extinction of the Jagellon line in 1574, the Diet elected the King, the crown was kept in the same family, and practically was hereditary. When Stephen Batory was elected by the whole body of freemen, he was chosen on condition of marrying Anne, the daughter of Sigismund I., just as William III. was chosen King of England, on condition of marrying into the Stuart family. Poland never had a greater king. The frontiers of Lithuania were at that time within a hundred and fifty English miles of Moscow, and the termination of the Polish question of that day would, had Batory met with more support from his nobles, have been the annexation of Muscovy to the Polish crown.

Afterwards, when Sigismund Wasa of Sweden became king (1587), he was chosen chiefly on the ground that he was a grandson of Sigismund I., through his daughter Catherine, sister of the late queen, so that the Jagellon family was still represented on the Polish throne. Sigismund Wasa (known as Sigismund III.), was succeeded by his son Ladislas, and Ladislas by his half-brother John Kasimir, who abdicated. The next king, Michael Wisnowięcki, was a Polish gentleman of small means, elected simply because the Poles believed, with justice, in his patriotism. The election of John Sobieski, on the death of Michael, surely needs no justification: this event took place in 1672. With Sobieski ended all the glory of ancient Poland, and from 1695, when Augustus II., Mr. Carlyle's "Man of Sin," ascended the

throne, until 1764, the date of Stanislas Augustı
Poniatowski's nomination by the Empress Cath
rine, the Polish elections were discreditable aı
disgraceful to the country. The surroundir
Powers would not, it is true, allow the Poles 1
choose a candidate after their own heart; but
was the Poles themselves who in the first instan
invited foreigners to the election field, and wl
suffered them to bring their troops on to Poli:
territory under pretence of watching their interesl
maintaining "freedom of election," and so o
The Poles, moreover, must have fallen very lo'
not only in a moral and political, but also in a mi
tary point of view, when, after having once mo
elected their own candidate, Stanislas Lesczinsl
they allowed a Russian general, at the head
7000 Russian troops, to enter Warsaw, and, wiı
an utter contempt for the will of the natio
give the crown to Augustus III. From th
moment, what had Poland to hope as long as
maintained the elective sovereignty? Whɛ
indeed, had it to hope under any circumstances
If, as its writers say, the mission of Poland was
keep off Russia, it failed strangely in that missi(
when it allowed an insignificant Russian force
enter its capital, and dispose of its crown—n
simply without consulting, but in the most ɑ
rect opposition to, the wishes of the whole natio
Abuses had crept not only into the political syste

of Poland, but into the moral system of the Poles as a people; and it is not to be wondered at that the most intelligent men in the country saw, as well as the surrounding despots, that the Constitution must be changed, or that it would fall to the ground and bring Poland down with it. There is not one instance of a Polish election having disturbed the tranquillity of neighbouring States; though it is quite true that during a period of sixty-nine years the elective sovereignty was a fruitful source of trouble and disgrace to Poland herself.*

It is easy to understand, then, that an historian of a republican turn of mind should have refused to reject republicanism because it had broken down in Poland during a corrupt period; for, as Lelewel himself has said, republicanism is a government for

* "In lamentable truth," says Mr. Cobden (*Russia, by a Manchester Manufacturer*), "almost every election became a signal for war, *which usually lasted during the greater portion of the next reign;* and thus, during the whole period from 1572 down to 1772, when the first partition was perpetrated by the three neighbouring Powers, Poland was the constant scene of anarchy and its attendant miseries — fire, bloodshed, and famine." The fact is, that during these two centuries only two elections out of eleven led to an appeal to arms,—that of Sigismund III., which led to an attack from Maximilian of Austria, his unsuccessful competitor, which lasted a few weeks, and that of Augustus III., after which the national candidate, Stanislas Lesczinski, was besieged for a few weeks in Dantzig by an army of Russians and Saxons. There is some difference between two months and two centuries.

T 2

brave and virtuous men; while despotism is a government for slaves and cowards. The modern democrat, as a rule, would scorn to base his views on the results of historical inquiry. Give him a pen and a sheet of paper, and he will improvise a perfect government, without any reference to the past and without much to the future. Lelewel, on the other hand, was a Conservative though a Republican; and in examining the three Polish Constitutions, with the view of devising a fourth, he asks himself at every step what is nationally and historically Polish in each. Poland, he says, grew up as a republican country, and it fell because the State machinery got out of order, and above all, because its republican liberties were not sufficiently extended—because a larger body of the population was not called upon to share them. He does not start from any assumption of his own that all men are equal, or that every man of twenty, twenty-one, or twenty-two years of age is by nature intended to vote, by ballot or otherwise, as he is evidently intended to eat and drink. But he finds that, by the Constitution of 1791, which having been accepted by the nation, he accepts himself, some thousands of non-noble Poles would have been ennobled or enfranchised from year to year, and that the peasants, with their landed possessions, would long before now have become free. He also observes that the Constitution of 1791 was to have been revised, or at least brought before the Diet for revision, every twenty-five years, and consequently, that to adopt that Constitution now in its original form would be to ignore the real intentions of its founders. Lelewel seldom loses an opportunity of expressing his contempt for the hereditary as compared with the elective principle; but his republicanism has always an historical basis, and he objects to the Czartoryskis, with their reform policy of 1764, not only because they were "aristocrats," but also, and above all, because they were innovators and wished to subvert a Constitution which he as an historian respected and admired. At a French democratic and socialist club, the learned Lelewel, the chief of the (so-called) Polish democratic party, among an essentially anti-democratic people, would soon have been regarded as a species of aristocrat.

After the capitulation of Warsaw, Lelewel, who had been a member of the Provisional Government, left with the Diet and the army, and went to Paris. Driven away from Paris, he proceeded to Arras, and driven from Arras, went on to Brussels, where he lived for many years, surrounded by his books and visited by numbers of his countrymen, who often in their travels made long circuits to have the opportunity of seeing and conversing with him. These visits were not always received in the spirit in which they were meant. Lelewel is said to have cared more for study than for communicating the results of his studies, and often became so absorbed in contemplation that it was painful to him to be interrupted. He seldom left his room, lived chiefly on his books, and wore the same green coat for a quarter of a century, until at last, thanks to constant patching, it exhibited as great a variety of greens as a forest which autumn is just beginning to turn yellow.

Lelewel's writings* are chiefly remarkable for the research and the analytical power that they exhibit. He is said, when printed and written testimony failed him, to have lighted up many obscure points in Polish history by the superior knowledge and discernment he brought to bear in the examination of antiquities of all kinds. A coin, a coat-of-arms, a monument, or a monumental inscription, the architecture of a church porch, the symbolical or characteristic decoration of a tomb, would serve to guide him in his difficult investigations. When he was appointed Professor of History at the University of Wilna, during the reign of Alexander I., he exercised an influence over the students which has been compared to that exercised by Abailard,

* *History of Poland, History of the Polish Kings, History of the Reign of Stanislaus Augustus, History of Lithuania and Ruthenia, Analysis and Parallel of the Three Polish Constitutions, History of Poland told by a Grandfather to his Grandchildren, Geography of the Middle Ages,* various works on Numismatics, *A Treatise on the Studies Serviceable and Necessary to the Writer of History, A Short Account of the Persecution of*

over the students of Paris. It is difficult for a foreigner to understand how this effect was produced—unless it was the subject itself, the history of their native land, that fascinated the youthful audience—for Lelewel seldom exhibits any of the warmth of enthusiasm; and there is wisdom, no doubt, in his occupying himself less with the glories and misfortunes of the Poles than with the facts of their history and their historical rights, which their enemies, now that they have violated them, seek to deny.

While he still occupied the historical chair at Wilna, he was elected Rector of the University by the Council of Professors, but the Government refused to sanction the appointment. After the failure of the insurrection of 1830, the Russian Government gave Lelewel a further proof of ill-will by sentencing him to death, while the French Government really injured him by separating him from his friends in Paris, and forcing him to take refuge in Belgium. There is one truly pathetic passage in Lelewel's preface, written in French, to the French translation of his pamphlet on the *Three Polish Constitutions*, dated from Arras. "I ought," he says, "to have looked over the translation, and to have recopied this preface. But time fails me. Pursued by an implacable enemy, I have only twenty-four hours given me to leave Arras, and forty-eight to leave France."

How this recalls the prophetic words of Skarga! "But whither shall we go? 'Go and die, those that are to die; go and suffer, those that are to suffer.'"

To return now to the "aristocratic" party. I repeat that, in Poland itself, I do not believe there are any political parties in the present day. But there were only too many in 1764; and it is of the reform party, the party headed by the Czartoryskis, which aimed at establishing an hereditary monarchy, supported by a powerful executive, that I have now to say a few words.

The Russians saw through the Czartoryski policy from the beginning, or nearly so. Catherine, in her instructions to the Russian ambassadors at Warsaw, Count Keyserling and Prince Repnin, when the election of Stanislas Augustus was being prepared, speaks of the Princes Czartoryski and their partizans as devoted to her interests. The Empress was for once in error. The Czartoryskis knew they could not attack Russia with success, and wished, in the first instance, to gain possession of all the principal offices in the State under Russian auspices. They then proposed to strengthen the executive, either by means of skilfully-prepared legislative enactments, which they hoped to pass through the Diet without raising any needless discussions upon them, or to do without any enactments at all, and simply trust to their own personal energy and ability. The army was to have been increased quietly, its organization reformed, and its direction confided to a minister of war. As Catherine had sufficient power to appoint her own candidate, whoever he might be, they determined to find one who would be acceptable to her. The Czartoryskis, Oginski, and Stanislas Poniatowski, were relations, and it seemed for some time uncertain which of them would be elevated to the throne. The position of Poland at this moment has been compared to that of Russia under the Tartars. The Grand Dukes of Moscow, though they more than once rose against the Tartars, found it impossible to throw off their yoke by force of arms. They were obliged to make use of them, to receive their investiture at their hands, and in the meanwhile to gather force so as to be able to attack them with success at the first favourable moment. The Czartoryskis felt keenly the position of their country —which, under Augustus III., was governed by a nominee of Russia, just as much as Muscovy, under the Grand Dukes, was ruled by a vassal of the Khan. Indeed, the position of Poland was worse than that of Muscovy, for the Grand Dukes were at least Muscovites, and accepted by the people, whereas Augustus III. had been imposed upon the Poles in spite of themselves.

The Czartoryskis had for some time to deal with a diplomatic fox, who succeeded in making himself pass for a diplomatic goose. The Chancellor Bestoujeff spoke and wrote French very imperfectly; his handwriting even was illegible; and when his diplomatic notes were sent back to him to be elucidated, it often suited his purpose to change the words he had originally written, or at least to give a new meaning to them. He was, moreover, deaf, and had a frightful impediment in his speech.

The Czartoryskis thought the man was imbecile; but he was profoundly cunning. When, meeting with the usual fate of Russian ministers, he fell into disgrace, he all at once contrived to hear, speak, and write perfectly well.

However, Stanislas Augustus being on the throne, the Czartoryski family, after fifty years' vain endeavours to get into power, had obtained the direction of affairs in Poland. An immense code of laws, which they took care not to call laws, but regulations and administrative articles, were voted in one session of the Diet. "When each of these articles is examined separately," says Miçkievicz, "it can be seen that they are the result of long meditation and great labour. They are all connected together, and all lead to the same point—kingly power."* For instance, a clause relating to the finances, empowered a commission to decide difficult questions connected with the treasury; and it is so worded, that the same commission can ad-

* *Miçkievicz, Cours de Littérature Slave*, vol. iii. p. 66.

minister the army, the post-office, and all the branches of the Government. All the proposed regulations were equally elastic and obscure, and the Diet voted the whole mass without understanding their real significance.

At the last moment—or rather just as the Czartoryskis were about to put their long-meditated projects in full action, they were found out. They could no longer conceal that they were working against Russia. The opposition was very slight at first; "but," says Miçkievicz, "there was something hard and harsh about it, and it became more terrible from having been so long suppressed." First of all, they refused to sign an offensive alliance proposed to them by Russia, and soon afterwards they proposed formally the abolition of the *veto* and the decision of questions in the Diet by majorities.

Then Frederic the Great saw the whole meaning of the Czartoryski's reforms; and from that moment vowed an implacable hatred to them, and to the King of Poland, who had hitherto been regarded as merely a Russian and Prussian agent, and who afterwards, from pusillanimity, but not from treachery or want of patriotism, was really not much better. The republican party—the republican Conservatives, who would have it that the old Constitution was perfect in spite of everything—also took alarm when they understood that the great object of the Czartoryskis was to strengthen the crown, and to abolish anarchy in the Diets. Russia and Prussia published a number of manifestoes, in which they attacked the despotic principle, explained the advantages of republicanism and the excellence of the *veto*, and took a solemn engagement to maintain Polish liberty in spite of the Poles themselves. The King was at the same time urged by the Czartoryskis to defend his position, and persist in carrying out the indispensable reforms, while, on the other hand, he was threatened by Russia and Prussia unless he abandoned the Czartoryskis altogether. He ended by throwing himself into the arms of Russia, and the Czartoryskis, after their fifty years' labours, found themselves deserted by their allies, and their country in a more dangerous position than ever.

The general opinion in England as regards Stanislas Poniatowski is, I believe, that he was always a willing instrument in the hands of Russia, and that he basely accepted the throne of Poland from Catherine with the intention of carrying out all her desires, and sacrificing his countrymen for the sake of his former mistress. For my part, I confess I was somewhat surprised to see his portrait in the print-shops of Warsaw at the end of the long line of Polish kings. He was undoubtedly a weak man, and held an undignified position; but it is not so certain that he could have saved the country had he possessed more vigour and energy. He resisted every concession which he made to

Russia for a time, and then justified his making it on the ground that it was indispensable not to provoke the wrath of the three Powers who had sworn to destroy Poland; that it was better to yield a little so as not to have to give up all. This is what his own countryman, Miçkievicz, says about him:—" More than once, he was seen to astonish the Court by the sallies of his wit, by the elegance of his conversation, by lively and joyous remarks; and after everyone had gone the unhappy King fell on the ground and rolled in the dust. Sometimes he was surprised kneeling at the side of his bed, with his hands stretched to heaven, and his eyes haggard, but he had not courage enough to avow to the nation his profound misery, to stretch his hands to heaven in the face of the Diet, to lay the national danger before them, and to seek a remedy for it in the enthusiasm of his people."

In another chapter we shall see what part the Czartoryskis played after their country had been partitioned, and their native province of Lithuania had passed under the Russian sceptre. The services which Prince Adam Czartoryski rendered to his country, even after it had ceased to be a country, were well summed up by a Russian Minister, Novosiltzoff, who, some years after the signing of the Treaty of Vienna, complained that Prince Adam had delayed the Russification of Lithuania by at least fifty years!

The Czartoryskis were defeated, routed; but not discouraged. Poland had been invaded by 100,000 Prussians and 10,000 Austrians, while 40,000 Russians were already in possession of all the strongholds of the country. England and France had been appealed to in vain, and much to the amusement of the magnanimous Frederic and his flatterer (when he was not his calumniator) Voltaire, who enjoyed immensely the hopeless struggles of the Poles for their liberty and national life. The first partition having been accomplished, there was nothing for the Poles to do but to remain quiet and prepare themselves, by concentrating their forces, to recover some day what they had lost. It was evident they had nothing to hope from foreign aid. I fancy they might have received some assistance had there been more unity in Poland, and had the Poles shown themselves resolved, as a nation, to defend their rights against any odds. If any one says that this was impossible, my reply is, that the Poles did not stop to count possibilities in 1794 or in 1830.

France did make an attempt to help Poland by sending officers and arms to the Confederates of Bar, who, however, were not the representatives of Poland, but only of the Polish republican party. Dumouriez found the Confederates without any organization,* and his account of their want of dis-

* "He found the Polish aristocrats corrupted by luxury, enervated by pleasures, employing in intrigues and fervent

cipline, of the readiness of everyone to command and no one to obey, corresponds closely enough with that given by Frederic the Great.

I have said that in the British Parliament the partition of Poland was not even made the subject of a question. It was alluded to vaguely in a speech from the throne as a territorial change without importance. That was not the opinion of the greatest statesman of the time; but Burke evidently considered the position of Poland quite hopeless, or he at least would have offered a protest in his place in the House of Commons against an act which he regarded as cruel, criminal, and dangerous in the highest degree to the future peace of all Europe. This is what Burke wrote about the partition of Poland in 1772 in the *Annual Register*:—

"The present violent dismemberment and partition of Poland, without the pretence of war, or even the colour of right, is to be considered as the first very great breach in the modern political system of Europe. It is not (say the politicians of the Continent) sapping by degrees the constitution of our

---

language the warmth of their patriotism. Sapieha, the principal leader, was massacred by his nobles. Pulaski and Micksenski were delivered up, wounded, to the Russians. Zaremba betrayed his country. He (Dumouriez) broke his sword, despairing for ever of this aristocracy without a people; calling it, as he quitted it, *the Asiatic nation of Europe.*"— *Lamartine's History of the Girondists*, vol. i. p. 404.

great Western Republic; it is laying the axe at once to the root in such a manner as threatens the total overthrow of the whole. . . . We now behold the destruction of a great kingdom, with the consequent disarrangement of power, and union, and commerce, with as total indifference and unconcern as we would read an account of the exterminating of one horde of Tartars by another in the days of Genghizan or Tamerlane. . . .

"The free states and cities of Germany seem to be more immediately affected by the present extraordinary transaction than any other part of Europe. Indeed, if the partition of Poland takes place in its utmost extent, the existence of the Germanic body in its present form for any length of time will be a matter rather to be wished than expected. The extraordinary power to which the houses of Austria and Brandenburg have risen within a few years, was already sufficiently alarming to the other parts of that body. Their natural jealousy and acquired animosity seemed, however, to counteract their ambition, and to afford a tolerable security that they would not join in any scheme destructive of other States, at the same time that their near equality made it impossible for one to be dangerous while opposed by the other. . . . Poland was the natural barrier of Germany as well as of the Northern Crowns, against the overwhelming power and ambition of Russia. Some small alterations in the system of Government, which might have been accomplished with little violence and infinite benefit to the Poles, would have made this barrier inexpugnable. . . . A great writer of a former age affirmed that if ever the Turks conquered Germany it must be through Poland; it may be with greater justice affirmed, that it is the road by which the Russians will enter Germany."

Five years afterwards, the *Annual Register* says of Poland: "Distracted and torn as this unhappy country continues, it has not, during this year, presented those shocking scenes of calamity which had long made it a spectacle as much of horror as of compassion. The vast armies with which it was covered having rendered all opposition impracticable, the pretences for cruelty were taken away, and the multitude of spectators, composed of different nations and under different commands, being a mutual check upon the enormities of each other, the rage for blood dwindles into regular oppression. Upon the whole, the condition of Poland is not worse than it has been."

Gradually, however, all except the Russian troops retired from the country, and when Wraxall and Coxe were at Warsaw, some fifteen years after the first partition, the Russian army in Poland numbered only ten thousand men, and there was a pretended understanding on both sides that the occupation was of a friendly character. Both Coxe and Wraxall had good sources of information open to them, but neither of them understood what was going on beneath the surface of society. Coxe understood that the Zamoyskis, Czartoryskis, and Chreptowiczs were emancipating their peasants; that a Ministry of Public Instruction—the first established in Europe—had been formed; that the national literature was being cultivated with great ardour; that the King was a great patron of art and science; but he had no idea that the great families of Poland were still fighting for the life of their country.

He saw in the Palace a map of Poland as the first partition had left it, and a portrait of the Empress Catherine hanging side by side with that of John Sobieski! The king's nephew gave him letters of introduction to great people in Moscow and St. Petersburg; and there seemed to him no reason to believe that the partition had not been at length acquiesced in. He little knew that the Poles who invited him to their houses, showed him over their estates, and talked pleasantly and learnedly about painting, poetry, and politics, were secretly preparing the Constitution of 1791. Every one who takes an interest in Polish affairs remembers Burke's eulogy on this Constitution,*

* *Appeal from the Old Whigs to the New.*

which has excited the admiration of honest politicians of all countries and of all shades of opinion, from Joseph Lemaistre, the Absolutist, to Lelewel, the Republican.

In laying it before the Diet, its authors remarked that, while retaining all the most essential principles of the ancient Polish Constitution, they had profited by a study of the Constitutions of England and the United States. The late Prince Adam Czartoryski appears to have been sent by his parents to England for the express purpose of studying our institutions. "The principal object of your visit," wrote Prince Adam, the General of Podolia, to the young Prince Adam in England, "must be to collect materials which you will be able to turn to account when the hour comes for you to pay to your country the tribute we all owe to it." *

The Constitution of the 3rd of May was introduced and voted with that scrupulous regard for legality which has always distinguished the Poles, and, before being adopted, it was submitted to the consideration not only of the deputies in the Diet, but to the electors at every Dietine or electoral college. The Czartoryskis and their adherents, together with Kollontay and Ignatius Potoçki, took an important part in preparing this

* *Le Prince Adam Czartoryski*, par le R. P. Félix, p. 35.

most important Act. This time the abolition not only of the *veto*, but of the elective sovereignty itself was formally decreed by the voice of the whole nation. Thirteen traitors alone protested against the measure, and on their behalf and once more in the interest of true republican liberty, the neighbouring despots interfered, and, with two blows — not this time unresisted — destroyed Poland.

CHAPTER XVII.

THE RESTORATION OF POLAND, ACCORDING TO KOSCIUSZKO, 1815; GENERAL CHLOPIÇKI, 1830; AND COUNT ANDREW ZAMOYSKI, 1862.

THE usual mode of ending an article or book on Poland is with a vague prophecy that the day of retribution must, sooner or later, arrive, and the cause of liberty and justice triumph. That is all very well; but I want to know who is to have the Polish provinces now incorporated with the Russian Empire. There can be no new Poland without them, the Poles will never renounce their claim to them, and, on the other hand, the Russians will never willingly give them up. They might be "cut away with the sword," as Mr. Carlyle says, but the sword would have to be a strong one, for the Russians will no more part with them than they would part with Smolensk or the city of Kieff. All other Polish territory has changed hands more than once since the partitions of the eighteenth century; but Russia alone, among the three Powers, has never surrendered the least corner of the provinces seized by her in 1772, 1793, and 1795. For a moment, when Napoleon passed through on his road to Moscow, these provinces became free, but as the French retreated, the Russians re-occupied them. Russia lost them as she lost her ancient capital; and she would almost as soon lose her ancient capital as lose them again.

But is it not very unjust for Russia to keep them, or rather, is it not very unjust and tyrannical for her to govern the inhabitants as Russians when she is bound by treaties to govern them as Poles, and to grant them a "national representation," which, under her government, they have never yet obtained? This is no doubt most unjust, and we have seen that a representation (a very mild one) was addressed to Russia on the subject by the British Government in 1831. The point, however, to consider is, that Russia will never give these provinces up of her own accord; that, unless the Russian Empire falls to pieces, the Poles cannot recover them; and that even in the improbable case of England and France uniting to require Russia, Austria, and Prussia to observe the treaties of 1815, we should not have the smallest right to demand a separation of these provinces from the Russian Empire. Of the manner in which the Russo-Polish provinces are now governed I shall afterwards have to speak. For the present, I will only remark that, barbarously as Russia has treated her Polish subjects during the greater part of the present century, and especially since the reign of Nicholas, yet, for a period of twenty years after the first partition (and it must not be forgotten that all the Russo-Polish provinces, as distinguished from the "Kingdom," were acquired by the partitions of the eighteenth century), the Poles who had passed under Russian dominion were treated with anything but severity. "The laws, language, property, and the religion of the inhabitants were respected," says a Polish author of great literary merit and remarkable impartiality,* "the administration of justice was maintained in Polish, and the principal local magistrates were elective. The taxes were moderate, and the new provinces remained free from military conscription during twenty years. The abuses of the Russian Administration were then less intolerable, the police of the districts as well as the local courts of justice being administered by magistrates elected by the landowners themselves. . . . . Poland being unable to make any attempt at regaining her lost provinces, no agitation for that purpose, and consequently no persecution on that score, took place. There was some religious persecution of the

* *Panslavism and Germanism*, by Count Valerian Krasinski. London, 1848.

peasantry belonging to the Greek Church united with Rome, but it was insignificant, and produced more by the bigotry of the local Greek bishops than by any regular system of the Government, and nothing at all in comparison to the persecution which the same Church has recently suffered."

Catherine had too much sense not to endeavour to conciliate the Poles when she had nothing to fear from them, and consequently nothing to gain by ill-treating them. When, however, Poland gave an alarming proof of vitality by adopting the Constitution of 1791, which rendered the crown hereditary, abolished the veto, liberated the peasants from serfdom, and placed the franchise within the reach of all classes—then the Allies fell with ferocity upon the re-invigorated State, which, if not at once destroyed, they knew would never rest until it had regained its former frontiers. But in 1796, a year after the third partition, Catherine died; and Paul, as soon as he became Emperor, visited Kosciuszko in his prison, liberated him, offered him a command in his army, which the Polish patriot of course could not accept, and assured him that if he had been on the throne at the time, the partition should never have taken place. He recalled from Siberia the Poles who had been exiled thither by Catherine, and gave them back their estates which she had confiscated. The reader knows that in the Kingdom of Poland everything Russian is abhorred; but in Austrian and Prussian Poland, where, if the Russians are not at all liked, Germans are very much hated, you may see in the shop windows engravings and photographs of a picture representing the interview of Paul with Kosciuszko in the St. Petersburg fortress. Paul only persecuted the Russians, especially the Russian nobility; and we know how this persecution was resented.

Only six years had elapsed since the third partition, when the Emperor Alexander ascended the throne, and spoke of the dismemberment of Poland as a crime, for which reparation must be made. Throughout his reign Alexander represented himself to the Poles as the future regenerator of their country. When Napoleon, in 1807, formed the Duchy of Warsaw out of the provinces recovered from Prussia, Alexander sought to negative the attraction exercised by this thoroughly Polish little State, by granting liberties and holding out hopes to the inhabitants of Lithuania and the other Polish provinces under his dominion.

Alexander, when his troops had taken possession of the Duchy of Warsaw in 1814, sincerely desired to be King of all Poland—an ambition which has never been entertained by a King of Prussia or, in modern times, by an Emperor of Austria. Only a few years before the first partition, the crown of Poland was offered to Frederic the Great for his brother Prince Henry.* Frederic at once refused it. He did not wish to revive Poland, but to build up Prussia at Poland's expense.

The Tsars of Russia, on the other hand, have desired to rule over Poland ever since the beginning of the sixteenth century, when (in 1506) the Tsar Vassili sent an ambassador to his sister, the Dowager Queen of Poland, begging her to induce the States of Poland and Lithuania to elect him for their monarch. Ivan the Terrible (son of Vassili), had he consented to be crowned in Cracow instead of Moscow, and to place the Polish before the Russian title in his designation, would probably have been elected King of Poland (1572). At least, he had a very strong party in his favour, who thought that in the event of Ivan ascending the throne, Polish institutions would be adopted by Muscovy, as they had been already adopted under similar circumstances by Lithuania.

Immediately afterwards, Stephen Batory sought to carry out the converse of Ivan's programme, and to unite, by force of arms, all Russia (or "Muscovy") to Poland.

In 1611, Ladislas, the son of Sigismund III. of Poland, was offered the Tsarate of Muscovy

* *Frédéric II., Catherine, et le Partage de la Pologne*, par Frederic de Smitt. Paris and Berlin.

THE CATHEDRAL OF CRACOW.

by the Council of Boyars, and would have reigned at Moscow as a constitutional monarch, but for the bigotry of his father, who would not give his consent to the guarantees demanded by the Boyars for their National Church.

Michael, the first of the Romanoffs, had enough to do to defend his own territory against the Poles; but Alexis, his son, was a candidate for the crown of Poland at the same time as Sobieski.

Peter the Great, son of Alexis, imposed two Kings on Poland, Augustus II. and Augustus III.; and the object of Russian policy, even at the beginning of Catherine's reign, was not to dismember Poland, but to gain the whole of it for the Russian Crown, or for a line of sovereigns to be nominated by Russia.

In short, the Poles know that they have nothing to hope from Prussia, and next to nothing from Austria; whereas from Russia they may expect almost anything short of complete independence, because Russia desires earnestly to govern all Poland, and to attain that end must, sooner or later, make terms with the Poles.

Count Skorupka, one of the representatives of Cracow in the Galician Diet, published a work last year,* in which he pointed out to the Austrian Government the advantage it would find in granting to Galicia a perfect system of self-government under the viceroyalty of an Austrian Grand Duke, so as to make it, and not the Kingdom, the centre of attraction for the Poles. Of course the Austrian Government has neither the foresight nor the energy to adopt this scheme.

Dombrowski, in 1794, when the Prussians were already in possession of Warsaw, begged Frederick William to declare himself King of all Poland;† promising him, if he would accept the throne, the support of the entire Polish nation, which then, as now, desired above all to be reunited, under no matter what sovereign. This, however, was far too dangerous a policy for Russia's jackal to embark upon.

We have seen, however, that it is a policy to which Russia has always been inclined; and she alone of the three partitioning Powers can hope to carry it out with success. The Russians are quite right in saying that Catherine II. never wished to dismember Poland. She wished to take it all; and when Frederic the Great forced the project of

* *Opocha* (The Corner-stone), by Count Leon Skorupka. Cracow and Leopol.
† Forster, *La Pologne.*

the first partition upon her, she had nothing to gain by accepting it, for a prince of her own choosing already occupied the Polish throne, the Russian ambassadors were all-powerful at Warsaw, and the whole of Poland was held in subjection by a force of not more than forty thousand Russian troops. Since the third partition, Russia has, on three occasions (in 1807, 1809, and 1815), gained fresh provinces at the expense of the German Powers; until now she finds herself in possession of at least four-fifths of the Poland of 1772, and has under her dominion about three-fourths of the entire population of the dismembered country. Russia may act with all possible good faith towards her neighbours, but the Emperor of Russia need only unite the whole of his Polish provinces into one constitutional kingdom, and declare himself *bonâ fide* King of Poland, to have the Galicians and the Poseners quite as much at his service as his own subjects. This was quite understood by Alexander I., who, when his Polish provinces appeared to be gravitating towards the little State formed by Napoleon out of the provinces reconquered from Prussia, was on the point of proclaiming himself King of Poland with a Constitution moulded on that of 1791. He appears to have had a good heart, but it is quite certain that he wished to attract the Duchy of Warsaw to his Crown, and defeat the plans of Napoleon. In this project the Emperor Alexander was encouraged by Prince Czartoryski* and by M. C. Oginski, who presented several valuable memoirs on the subject, which were approved of by His Majesty. "The re-establishment of Poland as you propose it," said the Emperor to Oginski on the 15th December, 1811, "is in no way contrary to the interests of Russia" .... "The Poles would be happy and contented if they had a Constitution. As for the title, why should I not call myself King of Poland if that will give pleasure to all the Poles?"

After the sudden invasion of Russia, when Napoleon was in full retreat, the Emperor said again to Oginski, on the 19th October, 1812: "As soon as I see him on his last legs, and unable to do any harm to the Poles, I will re-establish Poland. I will do it because it accords with my conviction, with the feelings of my heart, and even with the interests of my Empire. .... I know I shall meet with many difficulties and obstacles in carrying out my design; but, unless I die, I will realize it."

Not only did Prince Adam Czartoryski and M. C. Oginski look to the Emperor Alexander and

* See *L'Odyssée Polonaise*, par E. Regnault, *Les Mémoires d' Oginski*, and several extracts from the latter work in *D'Angeberg's Recueil des Traités*, &c., for the years 1811 and 1812.

to him alone for the re-establishment of Poland;
Kosciuszko did the same; and even Poniatowski,
Napoleon's most devoted follower, appears to have
hesitated one terrible night between his duty as a
soldier to the French Emperor, and as a Pole to his
native land. Alexander, during the French retreat, made a formal promise to restore Poland if
Poniatowski would only remain neutral with his
troops in the Duchy of Warsaw until the conclusion of the war. The temptation was so great that,
in his distress of mind, Poniatowski was on the
point of committing suicide, but ultimately he
sacrificed all other considerations to a feeling of
personal honour.*

As for Kosciuszko, he never believed in Napoleon's intention to re-establish Poland, and
refused to assist him in forming the Duchy of
Warsaw, from a just conviction that he would
attack and make peace with Russia and Austria
exactly as it might suit his own policy, and without
any reference to the interests of the Poles. This
did not prevent Napoleon from making a fraudu-
lent use of Kosciuszko's name in his proclamations†

* *L'Odyssée Polonaise*, par E. Regnault.
† By a strange omission, no documents bearing on this
important fact are published in D'Angeberg's valuable collection. On the contrary, a proclamation, signed by Dombrowski and Wybiçki, is published, announcing the speedy arrival
of Kosciuszko in Poland, though Kosciuszko had refused all
countenance to Napoleon's intrigues in the name of Polish

—a piece of baseness against which the Polish hero lost no time in protesting. Kosciuszko had only one idea of a revived Poland : the country as it existed before the partitions, under a Constitutional Government. For less than this he would not move; to obtain this he was ready, at any time, to lay down his life. Under a constitutional system, as long as the sovereign faithfully observes the Constitution, it matters comparatively but little who reigns. But in the peculiar case of Poland, it was evidently desirable that the crown should be given to a sovereign who would be able to defend it against all comers; and, as in 1814, Alexander had nearly the whole of ancient Poland in his possession, nothing seemed simpler than to beg him to re-establish the ancient limits and liberties of the country, and declare himself king. Twenty years had elapsed since the battle of Maciéiovicé, at which Kosciuszko, as he fell, did *not* exclaim, " *Finis Poloniæ!* " and now, for the first time, the undaunted patriot saw that there was an opportunity for his beloved country to recover its national existence.

" Everyone," says M. Guizot, speaking of the

independence. " If he will not allow us the use of his name, we must take it in spite of him," Napoleon had said. See, among other accounts of the formation of the Duchy of Warsaw, the one contained in Thiers' *History of the Consulate and the Empire*, and *L'Odyssée Polonaise*.

European Powers, " has made use of Poland. No one has ever assisted her." Accordingly, in seeking to regain her national unity, Poland would do well to consider, not which Power has persecuted her the most, or which has been the most ready to betray her, but simply which is the most interested, at the present moment, in, to some extent, furthering her views, and the most capable of carrying them out.

Let us go back once more: this time to the very beginning of the trials of Poland. They have now lasted a hundred years.

Ten years before the first partition, Frederic the Great and Peter III. signed a secret treaty binding them to maintain that curse of Poland, the elective sovereignty, and to oppose all attempts to make the crown hereditary. This treaty was renewed on behalf of Russia by Catherine II. in 1764; and the same year Prussia, Russia, and Austria made official declarations, through their ambassadors, in which they pledged themselves to maintain the integrity of Poland, and deprecated vigorously the guilty intentions already attributed to them. His Majesty of Prussia had heard of a shameful rumour to the effect that his court and that of Russia meditated the dismemberment of Poland, and he felt "justly indignant at these reports," more especially, as, " far from thinking of increasing his own dominions, he had always laboured, and always should labour, to maintain those of the Republic in their integrity." *

"If ever the spirit of lying invented a complete falsehood," wrote Catherine at the same time,† "it was when the report was audaciously spread" —that Catherine, in supporting the election of Stanislas Augustus, wished to prepare the way for the subjugation of Poland.

Until the very eve of the partition these protestations were renewed.

After the first partition, when Poland was reforming her Constitution, abolishing the *veto* and the elective sovereignty, enlarging the electoral body and liberating the peasants from serfdom, Prussia, under these circumstances, assured Poland of her sympathy and support, and a treaty of alliance between the two countries was signed at Warsaw on the 29th March, 1790. The year afterwards, when the Constitution of the 3rd of May had been adopted, Frederic William wrote to congratulate Stanislas Augustus, and to assure him of his continued friendship. Another year, and he was in league with Catherine II. to dis-

---

* *D'Angeberg*, p. 15.
† *Chodzko, La Pologne, Pitteresque et Illustrée*, t. iii. p. 142. *D'Angeberg*, p. 14.

member the territory of his ally, and pleading *"posteriora ligant"* as an excuse for his treachery. So much for the Prussian alliance.

As for Napoleon, he was always ready to abandon the Poles; at one time, to conciliate the Emperor Paul, to whom he actually proposed to forward Kosciuszko and a host of illustrious exiles in bran-new uniforms, as a sort of peace-offering;* at another for the sake of the friendship and co-operation of the Emperor Alexander, to whom he on two occasions ceded Polish territory,† and to whom he made a formal promise never to revive the name of Poland;‡ at another in order to retain Austria as an ally.

The Emperor Alexander, on his side, while he

* *L'Odyssée Polonaise*, par E. Regnault.
† Bialystock in 1807, and Tarnapol in 1809.
‡ M. Thiers denies that this promise was given, and so did Napoleon himself at St. Helena. It would be more correct to say that he was ashamed of having given it. See *L'Odyssée Polonaise*, par E. Regnault, who quotes the promise in writing. Napoleon was soliciting at the time the hand of a Russian Grand-duchess, and, as M. Regnault well says, "The sacrifice of Poland was to be his wedding-gift." Napoleon was always ready to give up the nation he had already betrayed for the sake of an advantageous legitimate union. That Napoleon really admired, perhaps even loved, Poland, is also certain; and the Poles apparently think that (to vary Tennyson)—

"'Tis better to be loved and lost,
Than never to be loved at all."

was leading Prince Czartoryski, his Minister of Foreign Affairs, and all the principal men of Lithuania, to believe that he was bent on the restoration of Poland in its integrity, was, during a portion of the time, carrying on a negotiation with Prussia; and, to do him justice, he did not conceal, in the year 1811, that, if he could make terms with Napoleon, he should not be in any hurry to carry out his Polish project at all.

"We must wait for events," he said to Oginski in December, 1811. "To-day I have received more satisfactory news, which gives me some hope that we shall not come to an open rupture with Napoleon." Nevertheless, although Alexander may not have wished to engage in a gigantic struggle for the sake of Poland, it is quite certain that when the retreat of the French left all the Polish provinces in his hands, he desired ardently to be proclaimed King of a united Poland, and that with the crown he was ready to accept a Constitution.

Here, however, the interests of the Western Powers were brought into play. Kosciuszko, after twenty years' retirement, during which his belief in the restoration of his native land never for a moment deserted him, begged Alexander to declare himself King of Poland, and to give the Poles a Constitution resembling that of England. Here is his letter ; a most valuable document for persons who wish not merely to have their interest and emotion excited by the history of the struggles of the Poles to regain their national existence, but who wish also to understand how that existence may be regained :—

Kosciuszko to the Emperor Alexander.
"*Berville, 9th of April,* 1814.

" SIRE,

"If from my obscure retreat I venture to address a prayer to a great monarch, a great captain, and, above all, a protector of humanity, it is because his generosity and magnanimity are well known to me.

" I ask three favours.

"The first is, that you will grant a general amnesty to the Poles without any restriction, and that the peasants who are dispersed in foreign countries may be regarded as free when they return home.

" The second is, that your Majesty will proclaim yourself King of Poland, with a free Constitution, like that of England [literally, "approaching that of England"], and establish schools, to be supported at the expense of the Government for the education of the peasants ; that the servitude of the peasants be abolished at the end of ten years; and that their possessions be made over to them as absolute property. If my prayers are granted, I will go personally, though I am an invalid, and throw myself at the feet of your Majesty to thank you, and to be the first to render homage to you as my Sovereign. If you can make any use of my abilities, such as they are, I will leave here instantly to rejoin my countrymen, to serve my country and my Sovereign with honour and fidelity.

"My third prayer, Sire, though of a private character, is of heartfelt interest to me. I have been living for the last fourteen years with the family of the estimable M. Zelltner, a Swiss by birth, and formerly the ambassador of his country in France. I am under a thousand obligations to him, but we are both of us poor, and he has a numerous family. I solicit for him some place of honour, either in the new French Government or in Poland. He is a man of ability, and I answer for his unbounded fidelity. I am, with the highest respect,

"Your Majesty's, &c."

This letter is very important, not only because it shows on what terms the Poles would gladly form a union with Russia, but also because Kosciuszko distinctly recognizes in it the right of the Polish peasants to the land held by them at that time as serfs, and which they now hold, not as free possessors, but as farmers. Whether the proprietors ought not to be compensated by the State, or what the amount of compensation ought to be, are different questions. It is useful to know that Kosciuszko, who certainly was not the enemy of the Polish nobility, thought the peasants ought to be liberated with their land. That was also the opinion of Miçkievicz, than whom no one had a higher respect for the great men of his country, and who lies buried at a village near Paris, side by side with Prince Adam Czartoryski and Niemcevicz. Indeed, Prince Adam Czartoryski, when he liberated the peasants on the one unconfiscated estate remaining to him in Galicia, gave up the whole of the peasants' land. This was an act of generosity no doubt, but it cannot be regarded as a concession to the spirit of communism. Indeed, the communists cry out for property which they know does not by any law, whether obsolete or in force, belong to them. Miçkievicz maintained that the land cultivated by the Polish serf for his own use *did* belong to him, in virtue of ancient contracts, which it was now necessary to modify, but not so as to weaken the absolute title of the peasant to his land. Kosciuszko, naturally, did not go into any arguments in his letter to the Emperor Alexander, but we may be sure that he, better than anyone, understood the true position of the Polish peasant, and knew the Polish traditions on the subject.

The Emperor Alexander's reply to Kosciuszko's letter was as follows:—

"*Paris, 3rd of May*, 1814.

"It is with great satisfaction, General, that I reply to your letter. Your dearest wishes will be accomplished. With the aid of the All-powerful I hope to bring about the regeneration of the brave and estimable nation to which you belong. I have taken a solemn engagement to do so; and its welfare has always occupied my thoughts. Political circumstances have alone raised obstacles which have prevented the execution of my designs. These obstacles no longer exist. Two years of a terrible but glorious struggle have removed them.

"A little time, and with prudence the Poles will recover their country and their name, and I shall have the happiness of convincing them that, forgetting the past, he whom they considered their enemy will realize all their wishes.

"What a satisfaction it will be to me to have you as my assistant in these salutary labours. Your name, your character, your talent, will be the best support I could have."

Now, if Kosciuszko's proposition had not only been accepted, but acted upon; if the Emperor Alexander could have proclaimed himself King of all Poland—of the Poland of 1772—the now insoluble Polish question would have been solved. It was not solved by the treaty of 1815, signed precisely a year after the date of Kosciuszko's letter; its solution was only postponed. The only settlement of the Polish difficulty which can ensure the happiness of the Poles, give peace to Russia, and relieve Europe of the disgrace which the present state of Poland reflects on all the European Powers, is the one proposed by Kosciuszko, accepted by Alexander I., and which the West of Europe alone prevented from being put into execution. If, the opportunity again presenting itself, England and France should still object to all Poland being annexed to Russia, on condition that the government be national and constitutional, then England and France must either cease to proclaim their sympathy for the Poles, or make some movement on behalf of Polish independence; which everyone, including every Pole of the least knowledge or experience, knows they will not and cannot do; which, during the Crimean war, when, according to all the rules of international law, they had the clearest right to raise up Poland, they carefully abstained from doing.

The objection to Kosciuszko's and Alexander's plan for restoring to Poland its national existence was reasonable enough, but not very noble. England and France felt a certain sympathy for Poland, but were very jealous indeed of Russia, and preferred, by far, that Poland should be cut up into five pieces, and, with the exception of the little "Kingdom" of Poland and the Free City of Cracow, left at the mercy of three despots, rather than that the Sovereign who ruled Russia absolutely should wear the crown of all Poland as Constitutional King.

Since 1830 it has often been said that it was impossible for the Russian Emperor to govern absolutely in Russia and constitutionally in Poland. The Poles were the first to make this observation in explaining and justifying the insurrection of 1830,[*] and the Russians, with their usual ingenuity, took it up, and founded on it an argument for withdrawing the Polish Constitution. It would be easy to show, from the history of Hungary, that the observation is untrue; and that if a sovereign can only be honest (for that, after all, appears to be the great difficulty), he can govern an absolute monarchy according to law, and a constitutional monarchy according to law, at the same time. Austria was never so strong as when the rights of Hungary were fully respected.

[*] *Manifesto of the Polish People*, written and sanctioned by the Diet of Poland, Warsaw, Dec. 20th, 1830. (*D'Angeberg*, p. 770.)

And Austria was rewarded for this by the unshakeable fidelity of Hungary during her wars against Napoleon. Is it certain that Hungary, with all her rights trampled upon, would be equally faithful if Austria should be attacked to-morrow by Napoleon III.?

Of course, if a sovereign placed in the position which Alexander I. held in Poland after 1815, tries to mix the two systems, he finds his position untenable. It was also untenable from a cause which would not have existed had France, England, and Austria not opposed the project arranged between Kosciuszko and Alexander; it was untenable not because Poland was ruled constitutionally and Russia despotically (for at that time the Russians pretended to like despotism), but because, under the same Crown, one part of Poland was endowed with free institutions, while another and a greater portion of the same country was subjected to absolute government.

At the present moment, too, it might be difficult to re-introduce constitutionalism into any part of Russian Poland, without publishing some sort of a Constitution for the whole of the Russian Empire. The Poles say, of course, that this is not their affair; that the treaties of 1815 did not bind them to wait for a representative government until the Emperor was ready to give one to all his Russian subjects. But, taking things as they are, and considering the legitimate aspirations of the educated classes in Russia* towards a constitutional system—I call them legitimate in the fullest sense of the word, because they have been encouraged and fostered by the Emperor—it might be inconvenient to give to the Poles only what Poles and Russians now demand alike. This may be a very good reason for raising the Russians to the lawful position of the Poles, but not for withholding from the Poles rights which the Russian Government is bound by treaty to grant them. And, as a question of expediency, it is becoming more evident every day that if the Russian Emperor finds it impossible to reconcile the parts of constitutional and despotic sovereign, it will be more than ever advantageous for him to abandon the latter character altogether.

Numbers of Poles would object, no doubt, to any arrangement that would leave them under the Russian Crown. But, in the absence of earthquakes, revolutions, and all sorts of stupendous occurrences not easily to be foreseen, what hope can they have of regaining their national existence by any other means, if they have nothing to support them but a strong internal conviction that their country will, some day, in some manner, recover its independent position? The Welsh had

* As to the constitutional movement in Russia, see vol. ii.

this conviction also; so also had the Irish; but we never hear now of a rational Irishman wishing for an independent Ireland, and it is centuries since any Welshman has thought of an independent Wales.

Nevertheless, no one can blame the Poles, and indeed, every one must applaud them, for refusing to accept a union with Russia, which would place them in the position held so long by Ireland with respect to England; but no one who has examined the difficulties of their situation will pity them for having to hold in the Russian Empire the high position that belongs to Scotland in the Empire of Great Britain. The most able and influential men among the Poles would rejoice to find themselves so circumstanced; and Kosciuszko in 1814, General Chlopiçki in 1830, and Count Andrew Zamoyski in 1862, asked for nothing more. Many readers will remember that, only last autumn, the principal landed proprietors of the Kingdom of Poland promised their loyal support to the Grand Duke Constantine, on condition that all Polish provinces in the possession of Russia were united into one constitutional kingdom. The address was not presented, but would have been had not Count Zamoyski been arrested and exiled for entertaining the *intention* of presenting it.

I am quite certain, for my part, that the above

solution of the Polish difficulty is the only one that the Poles will ever agree to, though, by fire and sword, the Russians may, of course, force them (at least, for a time) to submit unconditionally. The reader knows what Poland has demanded, on three important occasions, during the last fifty years, speaking in each case through a man whose right to represent the wishes of his country was undeniable. There is no difference between these demands, except that after 1815 it was impossible to ask the Russian Emperor to grant national and representative rights to provinces which were no longer in his power. If, however, Russia had granted the request contained in General Chlopicki's letter of 1830, or in Count Zamoyski's address of 1862, it was the hope of the Poles that negotiations would, sooner or later, be entered into with the Prussian and Austrian Governments for the cession of Posen and Galicia, subject to indemnification in territory (say, for Prussia in Germany, for Austria on the Danube).

It may now be interesting to consider what probability there is of conciliating the leading men of Poland, if the Russo-Polish provinces and the Kingdom are *not* reunited.

Since the scornful and tyrannical rejection of the demands contained in the address confided to

Count Zamoyski, the Poles of all Russian Poland have been governed more than ever like a conquered, or rather a half-conquered, people.

The rejection of Chlopiçki's propositions was followed by the war of 1831.

As for Kosciuszko's project, we have seen that Alexander, in the first instance, agreed to it with joy. When, through the natural objections of the Western Powers, who feared the increase of power it would give to Russia, it became impossible to carry it out, Kosciuszko, who was not a wild enthusiast, but, like other great heroes and patriots, a man of a very practical turn of mind, suggested that if the Emperor Alexander could not do all that he had originally intended for Poland, he might yet do as much as still lay within his power. He wrote a letter to the Emperor, asking this time *precisely* what Count Zamoyski asked the other day from Alexander II. The reader knows under what conditions all the best men in Poland, and, thanks to their influence and example, the whole of the Polish nation, would become the faithful subjects of the Russian Emperor ruling in Poland as Constitutional King. I will end this chapter by showing, from two letters of Kosciuszko, under what circumstances those who adopt him as their model must refuse to give the Russian Government in Poland their countenance and support.

1.

Kosciuszko to the Emperor Alexander.*

"*Vienna,* 10*th June,* 1815.

"Sire,

"Prince Czartoryski has made me acquainted with all the benefits which your Imperial and Royal Majesty is preparing for the Polish nation; I cannot find words to express the gratitude and admiration with which your conduct inspires me. One consideration alone troubles my mind and prevents my joy from being complete. I am a Lithuanian by birth, Sire, and I have only a few years to live; nevertheless, the veil of the future still covers the destinies of my native land, and of so many other of my country's provinces.† I do not forget the magnanimous promises in reference to them which Your Majesty deigned to make to me personally as well to many of my fellow-countrymen. My heart will never allow me to doubt the effect of those sacred words; but my soul, intimidated by such prolonged misfortunes, is in need of re-assurance. Listening only to the prompting of my own feelings, I now place the remainder of my

* *Hoffman, Alex. Ch., Coup d'Œil sur la Pologne de* 1815.
† At present, the Russians, by a chain of false historical and ethnological reasoning, prove the country of Kosciuszko, the Czartoryskis, Niemcevicz, Mickievicz, and Sobieski—that is to say, all Lithuania and Ruthenia—to be Russian.

existence at the service of your Majesty. Be my judge, Sire, in this juncture, so decisive for my conscience, and by one kind word deign to tell me that you approve of my determination. This word will be the fulfilment of the only wish that remains to me, that of descending to the tomb with the consoling conviction that all your Polish subjects will be called to bless you for your benefits. This conviction would, I confess, increase to an infinite degree my efforts and the energy of my zeal. I should never venture, Sire, to hurry you in the execution of your great projects. I will keep the secret of your intentions as a sacred trust reposed in me for the satisfaction of my own conscience, and will never make use of it without your express authorization. I shall wait here for your commands in reply to my humble prayer. It is my last, and I venture to lay it at your Majesty's feet with a feeling of confidence as firm as is, I am sure, your own magnanimity and your incomparable kindness."

2.

Letter from Kosciuszko to Prince Adam Czartoryski.*

"*Vienna, June* 13*th*, 1815.

"MY DEAR PRINCE,

"I attach great value to your friendship, your manner of thinking being in conformity

* *Hoffmann D'Angeberg*, p. 700.

with mine. You are, without doubt, convinced that the first of my desires is to serve my country efficaciously. The refusal of the Emperor to reply to my last letter from Vienna, of which I send you a copy, takes from me all possibility of attaining this aim. *I will not act without having some guarantee for my country, nor will I allow myself to be enticed by mere hope.* I have put in the same balance the interests of my country and those of the Emperor. I am incapable of separating them. Being unable to do anything more, I offered to give myself up to the service of my country, but not to see it restricted to that little piece of territory *emphatically decorated with the name of the Kingdom of Poland.*

"We have to thank the Emperor for having resuscitated the name of Poland; but a name alone does not constitute a nation. The extent of territory and the number of the population are also something. I do not know on what ground, unless it be our own desires, we are now to put faith in the guarantee he gave to us—to me, and so many others of our countrymen—that the frontiers of Poland should extend to the Dzwina and the Dnieper; which, in re-establishing a certain proportion of power and numbers, would have contributed to maintain between the Russians and ourselves mutual consideration and a stable friendship.

"With a liberal and quite separate Constitution, such as they have been led to expect, the Poles would have thought themselves happy to live with the Russians under the sceptre of so great a monarch. But at the very beginning I see quite a different order of things. The Russians are to fill concurrently with us the first places in the Government. This certainly cannot inspire the Poles with much confidence. They foresee, not without alarm, that in time the name of Pole will fall into contempt, and that the Russians will treat us soon as their subjects. And, indeed, how could a population so limited escape their preponderance? And those of our brothers who are kept under the Russian sceptre, can we forget them?

"Our hearts suffer at their not being reunited to us, and the Emperor gave us his sacred word that this union should be accomplished. Thus, a population of from fifteen to sixteen million souls would have been formed, which would have constituted the Kingdom of Poland; a kingdom which, having, like that of Hungary, its own constitution and laws, would have formed, under the same sceptre, one Empire with Russia.

"Here I must separate the generous and humane intentions of the Emperor from the policy of his Cabinet. I shall preserve till death a feeling of gratitude towards this prince for having resuscitated the name of Poland, though he has re-

icted the country to such narrow limits. May
ovidence direct you! As for me, as I can no
ıger serve my country usefully, I return to
ⁿitzerland. You know whether I have co-
erated as much as lay in my power for the
neral good."

In preparing the treaties of 1815, an endeavour
d been made—since Russia would not consent
 the independence of Poland, and France, Eng-
ıd, and Austria would not agree to the formation
 all Poland into one constitutional kingdom
der the Russian Crown—an endeavour had been
ıde, as if out of pity for the Poles, to secure, at
ıst, some sort of national existence for them.
 was expressly stipulated, both in the treaties
tween Russia, Austria, and Prussia, and in the
neral treaty signed by all the great Powers,
at all the Polish subjects of Russia, Austria, and
 ussia should enjoy a "national representation
d institutions." The Constitution given to the
-called "Kingdom of Poland" was a thing apart,
d Russian politicians now maintain that the
nperor Alexander granted it of his own free
ll. This is not precisely true. The Treaty of
enna sets forth that the Kingdom of Poland is
oined to Russia by its constitution." No con-
tution is specified, but every one knew that
ɜ constitution *meant* was the one which the

Emperor Alexander, assisted by Prince Czartoryski, had drawn up. Not to have seen this document at Vienna in 1815 was to have seen nothing, and its very exhibition, in a sort of private-public manner, gained for the Russian Emperor that reputation for "liberalism" which he retained for a long time afterwards, and which, but for the men who surrounded him, he no doubt would have justified. Soon after the promulgation of this constitution, the Emperor gave the Poles to understand that it was his intention to extend it to all the Polish provinces under his sceptre; and he continued to assure those who were in his confidence of this intention, and spoke of it as his "favourite project" until the last day of his reign. It was not until after the accession of the Emperor Nicholas that the Poles despaired of seeing their monarch's "favourite project" put into execution; and the certainty that it had been abandoned did more than anything else to bring about the insurrection of 1830.

At the present moment, it is looked upon as a crime on the part of the Poles to petition in the most respectful manner, and through perfectly legal channels, for the execution of the design known to have been entertained by Alexander I., and for the sake of which he had even caused a clause to be inserted in the Treaty of Vienna, empowering him to give the little Kingdom "the interior extension he might think fit." That is to say, the Emperor reserved to himself the right of extending the Polish Constitution to all the Polish provinces under the Russian sceptre not included in the Kingdom created by the Congress.

A few months ago, the nobles, or landed proprietors, of the Polish province of Podolia, adopted unanimously, at their triennial assembly, a petition, praying the Emperor not to grant a constitution, not to profit by the right which the Emperor Alexander had so significantly reserved—but simply to unite Podolia to the Kingdom, so that it might at least have a Polish administration, and that Polish might be the language of the Government offices, tribunals, and schools. The proprietors set forth plainly but respectfully the miserable effect which the forced substitution of Russian for Polish had had upon the civilization of the province; and the Government replied to the address by arresting the "marshals of the nobility," who had ventured to present it! * The marshals were accused of "attempting to destroy the integrity of the Empire," and, what is still more extraordinary, have been found guilty and condemned each to

---

* The Russo-Polish provinces are divided, like the provinces of Russia Proper, into districts, and the nobility of each district elect a "marshal" to represent them in their dealings with the Government.

fourteen months' imprisonment. The news of their condemnation is published in the English journals of February 16th.

Whatever the crime of these Polish noblemen may be in the eyes of the Russian Government, in the eyes of Europe their sole offence has been to solicit the observance of one of the clauses of a treaty sanctioned by all the European Powers. Lord Palmerston, as we have seen, reminded the Russian Government, in 1831, that this very stipulation had never been observed. The Russian Government now reminds all Europe that it not only does not mean to observe it, but that it is prepared to punish with severity any of its Polish subjects who, without citing the obnoxious clause itself, presume to ask, even in the humblest manner, for the natural rights which it was the object of that clause to secure for them.

In a few words, then, the great immediate object of the Kingdom of Poland and of the Polish provinces incorporated with the Russian Empire, is to become united so as to form one Polish kingdom. If this kingdom were endowed with a Constitution, the leading men of Poland are already pledged to serve the Emperor faithfully as his loyal subjects. But any arrangement which would enable the inhabitants of the Russo-Polish provinces to live and bring up their children as Poles, would be a blessing to them, and a consolation to the Poles of the existing "Kingdom." In the Polish provinces, incorporated with Russia, the inhabitants are reprimanded if they venture to speak of themselves as Poles, and thrown into prison if they dare to ask permission to use their native language. In respect to their nationality, they are as badly off as the Polish subjects of Prussia. As regards political rights, they are much in the same position as the Poles of the Kingdom: no position can be worse. They are far more unfortunately situated than any Russians, for they are not only the subjects of a despotism, but, what is infinitely worse, of a foreign despotism; not only of a foreign despotism, but of one which will not listen to them, nor in any way recognize their existence, unless they first of all reject all their past civilization, and make a vain, humiliating, really impossible attempt to transform themselves into foreigners.

APPENDIX.

No. I.

EXTRACT FROM "A STATEMENT OF FACTS AND ARGUMENTS ON THE SUBJECT OF POLAND."

Treaty of Vienna, 1815. WHEN, in 1815, the representatives of the great European Powers assembled at Vienna, to determine by a Treaty the future international relations of Europe, the first question to which they addressed themselves, was that of Poland. This question was at that time considered so important, that Prince Talleyrand, in the note forwarded by the French Government to the Congress, wrote in the following terms respecting it :—

Opinion of Prince Talleyrand. "Of all the questions which will come under the consideration of the Congress, the King would have looked upon that of Poland as the first, the greatest, the most eminently European, and beyond all comparison that which has the greatest claims to attention, were there any grounds for hoping that a people so deserving of the interest of all other nations by its antiquity, its valour, its misfortunes, and the services it rendered in past ages to Europe, could be restored to the full possession of her former independence. The partition which blotted her name from the list of nations was the prelude, and in part the cause, of the disorders which convulsed Europe, *and perhaps to a certain extent excused them.*" *

These last words convey a remarkable admission on the part of the Government of the Restoration. The partition of Poland must indeed have appeared in its eyes a hideous crime, to lead it to regard the revolutionary excesses which had overturned monarchy in France, and brought the head of Louis XVI. to the scaffold, as excusable.

The truth is, that in these words the cry of the conscience of Europe found a vent. The injustice done to Poland was too crying a fact to be denied or looked over. On the other hand, the three great Powers which had perpetrated this injustice were all-powerful in the Congress, and the respect which the Polish question inspired was not backed by power. Under these circumstances, it was thought necessary to compromise matters, by giving the partition of the Polish provinces the stamp of legality, on certain conditions, which guaranteed to all the Poles, under each of their

* *Klüber, Actes du Congrès de Vienne*, t. vii. p. 48.

rulers, a certain degree of autonomy. With this view the fourteen first Articles of the Treaty, which relate to Poland, were framed. The first of these, which is also the first of the Treaty, runs thus:—

<small>The fourteen first Articles of the Treaty.</small>

"The Duchy of Warsaw, with the exception of the provinces and districts which are otherwise disposed of by the following Articles, is united to the Russian Empire, to which it shall be irrevocably attached *by its Constitution*, and be possessed by His Majesty the Emperor of All the Russias, his heirs and successors, in perpetuity. His Imperial Majesty reserves to himself to give to this State, *enjoying a distinct Administration*, the exterior extension which he shall judge proper. He shall assume with his other titles that of Czar, King of Poland, agreeably to the form established for the titles attached to his other possessions.

"The Poles, who are respective subjects of Russia, Austria, and Prussia, *shall obtain a representation and national institutions*, regulated according to the degree of political existence that each of the Governments to which they belong shall judge expedient and proper to grant them." *

<small>The chief object the preservation of the existence of Poland.</small>

These words show clearly that it was the intention of the Congress to preserve the existence of the Polish nation. Poland was still to be one nation, though divided,

* *Neumann, Recueil des Traités*, t. ii. p. 673.

and is placed under separate States. This is even more stringently laid down in Art. 3 of the Treaty between Russia and Prussia, which, by Art. 118 of the general Treaty, is to be considered "part of the general enactments of the Congress, and is to have the same weight and value as if it had been inserted, word for word, in the general Treaty." The Article in question is as follows :—

"The Poles, subjects respectively of the high contracting parties, shall obtain institutions *which shall insure the preservation of their nationality*, in such form of political existence as each of the Governments to which they belong may think it useful and proper to grant them."

Again, in the 2nd Art. of the general Treaty, the boundary of the Grand Duchy of Posen is fixed, not only on the side of Russia, but also on that of Prussia, thus proving that although an appanage of Prussia, it was to be kept quite separate from it as a distinct State.

In other Articles of the Treaties of Vienna, liberty of navigation, circulation, and transit, was given to "Poland in her limits of 1772;" and certain advantages in commercial transactions were granted to Poles exclusively, Austrians, Prussians, and Russians being spoken of as "foreigners." This clearly establishes the intention of the Congress to recognize Poland as a distinct and separate nationality. Art. 14 of the general

Treaty thus summarizes the privileges here alluded to:—

<small>Free trade all over Poland (Art. 14.)</small> "The principles established for the free navigation of rivers and canals in the whole extent of ancient Poland (1772), as also the use of harbours, the circulation of products of the soil, and manufactures between the various Polish provinces, and commercial transit, as defined in Arts. 24, 25, 26, 28, and 29 of the Treaty between Austria and Russia, and Arts. 22, 23, 24, 25, 28, and 29 of the Treaty between Russia and Prussia, shall be invariably maintained."

The following, then, are the stipulations of the Treaty of Vienna relative to Poland:—

1st. Notwithstanding the political separation of the provinces, the national, civil, and commercial unity of the Poland of 1772 shall be preserved as an essential element of order and security in Europe.

2nd. The portions of Poland attached to the countries of Russia, Austria, and Prussia shall form distinct provinces, entirely separated from the Governments of those countries.

3rd. The Poles have not only a right to national representation and national institutions, but such institutions are to have for their object the maintenance and preservation of their nationality.

4th. Their rights are given the sanction, if not the guarantee, of Europe.

That the above is the interpretation that was given by the European Powers to the Articles of the Treaty which relate to Poland, is proved by the evidence of witnesses whose testimony is indisputable. The Emperor Alexander I. of Russia, in his proclamation to the Poles, granting them the Constitution of the 13th May, 1815, said,—

<small>Proclamation of Alexander I. to the Poles, 1815.</small>

"A Constitution appropriated to your wants and your character; the preservation, in public enactments, of your language; the restriction of public appointments to Poles; freedom of commerce and navigation; facility of communication with those parts of ancient Poland which are subject to other Powers; a national army; a guarantee that every means will be taken to perfect your laws; the free circulation of enlightenment in your country; such are the advantages you will enjoy under our rule and that of our successors, and which you will transmit as a patriotic legacy to your descendants." *

<small>His speech at the Diet in 1818.</small>

And further, three years afterwards, at the opening of the first Polish Diet at Warsaw, the Emperor Alexander held the same language:—

"*Your restoration is defined by solemn treaties,*" he said; "it is sanctioned by the constitutional

---

* *Archives Diplomatiques—Pologne*, par D'Angeberg, p. 693. Paris, Amyot, 1762-1862.

chart. *The inviolability of these* EXTERNAL *engagements* and of that fundamental law insures for Poland henceforth an honourable place among European nations." *

Indeed, so little did he doubt the guarantee of Europe for the preservation of the nationality of Poland, that, bent as he was on making the restoration of that country under his sceptre a means of furthering his own ambition, he boasted that he had obtained it by carrying all before him. "I have created this Kingdom," he said, "and I have established it on a very solid basis, for I have forced the European Powers to guarantee its existence by treaties."

<small>European guarantee.</small>

<small>Address of the King of Prussia to the inhabitants of Posen.</small> The King of Prussia addressed the inhabitants of Posen to the same effect in a proclamation published twelve days after the treaty:—

"You, too," he said, "have a fatherland, and I esteem you for having known how to defend it. You will be my subjects, without being compelled to deny your nationality on that account. Your religion shall be respected; your personal rights and your property regulated by laws which you will yourselves make. Your language shall be used on all public occasions, side by side with the German. You shall fill all the Government appointments in the Grand Duchy of Posen. My

* *Archives Diplomatiques—Pologne,* par D'Angeberg, p. 735. Paris, Amyot, 1762–1862.

viceroy, born in your country, shall reside among you." *

<small>Oath of Allegiance taken by Government employés in Posen.</small> The Oath of Allegiance taken by all functionaries was as follows:—

"I recognize His Majesty the King of Prussia as the only legitimate sovereign of this country, and that part of Poland which, in consequence of the Treaty of Vienna, has become a possession of the Royal House of Prussia, as my fatherland, which I am ready to defend against all invaders, under any circumstances, with my blood."

<small>Frederic William IV. of Prussia quotes the stipulations of the Treaty of Vienna relative to Poland, 1841.</small> And twenty-five years later, on dismissing the House of Representatives of 1841, Frederic William IV. quoted the same stipulations, though in less forcible terms, as being conscious of having violated them:—

"*In conformity with the stipulations of the Treaty of Vienna, we engage to respect in the Poles the love which every noble nation has for its language, its history, and its customs.*"

Such were the stipulations of the Treaty with regard to Poland, as they have been, and are, universally understood; and if the Poles <small>If the Poles have risen against the Governments forced upon them by the Treaty, it is because those Governments have violated it.</small> have since risen against the Governments which were forced upon them by that Treaty, it was because those Governments violated the conditions

* *Archives Diplomatiques — Pologne*, par D'Angeberg, p. 688. Paris, Amyot, 1762–1862.

on which it permitted them to retain their unjustly-acquired possessions. It is not the Poles, but the Governments which drive them to insurrection, that are revolutionists.

All their efforts tend to extinguish the nationality of Poland, in direct opposition to both the spirit and letter of the Treaty. The systematic violation of the Treaty by the three great Powers is matter of history, and has been acknowledged by our greatest statesmen. So far from "insuring the preservation of the nationality" of Poland, all the efforts of those Powers have tended to extinguish that nationality, by forbidding the use of the national language in public affairs, by filling all the posts of the State with foreigners, by suppressing the universities, and persecuting the national religion. Nor can the last paragraph of the first Article of the Treaty be pleaded as a justification of these proceedings. That paragraph, which grants to the Poles " a representation and national institutions, regulated according to the degree of political consideration that each of the Governments to which they belong shall judge expedient and proper to grant them," does not surely relieve those Governments of the obligation of preserving such representation and such national institutions. But the Power which chiefly signalized itself by the most flagrant violations of the Treaty was Russia. The *Russia in particular has repeatedly violated the Treaty.* Constitution alluded to in the first Article of the Treaty was that granted to Poland in 1815 by the Emperor

Alexander. Among its chief Articles were guarantees for the liberty of the subject and of the press, the Convocation of the Diet at least once in two years, and the submission of a Budget to the Diet once in four years. Each of these stipulations, during the fifteen years which preceded the insurrection of 1830, was violated. Many of the most eminent of the inhabitants of Warsaw were condemned, without even the form of a trial, to sweep the streets; the press was fettered; the Diet did not assemble for five years, and fifteen years elapsed without a Budget having been submitted to it. These illegal measures of the Government, combined with the well-known brutalities of the Grand Duke Constantine, produced the insurrection of 1830, which Russia endeavoured to make its excuse for the abolition, by the Organic Statute of the 26th February, 1832, of the Polish Constitution, the substitution of Provincial Councils for the National Diet, the confiscations, the transportations to Siberia, and the forced expatriation of thousands of families and children that followed it.

The British Government has refused to admit the Polish insurrection of 1830 as an excuse for further violations of the Treaty by Russia. But this excuse was not admitted by the British Government. The history of the correspondence that then took place between the two Governments was given by Lord Palmerston in the House of Commons on the 9th of July, 1833, in these terms:—

"The contracting parties to the Treaty of Vienna

have a right to require that the Constitution of Poland should not be touched—and this is an opinion which I have not concealed from the Russian Government previous to the taking of Warsaw —and when Warsaw fell, that opinion was again conveyed to the Russian Government. The Russian Government, however, took a different view of the question. They contended that, by the re-conquest of Poland, the Emperor was placed in the same situation in which he stood after the Treaty of Vienna, and before the granting of a Constitution to Poland, and that he was at liberty, the previously-existing institutions having been swept away, as they contended, by the Revolution, to determine by what sort of institutions they should be replaced. The reply of the English Government was to the following effect:—That having taken into full consideration all that the Russian Government had stated in support of their view of the case, they still adhered to the opinion previously expressed, that the true and fair interpretation of the Treaty of Vienna required that the Polish Constitution should remain as before the Revolution, and that Russia had no right to abolish it."

In the same debate, Lord John Russell expressed the same sentiments; and the Earl of Derby (then Lord Stanley) said :—

"If I am asked my own opinion as to the interpretation to be put upon the Treaty of Vienna, I am ready to say that it is that stated to be the opinion of the Government, and that I consider it has been violated by Russia."

<small>In 1842 Poland began to be governed and treated in all respects like a Russian province.</small> The Organic Statute, proclaimed in place of the Constitution, remained a dead letter. But the Kingdom of Poland still preserved some vestiges of a distinct Administration. In 1842, even these were removed by the abolition of the Council of State and Supreme Court of Justice in Poland, and the transfer of their functions to the Senate of St. Petersburg, which was followed by the organization of an elaborate system of denationalization. The Catholic clergy were dispossessed of a great part of their landed property, the Russian language was adopted in all public documents, and a Russian superintendent appointed to watch over the public education of Poland. In a word, Poland was governed in all respects like a Russian province, and the most strenuous efforts were made to complete the likeness by depriving the inhabitants of every special right, both personal and political.

No. II.

VISCOUNT PALMERSTON TO LORD HEYTESBURY.

Foreign Office, November 23, 1831.

MY LORD,

I have received your Excellency's despatches reporting the opinion which prevails in St. Petersburg that some considerable change is intended to be made in the Constitution of the Kingdom of Poland, explaining the arguments by which that supposed intention is defended, and asking for further instructions as to the course which your Excellency is to pursue with respect to the affairs of Poland in general.

His Majesty's Government have watched with unceasing interest and anxiety the progress of the contest in Poland. These feelings have been made known to your Excellency by the several communications which you have received from me, while they have not been concealed from the Representative of His Majesty the Emperor of Russia at the Court of London. You have also been apprized of the grounds upon which His Majesty's Government considered it not to be advisable to interfere directly in the contest between the Emperor of Russia and his Polish subjects.

The war being now over, and the authority of the Emperor as King being completely re-established in Poland, the time is come when His Majesty feels himself justified, both by his friendship for the Emperor of Russia and by the duty resulting from the obligations which he has contracted under the Treaty of Vienna, in addressing to His Imperial Majesty, in the most amicable tone, and with the deference which is due to his rights as an independent Sovereign, some observations as to the best mode of resettling the Kingdom of Poland under the dominion of the Emperor, on principles accordant with those on which its union with the Imperial Crown of Russia was originally formed, and in such a manner as may be most conducive to its future good government and tranquillity.

Your Excellency has already been instructed, by my despatch of the 22nd of March last, to express the confidence of His Majesty's Government that His Imperial Majesty would use his victory, when it should be obtained, with the moderation and mercy congenial with the high-minded and generous sentiments which are well known to animate the mind of his Imperial Majesty. It is, therefore, without any the slightest doubt of His Imperial Majesty's benevolent and merciful disposition, that I am commanded to instruct you to urge, whenever you may find a fit opportunity to do so, those considerations both of humanity and policy, which cannot fail to find advocates in His Imperial Majesty's own feelings, and which would recommend the greatest forbearance and lenity in the treatment of his Polish subjects who, by the success of His Majesty's arms, have been again reduced to obedience.

Above all, your Excellency is instructed to represent to the Russian Government how much severities of any kind, not authorized by the laws and Constitution of Poland, are to be avoided. If it should appear, therefore, that there is any intention of proceeding to measures of proscription and confiscation, as has been reported, you are instructed to represent to His Imperial Majesty's Government, the impolicy and injustice of proceedings that would violate the Constitution, which, according to the stipulation of the Treaty of Vienna, was granted by the Emperor Alexander to Poland, and by which it is provided that no man shall be punished except by virtue of existing laws, and no criminal banished except by process of law, and by which the penalty of confiscation is for ever abolished.

His Majesty's Government, indeed, under all the circumstances of the case, would earnestly recommend a full and complete amnesty, from which those persons only should be excepted who have been guilty of the crime of assassination, and whose punishment would be effected by the ordinary course of justice.

This measure would appear to be one of the soundest policy. It could not in any degree weaken His Imperial Majesty's authority, nor detract from his honour, being adopted at a moment when his power could no longer be resisted, and when such a measure could appear to be dictated only by the purest motives of benevolence and mercy. It could not fail to soothe the irritated feelings of the Poles, and to give them confidence in the Government, by preventing them from being exposed individually to vengeance; and it would do infinitely more than any harsh display of severity to reproduce among them those feelings of obedience to the Government which are necessary to its security and peace, and which cannot be expected under a system which might keep them in a state of continued insecurity and apprehension.

In this case, therefore, generosity and sound policy appear to go hand in hand, in suggesting that in order to make the possession of Poland conducive to the strength and prosperity of Russia, it is necessary for the Russian Government to conciliate the affections of the Poles, and to obliterate instead of perpetuating, the traces of the recent contest.

The Poles have displayed, during the late war, qualities both of intellect and courage which prove them capable of being either useful or dangerous subjects, according to the manner in which they may be governed. It is needless to point out the resources which may be drawn from 4,000,000 of people, full of activity, enterprise, and intelligence, provided they are attached to their sovereign, and contented with their political condition. But such a people must necessarily become a source of embarrassment and weakness if they are kept in a state of exasperation and discontent, which will only be controlled so long as no favourable opportunity shall occur to excite them into action.

Is it on the very frontier of an Empire, and in contact with military neighbours, that a wise Government would wish to place such elements of danger? Is it in the very outworks of defence that a prudent Administration would incur the risk of having a population disaffected to its Government, and ready to join any invader who might promise them a milder rule and a better fate?

It is, then, not more upon principles of humanity than upon a friendly regard for the interests and the honour of Russia that His Majesty's Government instruct you earnestly to press upon the Russian Government a general and complete amnesty; an act which is understood to have been spontaneously offered by the Emperor on more than one occasion during the war, and which His Majesty's Government have reason to believe is also recommended by other allies of His Imperial Majesty.

Your Excellency was instructed in a former despatch to state that His Majesty's Government could not see with indifference the Poles deprived of the advantages which had been secured to them by the Treaty of Vienna. These advantages consisted in a stipulation that a Constitution should be granted to them, and in the Constitution which, in consequence of that stipulation, they afterwards received from the Emperor Alexander.

His Majesty's Government is not unmindful of the arguments which you state to have been adduced to prove that the Polish Constitution is in no degree identified with the Treaty of Vienna; but the validity of this reasoning cannot, as it appears to them, be maintained.

The Treaty of Vienna declared that the Kingdom of Poland should be attached to Russia by its Constitution. A Constitution the Emperor of Russia accordingly gave; and it surely is no forced construction of the meaning of that Treaty to consider the Constitution so given as existing thenceforth under the sanction of the Treaty. But it is argued that the same Power which gave may modify or take away. This, however, is an assertion for which no proof is afforded. The Constitution, once given, became the link which, under the Treaty, binds the Kingdom of Poland to the Empire of Russia; and can that link remain unimpaired if the Constitution should not be maintained?

Had the Constitution reserved to the Sovereign a right to change or modify, no objection could then have been made to the exercise of a power which would legally have been his. But the Constitution carefully guards against any such acts of executive authority. It declares (Article 31) that the Polish nation shall for ever possess a national Representation, consisting of a Diet, composed of a King and two Chambers; it declares (Article 163) that the Organic Statutes and the Codes of Laws cannot be modified or changed, except by the King and two Chambers; it requires (Article 45) that every King of Poland shall swear before God and upon the Scriptures, to maintain the Constitution and cause it to be executed to the best of his power; and the Emperor Alexander, on the 27th November, 1815, formally gave this Constitution, and declared that he adopted it for himself and for his successors.

Such are the provisions of the Constitution,

which points out the authority by which any change or modification is to be made; and changes arbitrarily effected by the executive authority alone would obviously be violations of the Constitution.

It appears that some persons suppose the intention of the Russian Government to be to abolish the present form of government in Poland, consisting of a Diet composed of a King and two Chambers, and to substitute for the Chambers Provincial States such as those which have been established in Galicia and in some of the provinces of Prussia; and it is argued that such a change would still leave to Poland a Constitution sufficient to satisfy the stipulations of the Treaty of Vienna. But could such a form of government, fairly, and according either to the letter or the spirit of the Treaty of Vienna, be considered as placing Poland in the situation which was thereby contemplated? That Treaty clearly appears to draw a marked distinction between the system of government to be established in those parts of Poland which had been annexed as provinces to Austria, Prussia, and Russia, and had been incorporated in their respective dominions, and that part which was to form the separate Kingdom of Poland, and which was to be placed, as such, under the same Sovereign as Russia, and secured in the enjoyment of its distinct rights and privileges.

In the former provinces, accordingly, the grant of Provincial States was perfectly in accordance with the rights to be exercised by the Sovereign over provinces that were incorporated with his other dominions; while the Constitution given to the Kingdom of Poland was suited to the separate and distinct position in which it was placed in its relation to the Russian Empire.

But in the separate Kingdom of Poland, united according to the Treaty of Vienna by its Constitution with the Crown of Russia, to abrogate that Constitution, and to substitute Provincial States, expressly modelled after those which had been granted to the incorporated provinces of Austria and Prussia, would be, in effect, to reduce that Kingdom, though still nominally possessing a separate existence, to the state and condition of a province, deprived of all the rights and excluded from all the advantages which had been secured to it.

It cannot be admitted that the revolt of the Poles, and their violation of the Constitution by voting the separation of Poland from the Crown of Russia, can absolve the Emperor, after his authority has been re-established, from his obligation to adhere to that Constitution. Wrongs committed by one side are not to be punished by the commission of wrongs on the other. From the submission of the Poles to the arms of His Imperial Majesty, Europe looks for the reestablishment of law and justice, and not for acts of retaliation and vengeance; since, whatever excuse such acts may find in the troubles of an intestine war, they could not be palliated if resorted to by a Power which has subdued all opposition, and which cannot plead for its measures the necessity of any pressing emergency.

It has often been stated in the proclamations which have been issued by the Russian Government from time to time during the war, that only a part of the Poles had joined in the revolt, and that the majority of the nation remained faithful. If that be so, it affords a strong argument for not punishing the innocent for the offences of the guilty, by depriving all of the advantages which the Constitution confers upon them.

If, on the contrary, the whole of the nation should appear to have partaken in the revolt, such a general insurrection could only have proceeded from deeply-seated discontent, and such a feeling is not likely to be removed by a sweeping abrogation of the Constitution.

In pressing these considerations upon the Russian Government, your Excellency will be careful that while, on the one hand, you urge, as far as possible, the arguments which have been suggested, you do not, on the other, depart from that tone of friendly representation which is suited to the amicable relations existing between Great Britain and Russia.

I am, &c.
(Signed)   PALMERSTON.

No. III.

TRANSLATION FROM MIÇKIEVICZ, BY MRS. ELEANOR ORLEBAR.

Draw nigh : upon the bed of death
  Smiling, she falls asleep ;
Like the pale Dawn, when opal clouds
  Around her wheel and weep.
An aged priest is at the door,
  Her friends in mourning near ;
Her mother yet more sad, I see ;
  And a smother'd wail I hear.
He dares not on the dying gaze—
Her lover kneels apart, and prays.
The transient brightness of her eyes
By turns revives, and shines, and dies.
The rose is fading from her mouth ;
  Now for evermore 'tis flown,
And the repose of joy is there,
  And the violet there has blown.
She lifts her colourless brow, and gives
  To us, a loving smile ;
Then sees the weeping circle round,
  And sadly falls the while—

As white as is the sacred bread
The holy priest brings near her bed.
Her arms are stiff, her trembling breast
More slowly quivers—is at rest!
   O Mary! thou art dead!
Look at this latest pledge of love,
   A diamond bathed in flame;
Thus to her sapphire eyes, a ray
   Of her parting spirit came.
'Twas like the insect's silver wing
   That charms our summer shade,
Or the dew-drops by the tempest dimm'd,
   Upon the long grass laid.
No more resistance unto Death
   She made, than makes the flower
Unto the hand that gathers it—
   'Twas thus she met his power.
It fell on her like snow in spring
   On the first pale blossoms shed;
But we are left to weep alone:
   O Mary! thou art dead!

END OF VOL. I.

Woodfall and Kinder, Printers, Angel Court, Skinner Street, London.

www.ingramcontent.com/pod-product-compliance
Lightning Source LLC
Chambersburg PA
CBHW031418230426
43668CB00007B/344